An American Girl

Sara Jeannette Duncan

Alpha Editions

This edition published in 2024

ISBN : 9789366386317

Design and Setting By
Alpha Editions
www.alphaedis.com
Email - info@alphaedis.com

As per information held with us this book is in Public Domain. This book is a reproduction of an important historical work. Alpha Editions uses the best technology to reproduce historical work in the same manner it was first published to preserve its original nature. Any marks or number seen are left intentionally to preserve its true form.

Contents

PREFACE .... - 1 -
I .... - 2 -
II .... - 7 -
III .... - 16 -
IV .... - 23 -
V .... - 33 -
VI .... - 40 -
VII .... - 46 -
VIII .... - 54 -
IX .... - 63 -
X .... - 69 -
XI .... - 77 -
XII .... - 85 -
XIII .... - 93 -
XIV .... - 99 -
XV .... - 107 -
XVI .... - 113 -
XVII .... - 119 -
XVIII .... - 125 -
XIX .... - 132 -
XX .... - 139 -
XXI .... - 146 -
XXII .... - 154 -
XXIII .... - 158 -
XXIV .... - 166 -
XXV .... - 171 -

XXVI	- 176 -
XXVII	- 183 -
XXVIII	- 188 -
XXIX	- 191 -
XXX	- 197 -

PREFACE

FOR THE OTHER AMERICANS.

I have written this account only secondarily and at the instigation of publishers, for Americans. Primarily, I wrote it for the English people. I composed it in their country; it was suggested by their institutions, and it is addressed to them. You will see, if you read it, that I had reasons for doing this. The reasons are in the first chapter, at the very beginning. As you have not far to look for them, therefore, and as it is quite unnecessary to print a thing twice in the same book, I will not go over them again. The object of this preface is chiefly to draw your attention to the fact that I am not talking to you, dear compatriot, so that you will understand that there is no personal ground for any annoyance you may feel at what I say.

Notwithstanding this, one of the Miss Wastgoggles, of Boston, has already taken the trouble to send me a rather severely reproachful letter about my impressions and experiences, in which she says that she would have written hers, if it had ever occurred to her to do so, very differently. I have no doubt that this is true. She also begs me to remember that there are a great many different kinds of girls in America, numbers of whom are brought up "quite as they are in England." It is this remark of hers that makes me quote Miss Wastgoggles. I wish to say in connection with it that, while it is unreasonable to apologize for being only one kind of American girl, I do not pretend to represent the ideas of any more.

Mamie Wick.

No. 4000 Prairie Avenue, Chicago, Illinois,

November 20, 1890.

I

AM an American Girl. Therefore, perhaps, you will not be surprised at anything further I may have to say for myself. I have observed, since I came to England, that this statement, made by a third person in connection with any question of my own conduct, is always broadly explanatory. And as my own conduct will naturally enter more or less into this volume, I may as well make it in the beginning, to save complications.

It may be necessary at this point to explain further. I know that in England an unmarried person, of my age, is not expected to talk much, especially about herself. This was a little difficult for me to understand at first, as I have always talked a great deal, and, one might say, been encouraged to do it; but I have at length been brought to understand it, and lately I have spoken with becoming infrequency, and chiefly about the Zoo. I find the Zoo to be a subject which is almost certain to be received with approval; and in animal nature there is, fortunately, a good deal of variety. I do not intend, however, in this book, to talk about the Zoo, or anything connected with it, but about the general impressions and experiences I have received in your country; and one of my reasons for departing from approved models of discussion for young ladies and striking out, as it were, into subject-matter on my own account, is that I think you may find it more or less interesting. I have noticed that you are pleased, over here, to bestow rather more attention upon the American Girl than upon any other kind of American that we produce. You have taken the trouble to form opinions about her—I have heard quantities of them. Her behaviour and her bringing-up, her idioms and her 'accent'— above all her 'accent'—have made themes for you, and you have been good enough to discuss them—Mr. James, in your midst, correcting and modifying your impressions—with a good deal of animation, for you. I observe that she is almost the only frivolous subject that ever gets into your newspapers. I have become accustomed to meeting her there, usually at the breakfast-table, dressed in green satin and diamonds. The encounter had quite a shock of novelty for me at first, but that wore off in time; the green satin and diamonds were so invariable.

Being an American girl myself, I do not, naturally, quite see the reason of this, and it is a matter I feel a delicacy about inquiring into, on personal grounds. Privately, I should think that the number of us that come over here every summer to see the Tower of London and the National Gallery, and visit Stratford-upon-Avon, to say nothing of those who marry and stay in England, would have made you familiar with the kind of young women we are long ago; and to me it is very curious that you should go on talking about us. I can't say that we object very much, because, while you criticise us considerably as a class, you are very polite to us individually, and nobody minds being criticised as a noun of multitude. But it has occurred to me that, since so much is to be said about the American Girl, it might be permissible for her to say some of it herself.

'THAT IS HOW HE MADE HIS FORTUNE'

I have learned that in England you like to know a great deal about people who are introduced to you—who their fathers and mothers are, their grandfathers and grandmothers, and even further back than that.

So I will gratify you at once on this point, so far as I am able. My father is Mr. Joshua P. Wick, of Chicago, Ill.—you may have seen his name in connection with the baking-powder interest in that city. That is how he made his fortune—in baking-powder; as he has often said, it is to baking-powder that we owe everything. He began by putting it up in small quantities, but it is an article that is so much used in the United States, and ours was such a very good kind, that the demand for it increased like anything; and though we have not become so rich as a great many people in America, it is years since poppa gave his personal superintendence to the business. You will excuse my spelling it 'poppa'; I have called him that all my life, and 'papa' doesn't seem to mean anything to me.

Lately he has devoted himself to politics; he is in Congress now, and at the next election momma particularly wishes him to run for senator. There is a great deal of compliance about poppa, and I think he will run.

'I THINK HE WILL RUN'

Momma was a Miss Wastgaggle, of Boston, and she was teaching school in Chicago when poppa met her. Her grandfather, who educated her, was a manufacturer of glass eyes. There are Wastgaggles in Boston now, but they spell the name with one 'g,' and lately they have been wanting momma to write hers 'Mrs. Wastgagle-Wick; but momma says that since she never liked the name well enough to give it to any of her children, she is certainly not going to take it again herself. These Wastgagles speak of our great-grandfather as a well-known oculist, and I suppose, in a sense, he was one.

'SHE WAS TEACHING SCHOOL IN CHICAGO WHEN POPPA MET HER'

My father's father lived in England, and was also a manufacturer, poppa says, always adding, 'in a plain way;' so I suppose whatever he made he made himself. It may have been boots, or umbrellas, or pastry—poppa never states; though I should be disposed to think, from his taking up the baking-powder idea, that it was pastry.

I am sorry that I am not able to give you fuller satisfaction about my antecedents. I know that I must have had more than I have mentioned, but my efforts to discover them—and I have made efforts since I decided to introduce myself to you—have been entirely futile. I am inclined to think that they were not people who achieved any great distinction in life; but I have never held anything against them on that account, for I have no reason to believe that they would not have been distinguished if they could. I cannot think that it has ever been in the nature of the Wicks, or the Wastgaggles either, to let the opportunity for distinction pass through any criminal negligence on their part. I am perfectly willing to excuse them on this ground, therefore; and if I, who am most intimately concerned in the matter, can afford to do this, perhaps it is not unreasonable to expect it of you.

In connections we do better. A grand-aunt of some early Wastgaggles was burned as a witch in Salem, Mass.—a thing very few families can point back to, even in England, I should think; and a second cousin of momma's was the first wife of one of our Presidents. He was a Democratic President, though, and as poppa always votes the Republican ticket, we don't think much of that. Besides, as we are careful to point out whenever we mention the subject, she was in the cemetery years before he was in the White House. And there is Mrs. Portheris, of Half-Moon Street, Hyde Park, who is poppa's aunt by her first marriage.

We were all coming at first, poppa, and momma, and I—the others are still in school—and it had appeared among the 'City Personals' of the 'Chicago Tribune' that 'Colonel and Mrs. Joshua P. Wick, accompanied by Miss Mamie Wick'—I forgot to say that poppa was in the Civil War—'would have a look at monarchical institutions this summer.' Our newspapers do get hold of things so. But just a week before we were to sail something arose—I think it was a political complication—to prevent poppa's going, and momma is far too much of an invalid to undertake such a journey without him. I must say that both my parents are devoted to me, and when I said I thought I'd prefer going alone to giving up the trip, neither of them opposed it. Momma said she thought I ought to have the experience, because, though I'd been a good deal in society in Chicago, she didn't consider that that in itself was enough. Poppa said that the journey was really nothing nowadays, and he could easily get me a letter of introduction to the captain. Besides, in a shipful of two or three hundred there would be sure to be some pleasant people I could get acquainted with on the voyage. Mrs. Von Stuvdidyl, who lives next door to us, and has been to Europe several times, suggested that I should take a maid, and momma rather liked the idea, but I persuaded her out of it. I couldn't possibly have undertaken the care of a maid.

And then we all thought of Mrs. Portheris.

None of us had ever seen her, and there had been very little correspondence; in fact, we had not had a letter from her since several years ago, when she wrote a long one to poppa, something about some depressed California mining stock, I believe, which she thought poppa, as her nephew and an American, ought to take off her hands before it fell any lower. And I remember that poppa obliged her: whether as an American or as her nephew I don't know. After that she sent us every year a Christmas card, with an angel or a bunch of forget-me-nots on it, inscribed, 'To my nephew and niece, Joshua Peter and Mary Wick, and all their dear ones.' Her latest offering was lying in the card-basket on the table then, and I am afraid we looked at it with more interest than we had ever done before.

'I AM AFRAID WE LOOKED AT IT WITH MORE INTEREST THAN WE EVER HAD DONE BEFORE'

The 'dear ones' read so sympathetically that momma said she knew we could depend upon Mrs. Portheris to take me round and make me enjoy myself, and she wanted to cable that I was coming. But poppa said No, his aunt must be getting up in years now, and an elderly English lady might easily be frightened into apoplexy by a cablegram. It was a pity there was no time to write, but I must just go and see her immediately, and say that I was the daughter of Joshua P. Wick, of Chicago, and she would be certain to make me feel at home at once. But, as I said, none of us knew Mrs. Portheris.

II

I AM not much acquainted in New York, so I had only poppa and Mr. Winterhazel to see me off. Mr. Winterhazel lives there, and does business in Wall Street, where he operates very successfully, I've been told, for such a young man. We had been the greatest friends and regular correspondents for three or four years—our tastes in literature and art were almost exactly the same, and it was a mutual pleasure to keep it up—but poppa had never met him before. They were very happy to make each other's acquaintance, though, and became quite intimate at once; they had heard so much about each other, they said. We had allowed two days before the steamer sailed, so that I could make some purchases—New York styles are so different from Chicago ones; and, as poppa said afterwards, it was very fortunate that Mr. Winterhazel was there. Otherwise, I should have been obliged to go round to the stores alone; for poppa himself was so busy seeing people about political matters that he hadn't the thirtieth part of a second for me, except at meal-times, and then there was almost always somebody there. London is nothing to New York for confusion and hurry, and until you get accustomed to it the Elevated is apt to be very trying to your nerves. But Mr. Winterhazel was extremely kind, and gave up his whole time to me; and as he knew all the best stores, this put me under the greatest obligation to him. After dinner the first evening he took me to hear a gentleman who was lecturing on the London of Charles Dickens, with a stereopticon, thinking that, as I was going to London, it would probably be of interest to me—and it was. I anticipated your city more than ever afterwards. Poppa was as disappointed as could be that he wasn't able to go with us to the lecture; but he said that politics were politics, and I suppose they are.

Next day I sailed from North River Docks, Pier No. 2, a fresh wind blowing all the harbour into short blue waves, with the sun on them, and poppa and Mr. Winterhazel taking off their hats and waving their handkerchiefs as long as I could see them. I suppose I started for Great Britain with about as many comforts as most people have—poppa and Mr. Winterhazel had almost filled my state-room with flowers, and I found four pounds of caramels under the lower berth—but I confess, as we steamed out past Staten Island, and I saw the statue of Liberty getting smaller and smaller, and the waves of the Atlantic Ocean getting bigger and bigger, I felt very much by myself indeed, and began to depend a good deal upon Mrs. Portheris.

As to the caramels, in the next three hours I gave the whole of them to the first stewardess, who was kind enough to oblige me with a lemon.

Before leaving home I had promised everybody that I would keep a diary, and most of the time I did; but I find nothing at all of interest in it about the first three days of the voyage to London. The reason was that I had no opportunity whatever of making observations. But on the morning of the fourth day I was obliged to go on deck. The stewardess said she couldn't put up with it any longer, and I would never recover if I didn't; and I was very glad afterwards that I gave in. She was a real kind-hearted stewardess, I may say, though her manner was a little peremptory.

I didn't find as much sociability on deck as I expected. I should have thought everybody would have been more or less acquainted by that time, but, with the exception of a few gentlemen, people were standing or sitting round in the same little knots they came on board in. And yet it was very smooth. I was so perfectly delighted to be well again that I felt I must talk to somebody, so I spoke to one of a party of ladies from Boston who I thought might know the Wastgagles there. I was very polite, and she did not seem at all sea-sick, but I found it difficult to open up a conversation with her. I knew that the Bostonians thought a good deal of themselves—all the Wastgagles do—and her manner somehow made me think of a story I once heard of a Massachusetts milestone, marked '1 m. from Boston,' which somebody thought was a wayside tablet with the simple pathetic epitaph, 'I'm from Boston,' on it; and just to enliven her I told her the story. 'Indeed!' she said. 'Well, we *are* from Boston.'

I didn't quite know what to do after that, for the only other lady near me was English, I knew by her boots. Beside the boots she had grey hair and pink cheeks, and rather sharp grey eyes, and a large old-fashioned muff, and a red cloud. Only an Englishwoman would be wearing a muff and a cloud like that in public—nobody else would dare to do it. She was rather portly, and she sat very firmly and comfortably in her chair with her feet crossed, done up in a big Scotch rug, and being an English woman I knew that she would not expect anybody to speak to her who had not been introduced. She would probably, I thought, give me a haughty stare, as they do in novels, and say, with cold repression, 'You have the advantage of me, miss!'—and then what would my feelings be? So I made no more advances to anybody, but walked off my high spirits on the hurricane-deck, thinking about the exclusiveness of those Bostonians, and wondering whether, as a nation, we could be catching it from England.

You may imagine my feelings—or rather, as you are probably English, you can't—when the head steward gave me my place at the dinner-table immediately opposite the Bostonians, and between this lady and an unknown gentleman. 'I shall not make a single travelling acquaintance!' I said to myself as I sat down—and I must say I was disappointed. I began to realise how greatly we had all unconsciously depended upon my forming nice travelling acquaintances, as people always do in books, to make the trip pleasant, and I thought that in considering another voyage I should divorce myself from that idea beforehand. However, I said nothing, of course, and found a certain amount of comfort in my soup.

I remember the courses of that dinner very well, and if they were calculated to make interesting literary matter I could write them out. The Bostonians ostentatiously occupied themselves with one another. One of them took up a position several miles behind her spectacles, looked at me through them, and then said something to her neighbour about 'Daisy Miller,' which the neighbour agreed to. I know what they meant now. The gentleman, when he was not attending to his dinner, stared at the salt-cellar most of the time, in a blank, abstracted way; and the English lady, who looked much nicer unshelled than she did on deck, kept her head carefully turned in the other direction, and made occasional remarks to an elderly person next her who was very deaf. If I had not been hungry, I don't know how I should have felt. But I maintained an absolute silence and ate my dinner.

Gradually—perhaps because the elderly person was so extremely deaf, and my own behaviour comparatively unaggressive—the lady of England began to assume a less uncomfortable position. A certain repellent air went out of her right shoulder. Presently she sat quite parallel with the table. By the advent of the pudding—it was cabinet pudding—I had become conscious that she had looked at me casually three times. When the Gorgonzola appeared I refused it. In America ladies eat very little Gorgonzola.

'Don't you *like* cheese?' she said, suddenly, a little as if I had offended her. I was so startled that I equivocated somewhat.

'No'm, not to day, I think—thank you!' I said. The fact is, I never touch it.

'Oh!' she responded. 'But then, this is your first appearance, I suppose? In that case, you wouldn't like it.' And I felt forgiven.

She said nothing more until dessert, and then she startled me again. 'Have you been bad?' she inquired.

I didn't know quite what to say, it seemed such an extraordinary question, but it flashed upon me that perhaps the lady was some kind of missionary, in which case it was my duty to be respectful. So I said that I hoped not—that at least I hadn't been told so since I was a very little girl. 'But then,' I said, 'The Episcopalian Prayer-book says we're all miserable sinners, doesn't it?' The lady looked at me in astonishment.

'What has the Prayer-book to do with your being ill?' she exclaimed. 'Oh, I see!' and she laughed very heartily. 'You thought I meant naughty! Cross-questions and crooked answers! Mr. Mafferton, you will appreciate this!' Mr. Mafferton was the gentleman whom I have mentioned in connection with the salt-cellars; and my other neighbour seemed to know him, which, as they both came from England, did not surprise me then, although now I should be inclined to consider that the most likely reason of all why they shouldn't be acquainted. I didn't see anything so very humorous in it, but the lady explained our misunderstanding to Mr. Mafferton as if it were the greatest joke imaginable, and she had made it herself. 'Really,' she said, 'it's good enough for "Punch!"' I was unfamiliar with that paper then, and couldn't say; but now I think it was myself.

Mr. Mafferton coloured dreadfully—I omitted to say that he was a youngish gentleman—and listened with a sort of strained smile, which debouched into a hesitating and uncomfortable remark about 'curious differences in idioms.' I thought he intended it to be polite, and he said it in the most agreeable man's voice I had ever heard; but I could not imagine what there was to flurry him so, and I felt quite sorry for him. And he had hardly time to get safely back to the salt-cellar before we all got up.

Next morning at breakfast I got on beautifully with the English lady, who hardly talked to the elderly deaf person at all, but was kind enough to be very much interested in what I expected to see in London. 'Your friends will have their hands full,' she remarked, with a sort of kind acerbity, 'if they undertake to show you all that!' I thought of poor old Mrs. Portheris, who was probably a martyr to rheumatism and neuralgia, with some compunction. 'Oh!' I said, 'I shouldn't think of asking them to; I'll read it all up, and then I can go round beautifully by myself!'

'By *yourself!*' she exclaimed. 'You! This is an independent American young lady—the very person I went especially to the United States to see, and spent a whole season in New York, going everywhere, without coming across a single specimen! You must excuse my staring at you. But you'll have to get over that idea. Your friends will never in the world allow it—I suppose you *have* friends?'

'No,' I said; 'only a relation.'

The lady laughed. 'Do you intend that for a joke?' she asked. 'Well, they do mean different things sometimes. But we'll see what the relation will have to say to it.'

Mr. Mafferton occasionally removed his eyes from the salt-cellar during this meal, and even ventured a remark or two. The remarks were not striking in any way—there was no food for thought in them whatever; yet they were very agreeable. Whether it was Mr. Mafferton's voice, or his manner, or his almost apologetic way of speaking, as if he knew that he was not properly acquainted, and ought not to do it, I don't know, but I liked hearing him make them. It was not, however, until later in the day, when I was sitting on deck talking with the lady from England about New York, where she didn't seem to like anything but the air and the melons, that I felt the least bit acquainted with Mr. Mafferton. I had found out her name, by the way. She asked me mine, and when I told her she said: 'But you're old enough now to have a Christian name—weren't you christened Mary?' She went on to say that she believed in the good old-fashioned names, like Nancy and Betsy, that couldn't be babified—and I am not sure whether she told me, or it was by intuition, that I learned that hers was Hephzibah. It seems to me now that it never could have been anything else. But I am quite certain she added that her husband was Hector Torquilin, and that he had been dead fifteen years. 'A distinguished man in his time, my dear, as you would know if you had been brought up in an English schoolroom.' And just then, while I was wondering what would be the most appropriate thing to say to a lady who told you that her husband had been dead fifteen years, and was a distinguished man in his time, and wishing that I had been brought up in an English schoolroom, so that I could be polite about him, Mr. Mafferton came up. He had one of Mr. W. D. Howells' novels in his hand, and at once we glided into the subject of American literature. I remember I was surprised to find an Englishman so good-natured in his admiration of some of our authors, and so willing to concede an American standard which might be a high one, and yet have nothing to do with Dickens, and so appreciative generally of the conditions which have brought about our ways of thinking and writing. We had a most delightful conversation—I had no idea there was so much in Mr. Mafferton—and Mrs. Torquilin only interrupted once. That was to ask us if either of us had ever read the works of Fennimore Cooper, who was about the only author America had ever produced. Neither of us had, and I said I thought there were some others. 'Well,' she said, 'he is the only one we ever hear of in England.' But I don't think Mrs. Torquilin was quite correct in this statement, because since I have been in England I have met three or four people, beside Mr. Mafferton, who knew, or at least had heard of, several American writers. Then Mrs. Torquilin went to sleep, and when she woke up it was five o'clock, and her maid was just arriving with her tea. Mr. Mafferton asked me if he might get me some, but I said, No, thanks; I thought I would take a brisk walk instead, if Mrs. Torquilin would excuse me.

'Certainly,' she said; 'go and take some exercise, both of you. It's much better for young people than tea-drinking. And see here, my dear! I thought you were very sensible not to dress for dinner last night, like those silly young fools opposite. Silly young fools I call them. Now, take my advice, and don't let them persuade you to do it. An Atlantic steamer is no place for bare arms. Now run away, and have your walk, and Mr. Mafferton will see that you're not blown overboard.'

Mr. Mafferton hesitated a moment. 'Are you quite sure, he said, 'that you wouldn't prefer the tea?'

'Oh yes, sir!' I said; 'we always have tea at half-past six at home, and I don't care about it so early as this. I'd much rather walk. But don't trouble to come with me if *you* would like some tea.'

'I'll come,' he said, 'if you won't call me "sir."' Here he frowned a little and coloured. 'It makes one feel seventy, you know. May I ask why you do it?'

I explained that in Chicago it was considered polite to say 'ma'am' or 'sir' to a lady or gentleman of any age with whom you did not happen to be very well acquainted, and I had heard it all my life; still, if he objected to it, I would not use it in his case.

He said he thought he did object to it—from a lady; it had other associations in his ears.

So I stopped calling Mr. Mafferton 'sir'; and since then, except to very old gentlemen, I have got out of the way of using the expression. I asked him if there was anything else that struck him as odd in my conversation kindly to tell me, as of course I did not wish to be an unnecessary shock to my relation in Half-Moon Street. He did not say he would, but we seemed to get on together even more agreeably after that.

'WE SEEMED TO GET ON TOGETHER EVEN MORE AGREEABLY AFTER THAT'

Mr. Mafferton appeared to know nobody on board but Mrs. Torquilin; and I made acquaintance with hardly anybody else, so that we naturally saw a good deal of each other, usually in the afternoons, walking up and down the deck. He lent me all his books, and I lent him all mine, and we exchanged opinions on a great variety of subjects. When we argued, he was always very polite and considerate; but I noticed one curious thing about him—I never could bring him round to my point of view. He did not seem to see the necessity of coming, although I often went round to his. This was a new experience to me in arguing with a gentleman. And he always talked very impersonally. At first this struck me as a little cold and uninterested, but afterwards I liked it. It was like drinking a very nice kind of pure cold water—after the different flavours of personality I had always been accustomed to. Mr. Mafferton only made one exception to this rule that I remember, and that was the afternoon before we landed. Then he told me particularly about his father and mother, and their tastes and occupation, also the names and ages of his brothers and sisters, and their tastes and occupations, and where he lived. But I cannot say I found him as interesting that afternoon as usual.

I need not describe the bustle and confusion of landing at Liverpool Docks in the middle of a wet April afternoon. Mrs. Torquilin had told me at breakfast not on any account to let my relations take me away before she had given me her address; but when the time came I guess—if you will allow me—she must have forgotten, because the last time I saw her she was standing under a very big umbrella, which the maid held over her, a good deal excited, and giving a great many orders about her luggage to a nervous-looking man in livery.

I easily identified mine, and got off by train for London without any trouble to speak of. We arrived rather late, though, and it was still pouring.

'What has become of your people?' asked somebody at my elbow. I turned and saw Mr. Mafferton, who must have come down by the same train.

'I didn't expect my relation to meet me,' said; 'she doesn't expect *me*!'

'Oh!' said Mr. Mafferton; 'you did not write to her before you sailed?'

'No,' I said. 'There wasn't time.'

'Upon my word!' said Mr. Mafferton. Then, as I suppose I looked rather surprised, he added, hastily: "I only mean that it seems so—so uncommonly extraordinary, you know! But I would advise you, in that case, to give the bulk of your luggage into the hands of the forwarding agents, with instructions to send it early to-morrow to your friend's address. It is all you can do tonight,' said Mr. Mafferton, 'really. Of course, you will go there immediately yourself.'

'No,' I responded, firmly; 'I think not, Mr. Mafferton. My relation is very elderly, and probably in bad health. For all I know, she may have gone to bed. I must not disturb her so late. All the people I have ever known have stayed at the Métropole in London. I will go to the Métropole for to-night, and have my things sent there. To-morrow I will go and see my relation, and if she asks me to visit her I can easily telephone up for them. Thank you very much.'

Mr. Mafferton looked as sober as possible, if not a little annoyed. Then he went and got the agent's young man, and asked me to point out my things to him, which I did, and got receipts. Then he told a porter to call a cab, and put my smaller valises into it. 'I will put you in,' he said, and he gave me his arm and his umbrella, through the wettest rain I have ever experienced, to the hansom. I thanked him again very cordially, and before he said good-bye he very kindly gave me his card and address, and begged me to let him know if there was anything he could do for me.

Then I rattled away through the blurred lights of your interminable twisted streets to the Métropole, fancying I saw Westminster Abbey or St. Paul's through the rain at every turn.

When we stopped at last before the hotel, another hansom behind us stopped too, and though I am sure he didn't intend me to, I saw quite plainly through the glass—Mr. Mafferton. It was extremely kind of him to wish to be of assistance to a lady alone, especially in such weather, and I could easily understand his desire to see me to my hotel; but what puzzled me was, why he should have taken another cab!

And all night long I dreamed of Mrs. Portheris.

III

I ONCE visited the Wastgagles in Boston with momma. It was a visit of condolence, just after the demise of a grandmother of theirs. I was going to say, that never since that occasion had I experienced anything like the solemnity of my breakfast at the Métropole the morning after I arrived. As a sad-faced waiter with mutton-chop whiskers marshalled me across the room to an empty little white-and-silvery table beside one of the big windows, I felt, for the first time in my life, that I was being made imposing, and I objected to the feeling. The place itself did not impress me particularly—in America we are accustomed to gorgeousness in our hotels, and the mirrors and the gilding of the Métropole rather made me feel at home than otherwise; but it was the demeanour of everything that weighed upon me. My very chair lived up to its own standard of decorum; and the table seemed laid upon a pattern of propriety that it would never willingly depart from. There was an all-pervading sense of order in the air I couldn't make out exactly where it came from, but it was there, and it was fearful. The waiters spoke to each other in low tones, as if something of deep and serious importance were going on; and when I told one of them what I should like from the bill-of-fare, he bent down his ear and received my order as if it had been confidential State business I was asking him to undertake. When he came back, carrying the tray in front of him, it was almost processional. And in the interval, when I turned round to look out of the window, and saw another of those respectfully-subdued waiters standing behind my chair, quite motionless, I jumped. A great many people were getting their breakfasts, not with the cheerful alacrity which we use at home, but rather with a portentous deliberation and concentration which did not admit of much talking. The silence was broken only in one corner, where a group of Americans seemed to have got accustomed to the atmosphere. When the English breakfasters raised their eyes from their papers and eggs-and-toast, they regarded my talkative compatriots with a look which must have fairly chilled their tea. I hope nobody has ever looked at me like that in England. The Americans were from Virginia, as I could tell by their accent, and their 'c'y'arn't' and 'sis'r' and 'honey' and 'heap better.' But I have no doubt the English people, in their usual loftily comprehensive fashion, set the strangers down as 'Yankees,' and no amount of explanation could have taught them that the 'Yankees are the New Englanders, and that the name would once have been taken as an insult by a Southerner. But the Virginians were blissfully indifferent to the British estimate of themselves, and they talked as freely of their shopping and sight-seeing as they would in Delmonico's or the Brunswick. To be perfectly honest, a conviction came to me then that sometimes we don't care enough. But, for my part, I liked listening to that Virginian corner.

I'm afraid it was rather a late breakfast, and the lobby was full of people strolling in and out when I went through on my way to my room. I stood for a moment at the dining-room door looking at the lobby—I had heard so many Chicago people describe it—and I noticed in the seats that run around it, against the wall, two young women. They were leaning back nonchalantly, watching the comers and the goers. Both of them had their knees crossed, and one had her hands in her jacket pockets. A man in the seat next them, who might or might not have belonged to them, was smoking a large cigar. Two English ladies came out from breakfast behind me, stood waiting for somebody, and said one to the other: 'Look at those disgusting American girls!'

'"THOSE DISGUSTING AMERICAN GIRLS"'

But I had seen the young women's boots. Just to be satisfied, I walked up to one of them, and asked her if she could kindly tell me when I ought to post letters for New York.

'The American maiyel goes out Wednesdays an' Satuhdays, I fancy,' the young woman replied, 'but I'm not suah; it would be saifah to ask the clahk!'

She spoke quite distinctly, so that the English ladies must have heard her, and I am afraid they saw in my glance as I went upstairs that I had intended to correct their mistake.

I started to see Mrs. Portheris at eleven o'clock on the morning of the 9th of April—a lovely day, a day which augured brightly and hopefully. I waited carefully till eleven, thinking by that time my relation would have had her breakfast in bed and been dressed, and perhaps have been helped downstairs to her own particular sunny window, where I thought I might see her faded, placid, sweet old face looking up from her knitting and out into the busy street. Words have such an inspiring effect upon the imagination. All this had emanated from the 'dear ones,' and I felt confident and pleased and happy beforehand to be a dear one. I wore one of my plainest walking-dresses—I love simplicity in dress—so as to mitigate the shock to my relation as far as I could; but it was a New York one, and it gave me a great deal of moral support. It may be weak-minded in me, but I simply couldn't have gone to see my relation in a hat and gloves that didn't match. Clothes and courage have so much to do with each other.

The porter said that I had better take 'a'ansom,' or if I walked to Charing Cross I could get 'a 'Ammersmith 'bus' which would take me to Half-Moon Street, Piccadilly. I asked him if there were any street-cars running that way. 'D'ye mean growlers, miss?' he said. 'I can get ye a growler in 'arf a minute.' But I didn't know what he meant, and I didn't like the sound of it. A 'growler' was probably not at all a proper thing for a young lady to ride in; and I was determined to be considerate of the feelings of my relation. I saw ladies in hansoms, but I had never been in one at home, and they looked very tiltuppy. Also, they went altogether too fast, and as it was a slippery day the horses attached to them sat down and rested a great deal oftener than I thought I should like. And when the animals were not poor old creatures that were obliged to sit down in this precipitate way, they danced and pranced in a manner which did not inspire me with confidence. In America our cab-horses know themselves to be cab-horses, and behave accordingly—they have none of the national theories about equality whatever; but the London quadrupeds might be the greatest Democrats going from the airs they put on. And I saw no street-cars anywhere. So I decided upon the 'Ammersmith 'bus, and the porter pointed out the direction of Charing Cross.

It seems to me now that I was what you would call 'uncommonly' stupid about it, but I hadn't gone very far before I realised that I did not quite know what Charing Cross was. I had come, you see, from a city where the streets are mostly numbered, and run pretty much in rows. The more I thought about it, the less it seemed to mean anything. So I asked a large policeman— the largest and straightest policeman, with the reddest face I had ever seen: 'Mr. Officer,' I said, knowing your fondness for titles in this country, what is Charing Cross?'

He smiled very kindly. 'Wy, miss,' he said, 'there's Charing Cross Station, and there's Charing Cross 'Otel, and there's Charing Cross. Wot were you wanting pertickeler?'

'Charing Cross!' said I.

'There it lies, in front of you!' the policeman said, waving his arm so as to take in the whole of Trafalgar Square. 'It ain't possible for you to miss it,

Miss. And as three other people were waiting to ask him something else, I thought I ought not to occupy his attention any further. I kept straight on, in and out among the crowd, comparing it in my mind with a New York or Chicago crowd. I found a great many more kinds of people in it than there would be at home.

You are remarkably different in this country. We are a good deal the same. I was not at all prepared then to make a comparison of averages, but I noticed that life seemed to mean something more serious for most of the people I met than it does with us. Hardly anybody was laughing, and very few people were making unseemly haste about their business. There was no eagerness and no enthusiasm. Neither was there any hustling. In a crowd like that in Chicago everybody would have hustled, and nobody would have minded it.

'Where is Charing Cross?' I asked one of the flower-women sitting by the big iron entrances to the station. '*Right*'ere, miss, ware you be a-standin'! *Buy* a flower, miss? *Only* a penny! an' lovely they are! *Do* buy one, laidy!' It was dreadfully pathetic, the way she said it, and she had frightful holes in her shawl, and no hat or bonnet on. I had never seen a woman selling things out of doors with nothing on her head before, and it hurt me somehow. But I couldn't possibly have bought her flowers—they were too much like her. So I gave her a sixpence, and asked her where I could find an 'Ammersmith' bus. She thanked me so volubly that I couldn't possibly understand her, but I made out that if I stayed where I was an 'Ammersmith' bus would presently arrive. She went on asking me to buy flowers though, so I walked a little farther off. I waited a long time, and not a single 'bus appeared with 'Ammersmith on it. Finally, I asked another policeman. 'There!' he said, as one of the great lumbering concerns rolled up—'that's one of 'em now! You'll get it!' I didn't like to dispute with an officer of the law, but I had seen plenty of that particular red variety of 'bus go past, and to be quite certain I said: 'But isn't that a Hammersmith one?' The policeman looked quite cross. 'Well, isn't that what you're a-askin' for? 'Ammersmith an' 'Ammersmith—it's all the saime, dependin' on 'ow you pernounces it. Some people calls it 'Ammersmith, an' some people calls it '*Ammer*smith!' and he turned a broad and indignant back upon me. I flew for the 'bus, and the conductor, in a friendly way, helped me on by my elbow.

I did not think, before, that anything could wobble like an Atlantic steamer, but I experienced nothing more trying coming over than that Hammersmith 'bus. And there were no straps from the roof to hold on by—nothing but a very high and inconvenient handrail; and the vehicle seemed quite full of stout old gentlemen with white whiskers, who looked deeply annoyed when I upset their umbrellas and unintentionally plunged upon their feet. 'More room houtside, miss!' the conductor said—which I considered impertinent, thinking that he meant in the road. 'Is there any room on top?' I asked him, because I had walked on so many of the old gentlemen's feet that I felt uncomfortable about it. 'Yes, miss; that's wot I'm a-sayin'—lots o' room *hout*side!' So I took advantage of a lame man's getting off to mount the spiral staircase at the back of the'bus and take a seat on top. It is a pity, isn't it, that Noah didn't think of an outside spiral staircase like that to *his* ark. He might have accommodated so many more of the animals, providing them, of course, with oilskin covers to keep off the wet, as you do. But even coming from a bran new and irreverent country, where nobody thinks of consulting the Old Testament for models of public conveyances, anybody can see that in many respects you have improved immensely upon Noah.

It was lovely up there—exactly like coming on deck after being in a stuffy little cabin in the steamer—a good deal of motion, but lots of fresh air. I was a little nervous at first, but as nobody fell off the tops of any of the other 'buses, I concluded that it was not a thing you were expected to do, and presently forgot all about it looking at the people swarming below me. My position made me feel immeasurably superior—at such a swinging height above them all—and I found myself speculating about them and criticising them, as I never should have done walking. I had never ridden on the top of anything before; it gave me an entirely new revelation of my fellow-creatures—if your monarchical feelings will allow that expression from a Republican. I must say I liked it—looking down upon people who were travelling in the same direction as I was, only on a level below. I began to understand the agreeableness of class distinctions, and I wondered whether the arrangement of seats on the tops of the 'buses was not, probably, a material result of aristocratic prejudices.

Oh, I liked it through and through, that first ride on a London 'bus! To know just how I liked it, and why, and how and why we all like it from the other side of the Atlantic, you must be born and brought up, as most of us have been, in a city twenty-five or fifty years old, where the houses are all made of clean white or red brick, with clean green lawns and geranium beds and painted iron fences; where rows of nice new maple-trees are planted in the clean-shaved boulevards, and fresh-planed wooden sidewalks run straight for a mile or two at a time, and all the city blocks stand in their proper right angles—which are among our advantages, I have no doubt; but our advantages have a way of making your disadvantages more interesting.

Having been monarchists all your lives, however, you can't possibly understand what it is to have been brought up in fresh paint. I ought not to expect it of you. If you could, though, I should find it easier to tell you, according to my experience, why we are all so devoted to London.

There was the smell, to begin with. I write 'there was,' because I regret to say that during the past few months I have become accustomed to it, and for me that smell is done up in a past tense for ever; so that I can quite understand a Londoner not believing in it. The Hammersmith 'bus was in the Strand when I first became conscious of it, and I noticed afterwards that it was always more pronounced down there, in the heart of the City, than in Kensington, for instance. It was no special odour or collection of odours that could be distinguished—it was rather an abstract smell—and yet it gave a kind of solidity and nutriment to the air, and made you feel as if your lungs digested it. There was comfort and support and satisfaction in that smell, and I often vainly try to smell it again.

We find the irregularity of London so gratifying, too. The way the streets turn and twist and jostle each other, and lead up into nothing, and turn around and come back again, and assume *aliases*, and break out into circuses and stray into queer, dark courts, where small boys go round on one roller skate, or little green churchyards only a few yards from the cabs and the crowd, where there is nobody but the dead people, who have grown tired of it all.

'WHERE SMALL BOYS GO ROUND ON ONE ROLLER SKATE'

From the top of the Hammersmith 'bus, as it went through the Strand that morning, I saw funny little openings that made me long to get down and look into them; but I had my relation to think of, so I didn't.

Then there is the well-settled, well-founded look of everything, as if it had all come ages ago, and meant to stay for ever, and just go on the way it had before. We like that—the security and the permanence of it, which seems to be in some way connected with the big policemen, and the orderly crowd, and 'Keep to the Left' on the signboards, and the British coat of arms over so many of the shops. I thought that morning that those shops were probably the property of the Crown, but I was very soon corrected about that. At home I am afraid we fluctuate considerably, especially in connection with cyclones and railway interests—we are here to-day, and there is no telling where we shall be to-morrow. So the abiding kind of city gives us a comfortable feeling of confidence. It was not very long before even I, on the top of the Hammersmith 'bus, felt that I was riding an Institution, and no matter to what extent it wobbled it might be relied upon not to come down.

I don't know whether you will like our admiring you on account of your griminess, but we do. At home we are so monotonously clean, architecturally, that we can't make any aesthetic pretensions whatever. There is nothing artistic about white brick. It is clean and neat and sanitary, but you get tired of looking at it, especially when it is made up in patterns with red brick mixed in. And since you must be dirty, it may gratify you to know that you are very soothing to Transatlantic nerves suffering from patterns like that. But you are also misleading. 'I suppose,' I said to a workman in front of me as we entered Fleet Street, 'that is some old palace? Do you know the date of it?'

'No, miss,' he answered, 'that ain't no palace. Them's the new Law Courts, only built the last ten year!'

'The *new* Law Courts!' 'The Strand!' 'Fleet Street!' 'Ludgate Hill!' 'Cheapside!' and I was actually in those famous places, riding through them on a 'bus, part of their multitude. The very names on the street corners held fascination enough, and each of them gave me the separate little thrill of the altogether unexpected. I had unconsciously believed that all these names were part of the vanished past I had connected them with, forgetting that in London names endure. But I began to feel that I ought to be arriving. 'Conductor,' I said, as he passed, 'stop the 'bus, and let me get down at Half-Moon Street, Piccadilly.'

'We're goin' strait awai from it, miss; you get that red 'bus standin' over there—that'll taike you!'

So I went all the way back again, and on to my relation's, on the top of the red 'bus, not at all regretting my mistake. But it made it almost twelve o'clock when I rang the bell—Mrs. Portheris's bell—at the door of her house in Half-Moon Street, Piccadilly.

IV

'FROM THE OUTSIDE I DIDN'T THINK MUCH OF MRS. PORTHERIS'S HOUSE'

FROM the outside I didn't think much of Mrs. Portheris's house. It was very tall, and very plain, and very narrow, and quite expressionless, except that it wore a sort of dirty brown frown. Like its neighbours, it had a well in front of it, and steps leading down into the well, and an iron fence round the steps, and a brass bell-handle lettered 'Tradesmen.' Like its neighbours, too, it wore boxes of spotty black greenery on the window-sills—in fact, it was very like its neighbours, except that it had one or two solemn little black balconies that looked as if nobody ever sat in them running across the face of it, and a tall, shallow porch, with two or three extremely white stone steps before the front door. Half-Moon Street, to me, looked like a family of houses—a family differing in heights and complexions and the colour of its hair, but sharing all the characteristics of a family—of an old family. A person draws a great many conclusions from the outside of a house, and my conclusion from the outside of my relation's house was that she couldn't be very well off to be obliged to live in such a plain and gloomy locality, with 'Tradesmen' on the ground-floor; and I hoped they were not any noisy kind of tradesmen, such as shoemakers or carpenters, who would disturb her early in the morning. The clean-scrubbed stone steps reflected very favourably, I thought, upon Mrs. Portheris, and gave the house, in spite of its grimy, old-fashioned, cramped appearance, a look of respectability which redeemed it. But I did not see at any window, behind the spotty evergreens, the sweet, sad face of my relation, though there were a hand-organ and a monkey and a German band all operating within twenty yards of the house.

I rang the bell. The door opened a great deal more quickly than you might imagine from the time I am taking to tell about it, and I was confronted by my first surprise in London. It was a man—a neat, smooth, pale, round-faced man in livery, rather fat and very sad. It was also Mrs. Portheris's interior. This was very dark and very quiet, but what light there was fell richly, through a square, stained-glass window at the end of the hall, upon the red and blue of some old china above a door, and a collection of Indian spears, and a twisting old oak staircase that glowed with colour. Mrs. Portheris's exterior had prepared me for something different. I did not know then that in London everything is a matter of the inside—I had not seen a Duchess living crowded up to her ears with other people's windows. With us the outside counts so tremendously. An American duchess, if you can imagine such a person, would consider it only due to the fitness of things that she should have an imposing front yard, and at least room enough at the back for the clothes-lines. But this has nothing to do with Half-Moon Street.

'Does Mrs. Portheris live here?' I asked, thinking it was just possible she might have moved.

'Yes, miss,' said the footman, with a subdued note of interrogation.

I felt relieved. 'Is she—is she well?' I inquired.

'*Quite* well, miss,' he replied, with the note of interrogation a little more obvious.

'I should like to see her. Is she in?'

'I'll h'inquire, miss, 'n 'Oo shall I sai, miss?'

I thought I would prepare my relation gradually. 'A lady from Chicago,' said I.

'Very well, miss. Will you walk upstairs, miss?'

In America drawing-rooms are on the ground-floor. I thought he wanted to usher me into Mrs. Portheris's bedroom.

'No, sir,' I said; 'I'll wait here.' Then I thought of Mr. Mafferton, and of what he had said about saying 'sir' to people, and my sensations were awful. I have never done it once since.

The footman reappeared in a few minutes with a troubled and apologetic countenance. 'Mrs. Portheris says as she doesn't want anythink, miss! I told her as I didn't understand you were disposin' of anythink; but that was 'er message, miss.'

I couldn't help laughing—it was so very funny to think of my being taken for a lady-pedlar in the house of my relation. 'I'm very glad she's in,' I said. 'That is quite a mistake! Tell her it's Miss Mamie Wick, daughter of Colonel Joshua R. Wick, of Chicago; but if she's lying down, or anything, I can drop in again.'

He was away so long that I began to wonder if my relation suspected me of dynamite in any form, and he came back looking more anxious than ever. 'Mrs. Portheris says she's very sorry, miss, and will you please to walk up?' 'Certainly,' I said, 'but I hope I won't be disturbing her!'

And I walked up.

It was a big square room, with a big square piano in it, and long lace curtains, and two or three gilt-framed mirrors, and a great many old-fashioned ornaments under glass cases, and a tinkling glass chandelier in the middle. There were several oil-paintings on the walls—low-necked portraits and landscapes, principally dark-green and black and yellow, with cows, and quantities of lovely china. The furniture was red brocade, with spindly legs, and there was a tall palm in a pot, which had nothing to do with the rest of the room, by itself in a corner. I remembered these things afterwards.

'THEY SAT UP VERY NICELY INDEED'

At the time I noticed chiefly two young persons with the pinkest cheeks I ever saw, out of a picture-book, sitting near a window. They were dressed exactly alike, and their hair hung down their backs to their waists, although they must have been seventeen; and they sat up very nicely indeed on two of the red chairs, one occupied with worsted work, and the other apparently reading aloud to her, though she stopped when I came in. I have seen something since at Madame Tussaud's—but I daresay you have often noticed it yourself. And standing in the middle of the room, with her hand on a centre-table, was Mrs. Portheris.

My first impression was that she had been standing there for the last hour in that immovable way, with exactly that remarkable expression; and it struck me that she could go on standing for the next without altering it, quite comfortably—she seemed to be so solidly placed there, with her hand upon the table. Though I wouldn't call Mrs. Portheris stout, she was massive—rather, of an impressive build. Her skirt fell in a commanding way from her waist, though it hitched up a little in front, which spoiled the effect. She had broad square shoulders, and a lace collar, and a cap with pink ribbons in it, and grey hair smooth on each side of her face, and large well-cut features, and the expression I spoke of. I've seen the expression since among the Egyptian antiquities in the British Museum, but I am unable to describe it. 'Armed neutrality' is the only phrase that occurs to me in connection with it, and that by no means does it justice. For there was curiosity in it, as well as hostility and reserve—but I won't try. And she kept her hand—it was her right hand—upon the table.

'Miss *Wick*' she said, bowing, and dwelling upon the name with strong doubt. 'I believe I have a connection of that name in America. Is your father's name Joshua *Peter*?'

'Yes, Mrs. Portheris,' I replied; 'and he says he is your nephew. I've just come. How do you do?' I said this because it was the only thing the situation seemed to warrant me saying.

'Oh, I am quite in my usual health, thank you! My nephew by marriage—a former marriage—a very distant connection.'

'Three thousand five hundred miles,' said I; 'he lives in Chicago. You have never been over to see us, Mrs. Portheris. At this point I walked across to one of the spindly red chairs and sat down. I thought then that she had forgotten to ask me; but even now, when I know she hadn't, I am not at all sorry I sat down. I find it is possible to stand up too much in this country.

'THE OLD LADY GATHERED HERSELF UP AND LOOKED AT ME'

The old lady gathered herself up and looked at me. 'Where are your father and mother?' she said.

'In Chicago, Mrs. Portheris. All very well, thank you! I had a cable from them this morning, before I left the hotel. Kind regards to you.'

Mrs. Portheris looked at me in absolute silence. Then she deliberately arranged her back draperies and sat down too—not in any amiable way, but as if the situation must be faced.

'Margaret and Isabel,' she said to the two young pink persons, 'go to your rooms, dears!' And she waited till the damsels, each with a little shy smile and blush, gathered up their effects and went, before she continued the conversation. As they left the room I observed that they wore short dresses, buttoned down the back. It began to grow very interesting to me, after the first shock of finding this kind of relation was over. I found myself waiting for what was to come next with the deepest interest. In America we are very fond of types—perhaps because we have so few among ourselves—and it seemed to me, as I sat there on Mrs. Portheris's spindly red chair, that I had come into violent contact with a type of the most valuable and pronounced description. Privately I resolved to stay as long as I could, and lose no opportunity of observing it. And my first observation was that Mrs. Portheris's expression was changing—losing its neutrality and beginning to radiate active opposition and stern criticism, with an uncompromising sense of duty twisted in at the corners of the mouth. There was no agitation whatever, and I thought with an inward smile of my relation's nerves.

'Then I suppose,' said Mrs. Portheris—the supposition being of the vaguest possible importance—'that you are with a party of Americans. It seems to be an American idea to go about in hordes. I never could understand it—to me it would be most obnoxious. How many are there of you?'

'One, Mrs. Portheris—and I'm the one. Poppa and momma had set their hearts on coming. Poppa thought of getting up an Anglo-American Soda Trust, and momma wanted particularly to make your acquaintance—your various Christmas cards have given us all such a charming idea of you—but at the last minute something interfered with their plans and they had to give it up. They told me to tell you how sorry they were.'

'Something interfered with their plans! But nothing interfered with *your* plans!'

'Oh, no; it was some political business of poppa's—nothing to keep me!'

'Then do I actually understand that your parents, of their *own free will*, permitted you to cross the Atlantic *alone?*'

'I hope you do, Mrs. Portheris; but if it's not quite clear to you, I don't mind explaining it again.'

'Upon my word! And you are at an hotel—which hotel?' When I told Mrs. Portheris the Métropole, her indignation mounted to her cap, and one of the pink ribbons shook violently.

'It is very American!' she said; and I felt that Mrs. Portheris could rise to no more forcible a climax of disapproval.

But I did not mind Mrs. Portheris's disapproval; in fact, according to my classification of her, I should have been disappointed if she had not disapproved—it would have been out of character. So I only smiled as sweetly as I could, and said, 'So am I.'

'Is it not very expensive?' There was a note of angry wonder as well as horror in this.

'I don't know, Mrs. Portheris. It's very comfortable.' 'I never heard of such a thing in my life!' said Mrs. Portheris. 'It's—it's outrageous! It's—it's not customary!

I call it criminal lenience on the part of my nephew to allow it, he must have taken leave of his senses!'

'Don't say anything nasty about poppa, Mrs. Portheris,' I remarked; and she paused.

'As to your mother——'

'Momma is a lady of great intelligence and advanced views,' I interrupted, 'though she isn't very strong. And she is very well acquainted with me.'

'Advanced views are your ruin in America! May I ask how you found your way here?'

'On a 'bus, Mrs. Portheris—the red Hammersmith kind. On two 'buses, rather, because I took the wrong one first, and went miles straight away from here; but I didn't mind it—I liked it.'

'*In* an omnibus I suppose you mean. You couldn't very well be *on* it, unless you went on the top!' And Mrs. Portheris smiled rather derisively.

'I did; I went on the top,' I returned calmly. 'And it was lovely.'

Mrs. Portheris very nearly lost her self-control in her effort to grasp this enormity. Her cap bristled again, and the muscles round her mouth twitched quite perceptibly.

'Careering all over London on the top of an omnibus!' she ejaculated. 'Looking for my house! And in that frock!' I felt about ten when she talked about my 'frock.' 'Couldn't you *feel* that you were altogether too smart for such a position?'

'No, indeed, Mrs. Portheris!' I replied, unacquainted with the idiom. 'When I got down off the first omnibus in Cheapside I felt as if I hadn't been half smart enough!'

She did not notice my misunderstanding. By the time I had finished my sentence she was rapping the table with suppressed excitement.

'Miss Wick!' she said—and I had expected her to call me Mamie, and say I was the image of poppa!—'you are the daughter of my nephew—which can hardly be called a connection at all—but on that account I will give you a piece of advice. The top of an omnibus is not a proper place for you—I might say, for any connection of mine, however distant! I would not feel that I was doing my duty toward my nephew's daughter if I did not tell you that you *must not* go there! Don't on any account do it again! It is a thing people *never* do!'

'Do they upset?' I asked.

'They might. But apart from that, I must ask you, on personal—on family grounds—*always* to go inside. In Chicago you may go outside as much as you like, but in London——'

'Oh, no!' I interrupted, 'I wouldn't for the world—in Chicago!' which Mrs. Portheris didn't seem to understand.

I had stayed dauntlessly for half an hour—I was so much interested in Mrs. Portheris—and I began to feel my ability to prolong the interview growing weaker. I was sorry—I would have given anything to have heard her views upon higher education and female suffrage, and the Future State and the Irish Question; but it seemed impossible to get her thoughts away from the appalling Impropriety which I, on her spindly red chair, represented I couldn't blame her for that—I suppose no impropriety bigger than a spider had ever got into her drawing-room before. So I got up to go. Mrs. Portheris also rose, with majesty. I think she wanted to show me what, if I had been properly brought up, I might have expected reasonably to develop into. She stood in the midst of her red brocaded furniture, with her hands folded, a model of what bringing up can do if it is unflinchingly persevered in, and all the mirrors reflected the ideal she presented. I felt, beside her, as if I had never been brought up at all.

'Have you any friends in London?' she asked, with a very weak solution of curiosity in her tone, giving me her hand to facilitate my going, and immediately ringing the bell.

'I think not,' I said with, decision.

'But you will not continue to stay at the Métropole! I *beg* that you will not remain another *day* at the Métropole! It is not usual for young ladies to stay at hotels. You must go to some place where only ladies are received, and as soon as you are settled in one communicate at once with the rector of the parish—alone as you are, that is *quite* a necessary step, lights and fires will probably be extra.'

'I thought,' said I, 'of going to the Lady Guides' Association—we have heard of it in Chicago through some friends, who went round every day for three weeks with lady-guides, and found it simply fascinating—and asking them to get me a private family to board with. I particularly wished to see what a private family is like in England.'

Mrs. Portheris frowned. 'I could never bring myself to approve of lady-guides,' she said. 'There is something in the idea that is altogether too—American.' I saw that the conversation was likely to grow personal again, so I said: 'Well, good-bye, Mrs. Portheris!' and was just going, when 'Stop!' said my relation, 'there is Miss Purkiss.'

'Is there?' said I.

'Certainly—the very thing! Miss Purkiss is a very old friend of mine, in reduced circumstances. I've known her thirty-five years. She is an excellent woman, with the most trustworthy views upon all matters. In so far as our widely different social positions have permitted, Miss Purkiss and I have been on terms, I may say, of sisterly intimacy since before you were born. She has no occupation now, having lost her position as secretary to the Home for Incurable Household Pets through ill-health, and a very limited income. She lives in an excessively modest way in Upper Baker Street—very convenient to both the omnibuses and Underground—and if you cast in your lot with hers while you are in England, Miss Wick'—here Mrs. Portheris grew almost demonstrative—'you need never go out alone. I need not say that she is a lady, but her circumstances will probably necessitate her asking you rather more than the usual rate for board and lodging, in compensation for her chaperonage and companionship. All I can say is, that both will be very thorough. I will give you Miss Purkiss's address at once, and if you drive there immediately you will be sure to find her in. John, call a hansom!' And Mrs. Portheris went to her writing-table and wrote the address.

'There!' she said, folding it up and giving it to me. 'By all means try to arrange with Miss Purkiss, and she, being a friend of my own, some afternoon, perhaps—I must think about it—I may ask her to bring you to tea! Good-bye!'

As the door closed behind me I heard Mrs. Portheris's voice on the landing. 'Margaret and Isabel,' it said, 'you may come down now!'

'Ware to, miss?' said the driver.

'Hôtel Métropole,' said I. And as we turned into Piccadilly a little flutter of torn white paper went back on the wind to Mrs. Portheris. It was Miss Purkiss's address.

'SPENT HALF AN HOUR IN THE MIDST OF MY TRUNKS'

After lunch I made careful notes of Mrs. Portheris, and then spent half an hour in the midst of my trunks, looking in the 'Board and Lodging' column of the 'Morning Post' for accommodation which promised to differ as radically as possible from Miss Purkiss's.

V

MY principal idea was to get away as soon as possible from the Métropole. So long as I was located there I was within the grasp of my relation; and as soon as she found out my insubordination in the matter of her advice, I had no doubt whatever that my relation would appear, with Miss Purkiss, all in rusty black, behind her—a contingency I wished to avoid. Miss Purkiss, I reflected, would probably be another type, and types were interesting, but not to live with—my relation had convinced me of that. And as to Mrs. Portheris herself, while I had certainly enjoyed what I had been privileged to see of her, her society was a luxury regarding which I felt that I could exercise considerable self-denial. I did not really contemplate being forced into Miss Purkiss and Upper Baker Street by Mrs. Portheris against my will, not for a moment; but I was afraid the situation would be presented on philanthropic grounds, which would be disagreeable. Miss Purkiss as a terror I felt equal to, but Miss Purkiss as an object of charity might cow me. And Miss Purkiss in any staying capacity was not, I felt, what I came to Great Britain to experience. So I studied the columns of the 'Morning Post' diligently for a haven of refuge from Miss Purkiss.

I found it difficult to make a selection, the havens were so very different, and all so superior. I believe you talk about the originality of American advertising. I never in my life saw a newspaper page to compare in either imagination or vocabulary with the one I scanned that day at the Métropole. It seemed that I could be taken all over London, at prices varying from one 'g.' to three 'gs.' per week, although the surprising cheapness of this did not strike me until I had laboriously calculated in dollars and cents the exact value of a 'g.' I know now that it is a term of English currency exclusively employed in Bond Street, Piccadilly, Regent and Oxford Streets—they never give you a price there in any other. And the phrases descriptive of the various homes which were awaiting me were so beautiful. 'Excellent meat breakfast,' 'a liberal and charmingly-refined home,' 'a mother's devoted supervision,' 'fresh young society,' 'fashionably situated and elegantly furnished,' 'just vacated by a clergyman,' 'foreign languages understood'—which would doubtless include American—'a lofty standard of culture in this establishment.' I wondered if they kept it under glass. I was struck with the number of people who appeared in print with 'offerings' of a domiciliary nature. 'A widow lady of cheerful temperament and artistic tastes offers——' 'The daughter of a late Civil Servant with a larger house than she requires offers——' This must have been a reference put in to excite sympathy, otherwise, what was the use of advertising the gentleman after he was dead? Even from the sympathetic point of view, I think it was a mistake, for who would care to go and settle in a house the minute the crape was off the door? Nobody.

Not only original advertisements of the kind I was looking for, but original advertisements of kinds I wasn't looking for, appealed to my interest and took up my time that afternoon.

'Would any one feel disposed to lend an actress five pounds?

'Temporary home wanted, with a family of quiet habits, in a healthful neighbourhood, who can give best references, for a Persian cat.' 'An elderly country rector and his wife, in town for a month's holiday, would be glad of a little pleasant society.'

'A young subaltern, of excellent family, in unfortunate circumstances, implores the loan of a hundred pounds to save him from ruin. Address, care of his solicitors.' 'A young gentleman, handsome, an orphan, of good education and agreeable address, wishes to meet with elderly couple with means (inherited) who would adopt him. Would make himself pleasant in the house. Church of England preferred, but no serious objection to Nonconformists.'

We have nothing like this in America. It was a revelation to me—a most private and intimate revelation of a social body that I had always been told no outsider could look into without the very best introductions. Of course, there was the veil of 'A. B.' and 'Lurline,' and the solicitors' address, but that seemed as thin and easily torn as the 'Morning Post,' and much more transparent, showing all the struggling mass, with its hands outstretched, on the other side. And yet I have heard English people say how 'personal' our newspapers are!

My choice was narrowed considerably by so many of the addresses being other places than London, which I thought very peculiar in a London newspaper. Having come to see London, I did not want to live in Putney, or Brixton, or Chelsea, or Maida Vale. I supposed vaguely that there must be cathedrals or Roman remains, or attractions of some sort, in these places, or they would not be advertised in London; but for the time being, at any rate, I intended to content myself with the capital. So I picked out two or three places near the British Museum—I should be sure, I thought, to want to spend a great deal of time there—and went to see about them.

They were as much the same as the advertisements were different, especially from the outside. From the outside they were exactly alike—so much so that I felt, after I had seen them all, that if another boarder in the same row chose to approach me on any occasion, and say that she was me, I should be entirely unable to contradict her. This in itself was prejudicial. In America, if there is one thing we are particular about, it is our identity. Without our identities we are in a manner nowhere. I did not feel disposed to run the risk of losing mine the minute I arrived in England, especially as I knew that it is a thing

Americans who stay here for any length of time are extremely apt to do. Nevertheless, I rang the three door-bells I left the Métropole with the intention of ringing; and there were some minor differences inside, although my pen insists upon recording the similarities instead. I spent the same length of time upon the doorstep, for instance, before the same tumbled and apologetic-looking servant girl appeared, wiping her hands upon her apron, and let me into the same little dark hall, with the same interminable stairs twisting over themselves out of it, and the smell of the same dinner accompanying us all the way up. To be entirely just, it was a wholesome dinner, but there was so much of it in the air that I very soon felt as if I was dining unwarrantably, and ought to pay for it. In every case the stair-carpet went up two flights, and after that there was oilcloth, rather forgetful as to its original pattern, and much frayed as to its edges—and after that, nothing. Always pails and brushes on the landings—what there is about pails and brushes that should make them such a distinctive feature of boarding-house landings I don't know, but they are. Not a single elevator in all three. I asked the servant-girl in the first place, about half-way up the fourth flight, if there was no elevator? 'No, indeed, miss,' she said: 'I wishes there was! But them's things you won't find but very seldom 'ere. We've 'ad American ladies 'ere before, and they allus asks for 'em, but they soon finds out they ain't to be 'ad, miss.'

Now, how did she know I was an 'American lady'? I didn't really mind about the elevator, but this I found annoying, in spite of my desire to preserve my identity. In the course of conversation with this young woman, I discovered that it was not my own possibly prospective dinner that I smelt on the stairs. I asked about the hour for meals. 'Aou, we never gives meals, miss!' she said. 'It's only them boardin' 'ouses as gives meals in! Mrs. Jones, she only lets apartments. But there's a very nice restirong in Tottinim Court Road, quite convenient, an' your breakfast, miss, you could 'ave cooked 'ere, but, of course, it would be hextra, miss.'

Then I remembered all I had read about people in London living in 'lodgings,' and having their tea and sugar and butter and eggs consumed unrighteously by the landlady, who was always represented as a buxom person in calico, with a smut on her face, and her arms akimbo, and an awful hypocrite. For a minute I thought of trying it, for the novelty of the experience, but the loneliness of it made me abandon the idea. I could not possibly content myself with the society of a coal-scuttle and two candlesticks, and the alternative of going round sightseeing by myself. Nor could I in the least tell whether Mrs. Jones was agreeable, or whether I could expect her to come up and visit with me sometimes in the evenings; besides, if she always wore smuts and had her arms akimbo, I shouldn't care about asking her. In America a landlady might as likely as not be a member of a Browning Society, and give 'evenings,' but that kind of landlady seems indigenous to the United States. And after Mrs. Portheris, I felt that I required the companionship of something human.

In the other two places I saw the landladies themselves in their respective drawing-rooms on the second floor. One of the drawing-rooms was 'draped' in a way that was quite painfully aesthetic, considering the paucity of the draperies. The flower-pots were draped, and the lamps; there were draperies round the piano-legs, and round the clock; and where there were not draperies there were bows, all of the same scanty description. The only thing that had not made an effort to clothe itself in the room was the poker, and by contrast it looked very nude. There were some Japanese ideas around the room, principally a paper umbrella; and a big painted palm-leaf fan from India made an incident in one corner. I thought, even before I saw the landlady, that it would be necessary to live up to a high standard of starvation in that house, and she confirmed the impression. She was a Miss Hippy, a short, stoutish person, with very smooth hair, thin lips, and a nose like an angle of the Pyramids, preternaturally neat in her appearance, with a long gold watch-chain round her neck. She came into the room in a way that expressed reduced circumstances and a protest against being obliged to do it. I feel that the particular variety of smile she gave me with her 'Good morning!'—although it was after 4 P.M.—was one she kept for the use of boarders only, and her whole manner was an interrogation. When she said, 'Is it for yourself?' in answer to my question about rooms, I felt that I was undergoing a cross-examination, the result of which Miss Hippy was mentally tabulating.

'We have a few rooms,' said Miss Hippy, 'certainly.' Then she cast her eyes upon the floor, and twisted her fingers up in her watch-chain, as if in doubt. 'Shall you be long in London?'

I said I couldn't tell exactly.

'Have you—are you a professional of any kind?' inquired Miss Hippy. 'Not that I object to professional ladies—they are often very pleasant. Madame Solfreno resided here for several weeks while she was retrenching; but Madame Solfreno was, of course, more or less an exceptional woman. She did not care—at least, while she was retrenching—for the society of other professionals, and she said that was the great advantage of my house—none of them ever would come here. Still, as I say, I have no personal objection to professionals. In fact, we have had head-ladies here; and real ladies, I must say, I have generally found them. Although hands, of course, I would not take!'

I said I was not a professional.

'Oh!' said Miss Hippy, pitiably baffled. 'Then, perhaps, you are not a—a young lady. That is, of course, one can see you are that; but you are—you are married, perhaps?'

'I am not married, madame,' I said. 'Have you any rooms to let?'

Miss Hippy rose, ponderingly. 'I might as well show you what we have,' she said.

'I think,' I replied, 'that you might as well. Otherwise I will not detain you any longer.' At which, curiously enough, all hesitation vanished from Miss Hippy's manner, and she showed me all her rooms, and expatiated upon all their advantages with a single eye to persuading me to occupy one of them. So comprehensively voluble was she, indeed, and so impenetrably did she fill up the door with her broad person when we came down again, that I found no loophole of escape anywhere, and was obliged to descend to equivocal measures. 'Have you any rooms, Miss Hippy,' I inquired, 'on the ground floor?'

'That,' returned Miss Hippy, as if I had put her the only possible question that she was not prepared for, 'I have not. A gentleman from the West Indies'—Miss Hippy went on impressively—'hardly ever without inflammatory rheumatism, which you will admit makes stairs an impossibility for him, occupies my only ground-floor bedroom—just off the dining-room!'

'That is unfortunate,' I said, 'since I think in this house I would prefer a room on the ground-floor. But if I decide to take one of the others I will let you know, Miss Hippy.'

Miss Hippy's countenance fell, changed, and again became expressive of doubt—this time offensively.

'I've not asked for any references,' though, of course, it is my custom——'

'You will receive references,' I interrupted, 'as soon as you require them. Good afternoon!' We were standing in the hall, and Miss Hippy, from force of circumstances, was obliged to unfasten the door; but I did not hear from her, as I passed out into the street, any responsive 'Good afternoon!'

My third experience was quite antipodal to Miss Hippy. Her parlour was Japanesy, too, in places, but it was mostly chipped; and it had a great many rather soiled fat cushions in it, quite a perceptible odour of beer and tobacco, and a pair of gentleman's worked slippers under the sofa. The atmosphere was relaxing after Miss Hippy, and suggested liberality of all sorts; but the slippers, to say nothing of the odours, which might have floated in from other regions, made it impossible. I waited for the lady of the house a conscious hypocrite.

"I WAITED FOR THE LADY OF THE HOUSE A CONSCIOUS HYPOCRITE"

She came in at last voluminously, rather out of breath, but with great warmth of manner. 'Do sit down!' she said.

'Now, it does seem strange! Only las' night, at the table, we were sayin' how much we wanted one more lady boarder! You see, I've got four young gentlemen in the City here, and of us ladies there's just four, so we sometimes get up a little dance amongst ourselves in the evenin's. It amuses the young people, and much better wear out carpets than pay doctors' bills, say I. Now, I generally play, an' that leaves only three ladies for the four gentlemen, you see! Now, isn't it a curious coincidence,' she said, leaning forward with a broad and confident smile, 'that you should have come in to-day, just after we were sayin' how nice it would be if there were enough to get up the Lancers!'

I bowed my acknowledgments.

'You want a room for yourself, I suppose,' my hostess went on, cheerfully. 'My top flat, I'm sorry to say, is every bit taken. There isn't an inch of room up there; but I've got a beautiful little apartment on the ground-floor you could use as a bed-sittin' room, lookin' out on what green grass we have. I'll show it to you!'—and she led me across the hall to a dismantled cupboard, the door of which she threw open. 'That,' she said, 'you could have for twenty-five shillin's a week. Of course, it is small, but then—so is the price!' and she smiled the cheerful, accustomed smile that went with the joke. 'I've another up here,' she said, leading the way to the first landing, 'rather bigger—thirty shillin's. You see, they're both bein' turned out at present, so it's rather unfavourable!'—and the lady drew in the deep breath she had lost going up the stairs.

I could think of only one thing to say: 'I believe you said your top flat was all taken,' I remarked amiably. She was such a good-natured soul, I couldn't bear to say anything that would hurt her feelings. 'That is unfortunate. I particularly wanted a room in a top flat. But if I decide on one of these others I'll let you know!' There were two fibs, and diametrically opposed fibs, within half an hour, and I know it's excessively wrong to fib; but, under the circumstances, what could you say?

'Do, miss. And, though I wouldn't for the world persuade you, I certainly hope you will, for I'm sure you'd make a very pleasant addition to our party. I'll just let you out myself.' And she did.

VI

I DROVE straight back to the Métropole, very thankful indeed that that was evidently the thing to do next. If there had been no evident thing to do next, I was so depressed in my mind that I think I would have taken a ticket to Liverpool that night, and my passage to New York on the first steamer that was leaving. I won't say what I did in the cab, but I spoilt a perfectly new veil doing it. London seemed dingy and noisy, and puzzling and unattractive, and always going to rain. I thought of our bright clear air in Chicago, and our nice clean houses, and our street-cars, and our soda-water fountains, and poppa and momma, and always knowing everybody and what to do under every circumstance; and all the way to the Métropole I loved Chicago and I hated London. But there *was* the Métropole, big and solid and luxurious, and a fact I understood; and there was the nice respectful housemaid on my corridor—it would be impossible to convince you how different servants are with us—and a delightful little fire in my room, and a tin pitcher of hot water smoking in the basin, and a sort of air of being personally looked after that was very comforting to my nerves. While I was getting ready for dinner I analysed my state of mind, and blamed myself severely, for I found that I could not justify one of the disagreeable things I had been thinking in any philosophical way. I had simply allowed the day's experiences, capped by my relation in the morning, to overcome my entire nerve-system, which was childish and unreasonable. I wished then, and often since, that Providence had given us a more useful kind of nerve-system on our side of the Atlantic—something constructed solidly, on the British plan; and just as I was wishing that there came a rap. A rap has comparatively no significance until it comes at your bedroom door when you are alone in a big hotel two thousand five hundred miles from home. Then it means something. This one meant two cards on a salver and a message. One of the cards read: '*Mrs. Cummers Portheris,*' with '*Miss Purkiss*' written under it in pencil; the other, '*Mr. Charles Mafferton,*' with '49, *Hertford Street. Mayfair,*' in one corner, and '*The Isthmian Club*' in the other.

'Is she there now?' I asked the servant in acute suspense.

'No, miss. The ladies, they called about 'alf-past three, and we was to say that one lady was to be 'ere again to-morrow mornin' at ten, miss. The gentleman, he didn't leave no message.'

Then my heart beat again, and joyfully, for I knew that I had missed my relation and Miss Purkiss, and that the way of escape was still open to me, although ten o'clock in the morning was rather early to be obliged to go out. I must say I thought it extremely foolish of Miss Purkiss to have mentioned the hour—it was like a fox making an appointment with a rabbit, a highly improbable thing for the rabbit to keep. And I went downstairs feeling quite amused and happy, and determined to stay amused and happy. My unexpected reward for this came at dinner, when I discovered my neighbours to be two delightful ladies from St. Paul, Minn., with whom I conversed sociably there, and later in the drawing-room. They had known Dr. Oliver Wendell Holmes; but what to my eyes gave them an added charm was their amiable readiness to know me. I was made to promise that I would send them my address when I was settled, and to this day I suffer from unquieted pangs of conscience because I failed to keep my word.

By ten o'clock next morning I was in Cockspur Street, Pall Mall, looking for the 'Lady Guides' Association.' The name in white letters on the window struck me oddly when I found it. The idea, the institution it expressed, seemed so grotesquely of to-day in the heart of old London, where almost everything you see talks of orthodoxy and the approval of the centuries. It had the impertinence that a new building has going up among your smoky old piles of brick and mortar. You will understand my natural sympathy with it. The minute I went in I felt at home.

There were several little desks in several little adjoining compartments, with little muslin curtains in front of them, and ladies and ink-bottles inside, like a row of shrouded canary-cages. Two or three more ladies, without their things on, were running round outside, and several others, with their things on, were being attended to. I saw only one little man, who was always getting out of the ladies' way, and didn't seem properly to belong there. There was no label attached, so I couldn't tell what use they made of him, but I should like to have known.

The desks were all lettered plainly—one 'Lady Guides,' the next 'Tickets for the Theatre,' and so on; but, of course, I went to the first one to inquire, without taking any notice of that—people always do. I think, perhaps, the lady was more polite in referring me to the proper one than the man would have been. She smiled, and bowed encouragingly as she did it, and explained particularly, 'the lady with the eyeglasses and her hair done up high—do you see?' I saw, and went to the right lady. She smiled too, in a real winning way, looking up from her entrybook, and leaning forward to hear what I had to say. Then she came into my confidence, as it were, at once. 'What you want,' she said, 'is a boarding-house or private hotel. We have all the best private hotels on our books, but in your case, being alone, what I should advise would be a thoroughly well-recommended, first-class boarding-house.'

I said something about a private family—'Or a private family,' added the lady, acquiescently. 'Now, we can give you whichever you prefer. Suppose,' she said, with the kindly interested counsel of good-fellowship, dropping her voice a little, 'I write you out several addresses *of both kinds*, then you can just see for yourself'—and the lady looked at me over her eyeglasses most agreeably.

'Why, yes!' I said. 'I think that's a very good idea!'

'Well now, just wait a minute!' the lady said, turning over the pages of another big book. 'There's a great deal, as you probably know, in *locality* in London. We must try and get you something in a nice locality. Piccadilly, for instance, is a very favourite locality—I think we have something in Half-Moon Street—'

'Gracious!' I said. 'No! not Half-Moon Street, please. I—I've been there. I don't like that locality!'

'Really!' said the lady, with surprise. 'Well, you wouldn't believe what the rents are in Half-Moon Street! But we can easily give you something else—the other side of the Park, perhaps!'

'Yes.' I said, earnestly. 'Quite the other side, if you please!'

'Well,' returned the lady, abstractedly running her finger down the page, 'there's Mrs. Pragge, in Holland Park Gardens—have you any objection to children?—and Miss Camblewell, in Lancaster Gate, *very* clean and nice. I think we'll put *them* down. And then two or three private ones—excuse me *one* minute. There! I think among those,' with sudden gravity, 'you ought to find something suitable at from two to three-and-a-half guineas per week; but if you do not, be sure to come in again. We always like to give our clients satisfaction.' The lady smiled again in that pardonable, endearing way; and I was so pleased with her, and with myself, and with the situation, and felt such warm comfort as the result of the interview, that I wanted badly to shake hands with her when I said Good-morning. But she was so engaged that I couldn't, and had to content myself with only saying it very cordially. As I turned to go I saw a slightly blank expression come over her face, and she coughed with some embarrassment, leaning forward as if to speak to me again. But I was too near the door, so one of the ladies who were running about detained me apologetically.

'There is a—a charge,' she said, 'of two-and-sixpence. You did not know.' So I went back uncomfortably and paid. 'Thanks, yes!' said the lady in the cage. '*Two-and-six!* No, that is two shillings, a florin, you see—and that is four—it's half-a-crown we want, isn't it?' very amiably, considering all the trouble I was giving her. 'Perhaps you are not very well accustomed to our English currency yet,' as I finally counted out one shilling, two sixpences, a threepence, and six halfpennies. If there *is* a thing in this country that needs reforming more than the House of Lords—but there, it isn't to be supposed that you would like my telling you about it. At all events, I managed in the end to pay my very proper fee to the Lady Guides' Association, and I sincerely hope that any of its members who may happen to read this chapter will believe that I never endeavoured to evade it. The slight awkwardness of the mistake turned out rather pleasantly for me, because it led me into further conversation with the lady behind the eyeglasses, in which she asked me whether I wouldn't like to look over their establishment. I said Yes, indeed; and one of the outside ladies, a very capable-looking little person, with a round face and short, curly hair, was told off to take me upstairs. I hadn't been so interested for a long time. There was the club-room, where ladies belonging to the Association could meet or make appointments with other people, or write letters or read the papers, and the restaurant, where they could get anything they wanted to eat. I am telling you all this because I've met numbers of people in London who only know enough about the Lady Guides' Association to smile when it is mentioned, and to say, 'Did you go *there?*' in a tone of great amusement, which, considering it is one of your own institutions, strikes me as curious. And it is such an original, personal, homelike institution, like a little chirping busy nest between the eaves of the great unconcerned City offices and warehouses, that it is interesting to know more about than that, I think. The capable little lady seemed quite proud of it as she ushered me from one room into the next, and especially of the bedrooms, which were divided from one another by pretty chintz hangings, and where at least four ladies, 'arriving strange from the country, and elsewhere,' could be tucked away for the night. That idea struck me as perfectly sweet, and I wished very sincerely I had known of it before. It seemed to offer so many more advantages than the Métropole. Of course, I asked any number of questions about the scope and working of the Association, and the little lady answered them all with great fluency. It was nice to hear of such extended usefulness—how the Lady Guides engage governesses, or servants, or seats at the theatre, and provide dinners and entertainments, and clothes to wear at them, and suitable manners; and take care of children by the day—I do not remember whether the little lady said they undertook to bring them up—and furnish eyes and understanding, certified, to all visitors in London, at 'a fixed tariff'—all except gentlemen unaccompanied by their families. 'Such clients,' the little lady said, with a shade of sadness, I fancied, that there should be any limitation to the benevolence of the Association, 'the Lady Guide is compelled to decline. It is a great pity—we have so many gentleman-applicants, and there would be, of course, no necessity for sending *young* lady-guides out with them—we have plenty of elderly ones, widows and so on; but'—and here the little lady grew confidentially deprecating—'it is thought best not to. You see, it would get into the papers, and the papers might chaff, and, of course, in our position we can't afford to be made ridiculous. But it is a great pity!'—and the little lady sighed again. I said I thought it was, and asked if any special case had been made of any special entreaty. 'One,' she admitted, in a justifying tone. 'A gentleman from Japan. He told us he never would have come to England if he had not heard of our Association, being a perfect stranger, without a friend in the place.'

'And unacquainted with English prejudices,' I put in.

'Quite so. And what could we do?'

'What did you do?' I inquired.

'We sent *two!*' responded the little lady, triumphing once more over the situation. 'Nobody could say a thing to that. And he *was* such a pleasant little man, and thanked us so cordially.'

' " WE SENT TWO " '

'Did you find him intelligent?' I asked.

'Very.' But the little lady's manner was growing rather fidgety, and it occurred to me that perhaps I was taking more information than I was entitled to for two-and-six. So I went reluctantly downstairs, wishing there was something else that the lady-guides could do for me. A little black-eyed woman down there was giving some very businesslike orders. 'Half a day's shopping? I should say send Miss Stuart Saville. And tell her to be very particular about her accounts. Has Mrs. Mason got that private ward yet?'

'That,' said my little cicerone, in a subdued tone, 'is our manageress. She planned the whole thing. Wonderful head!' 'Is that so?' I remarked. 'I should like to congratulate her.'

'I'm afraid there isn't time,' she returned, looking flurried; 'and the manageress doesn't approve of anybody wasting it. Will you write your name in our visitors' book?'

'With pleasure,' I said; 'and I'll come again whenever I feel that I want anything.' And I wrote my name—badly, of course, as people always do in visitors' books, but with the lively satisfaction people always experience in writing their names—why, I've never been able to discover. I passed the manageress on my way out. She was confronting a pair of ladies, an old and a young one, in black, who leaned on their parasols with an air of amiable indecision, and falteringly addressed her: 'I had a day and a half last week,' one of them said, rather weakly; 'is there?—do you want me for anything this——?'

The manageress looked at her with some impatience. 'If I want you I'll send for you, Miss Gypsum,' she said. The door closed upon me at that moment, so I don't know how Miss Gypsum got away.

As for me, I walked through Cockspur Street and through Waterloo Place, and so into Piccadilly, reflecting upon Mrs. Pragge, and Miss Camblewell, and all their uncertainties. Standing in the lee of a large policeman on one of your valuable iron refuges in the middle of the street, a flounced black-and-white parasol suddenly shut down almost in my face. The lady belonging to it leaned over her carriage and said: 'How d'ye do, Miss——? Dear me, how stupid I am about names! Miss Chicago-young-lady-who-ran-away-without-getting-my-address? Now I've found you, just pop in——'

'I must ask you to drive on, madam,' the policeman said.

'As soon as this young lady has popped in. There! Now, my dear, what did the relation say? I've been longing to know.'

And before I realised another thing I was rolling up Regent Street statefully in the carriage of Mrs. Torquilin.

VII

"I CAN DROP YOU ANYWHERE YOU LIKE."

ARE you going there now?' Mrs. Torquilin went on. 'Because I'm only out for an airing, I can drop you anywhere you like.' 'Oh, by no means, thank you, Mrs. Torquilin,' I said; 'I've been there already.'

Mrs. Torquilin looked at me with an extraordinary expression. On top it was conscientiously shocked, underneath it was extremely curious, amused by anticipation, and, through it all, kindly.

'You don't get on,' she said. 'What did I tell you? "Mark my words," I said to Charlie Mafferton, "that child knows *nothing* of what is ahead of her!" But pray go on. What happened?'

I went on, and told Mrs. Torquilin what happened a good deal as I have told you, but I am afraid not so properly, because she was very much amused; and I suppose if the story of my interview with Mrs. Portheris excited any feeling in your mind, it was one of sympathy for me. At least, that was what I intended. But I was so happy in Mrs. Torquilin's carriage, and so delighted to be talking to somebody I knew, that I made as funny an account of the tender greetings of my relation as I could, and it lasted all the way to the Métropole, where I was to be dropped. I referred to her always as 'my relation,' because Mrs. Torquilin seemed to enjoy the expression. Incidentally, too, I told her about my plans, and showed her the addresses I had from the lady-guide, and she was kind enough to say that if I did not find them satisfactory I must let her know, and she could send me to a person of her acquaintance, where I should be 'very comfy, dear'; and I believed her. 'You see,' she said, 'I should like to take a little interest in your plans, because you seem to be the only

- 46 -

really American girl I've come upon in the whole course of my travels. The New York ones were all English imitations—I had no patience with them.'

'Oh!' I responded, cheerfully, 'that's only on the outside, Mrs. Torquilin. If you ran down the Stars and Stripes I guess you would find them pretty American.'

'Well, yes,' Mrs. Torquilin admitted, 'I remember that *was* the case'; but just then we stopped in front of the Métropole, and I begged her to come in and lunch with me. 'Dear me, child, no; I must be off!' she said; but I used all the persuasion I could, and represented how dreadfully lonely it was for me, and Mrs. Torquilin hesitated. At the moment of her hesitation there floated out from the dining-room a most appetising suggestion of fried soles. What small matters contribute to important results! I don't know anything that I have more cause to be grateful to than that little wandering odour. For Mrs. Torquilin, encountering it, said, with some feeling, 'Poor child. I've no doubt it is lonely for you. Perhaps I really ought to cheer you up a bit—I'll come!'

And Mrs. Torquilin and I pursued the wandering odour into the dining-room.

We had a particularly good lunch, and we both enjoyed it immensely, though Mrs. Torquilin made a fuss about my ordering champagne, and said it was simply ruinous, and I really ought to have somebody to look after me. 'By the way,' she said, 'have you seen anything of the Maffertons?' I told her that Mr. Mafferton had left his card the afternoon before, but I was out. 'You were out?' said Mrs. Torquilin. 'What a pity!' I said no; I wasn't very sorry, because I felt so unsettled in my mind that I was sure I couldn't work myself up to an intelligent discussion of any of Mr. Mafferton's favourite subjects, and he would hardly have found much pleasure in his visit. 'Oh! I think he would,' said Mrs. Torquilin. 'What on earth has "intelligent discussion" to do with it? I know the Maffertons very well,' she went on, looking at me quite sharply. 'Excellent family—cousins of Lord Mafferton of Mafferton. Charlie has enough, but not too much, I should say. However, that's neither here nor there, for he has no expensive habits, to *my* knowledge.'

'Just imagine,' I said, 'his being cousin to a lord! And yet he's not a bit haughty! Have you ever seen the lord, Mrs. Torquilin?'

'Bless the child, yes! Gone down to dinner with him more than once! Between ourselves,' said Mrs. Torquilin, confidentially, 'he's an old brute—neither more nor less! But one can't be rude to the man. What he'll have to say to it heaven only knows! But Charlie is quite capable of snapping his fingers at him. Do have one of these ices.'

I was immensely interested. 'What has Mr. Mafferton been doing?' I asked.

'I've no reason to believe he's done it yet,' said Mrs. Torquilin, a little crossly I thought. 'Perhaps he won't.'

'I'm sure I hope not,' I returned. 'Mr. Mafferton is so nice that it would be a pity if he got into trouble with his relations, especially if one of them is a lord.'

'Then don't let him!' said Mrs. Torquilin, more crossly than before.

'Do you think I would have any influence with him?' I asked her. 'I should doubt it very much. Mr. Mafferton doesn't strike me as a person at all susceptible to ladies' influence. But, if I knew the circumstances, I might try.'

'Oh, come along, child!' Mrs. Torquilin returned, folding up the napkin. 'You're *too* stupid. I'll see the Maffertons in a day or two, and I'll tell them what I think of you. Is there nothing else you'll have? Then let us depart, and make room for somebody else.' And I followed Mrs. Torquilin out of the room with a vague consciousness that she had an important voice in the management of the hotel, and had been kind enough to give me my lunch.

My friend did not take leave of me in the hall. 'I'd like to see the place,' she said. 'Take me up into the drawing-room.'

Mrs. Torquilin admired the drawing-room very much. 'Sumptuous!' she said, 'Sumptuous!' And as I walked round it with her I felt a particular kind of pleasure in being the more familiar with it of the two, and a little pride, too, in its luxury, which I had always been told was specially designed to suit Americans. I was so occupied with these feelings and with Mrs. Torquilin's remarks, that I did not observe two ladies on a sofa at the end of the room until we were almost in front of them. Then I noticed that one of the ladies was sitting bolt upright, with a stern, majestic eye fixed full upon me, apparently frozen with indignation; I also noticed that it was Mrs. Portheris. The other lady, in rusty black, as I knew she would be, occupied the farther end of the sofa, very much wilted indeed.

'Miss Wick.' said Mrs. Portheris, portentously, standing up, 'I have been shopping in the interval, but my friend Miss Purkiss—this is Miss Purkiss; Miss Purkiss, this is Miss Wick, the connection from Chicago whom you so kindly consented to try to befriend—Miss Purkiss has been here since ten o'clock. You will excuse her rising—she is almost, I might say, in a state of collapse!'

I turned round to Mrs. Torquilin.

'Mrs. Torquilin,' I said, 'this is my relation, Mrs. Portheris. Mrs. Portheris—Mrs. Torquilin.' In America we always introduce.

'ONE OF THE LADIES WAS SITTING BOLT UPRIGHT, WITH A STERN, MAJESTIC EYE'

But I was astonished at the change in Mrs. Torquilin. She seemed to have grown quite two inches taller, and she was regarding Mrs. Portheris through a pair of eyeglasses on a stick in the most inexplicable manner, with her mouth set very firmly indeed in a sort of contemptuous smile.

'Mrs. Cummers Portheris!' she said. 'Yes, I think Mrs. Cummers Portheris knows me. You did not tell me, dear, that Mrs. Portheris was your relation—but you need not fear that I shall think any the less of you for that.'

'Heppy,' said Mrs. Portheris, throwing up her chin, but looking distinctly nervous, 'your temper is much the same, I am sorry to see, as it always was.'

Mrs. Torquilin opened her mouth to reply, but closed it again resolutely, with an expression of infinite disdain. Then, to my surprise, she took a chair, in a way that told me distinctly of her intention not to desert me. I felt at the moment that I would have given anything to be deserted—the situation was so very embarrassing. The only thing I could think of to do was to ask Miss Purkiss if she and Mrs. Portheris wouldn't have some lunch. Miss Purkiss looked quite cheerful for a moment, and began to unbutton her glove; but her countenance fell when my unfeeling relation forbade her with a look, and said: 'Thank you, *no*, Miss Wick! Having waited so long, we can easily manage without food a little longer. Let us get to our arrangements. Perhaps Miss Purkiss will tell Miss Wick what she has to offer her.' Mrs. Portheris was evidently trying to ignore Mrs. Torquilin, and sat offensively, and sideways to her; but she could not keep the apprehension out of her eye.

'Certainly!' I said; 'but Miss Purkiss must have something.' I was determined to decline, but I wished to do it as mercifully as possible. 'Tell somebody,' I said to a servant who had come up to poke the fire, 'to bring up some claret and crackers.'

'Biscuits, child,' put in Mrs. Torquilin, 'is what you mean. Biscuits the young lady means'—to the servant—'and be sharp about it, for we want to go out immediately.' Then—'May I ask what arrangements you were thinking of offering Miss Wick?'—to Miss Purkiss.

Miss Purkiss began, quaveringly, that she had never done such a thing in her life before, but as Mrs. Portheris particularly wished it——

'For your own good, Jane,' interrupted Mrs. Portheris; 'entirely for your own good. I don't call that gratitude.'

Miss Purkiss hastily admitted that it *was* for her own good, of course, and that Mrs. Portheris knew her far too well to believe for a moment that she was not grateful; but I could have a nice back bedroom on the second floor, and the use of her sitting-room all day, and I, being recommended by Mrs. Portheris, she wouldn't think of many extras. Well, if there were fires, lights, the use of the bath and piano, boots, and friends to meals, that would be *all*.

'It is quite impossible!' said Mrs. Torquilin. 'I'm sorry you had the trouble of coming. In the first place, I fear *my young friend*,' with emphasis and a cursory glance at Mrs. Portheris's chair, 'would find it dull in Upper Baker Street. In the second'—Mrs. Torquilin hesitated for a moment, and then made the plunge—'I have taken a flat for the season, and Miss Wick is coming to me. I believe that is our little plan, my dear'—with a meaning smile to me. Then Mrs. Torquilin looked at Mrs. Portheris as if she were wondering whether there could be any discoverable reason why my relation should stay any longer. Mrs. Portheris rose, routed, but with a calm eye and a steady front. 'In that case I *hope* you will be forbearing with her, Heppy,' she said. 'Remember that she is a stranger to our ways of thinking and doing, and has probably never had the advantages of up-bringing that you and I have. I have no doubt, however, that my nephew, Colonel Wick, has done his best for her. *As you are probably aware*, he is worth his million.'

Mrs. Torquilin missed the sarcasm. 'Not I!' she returned, coolly; 'but I'm sure I'm very glad to hear it, for Miss Wick's sake. As to my temper, I've noticed that those know most about it who best deserve it. I don't think you need *worry* yourself about your young connection, Mrs. Cummers Portheris.'

'No,' said I, meekly; 'I should hate to be a weight on your mind.'

Mrs. Portheris took my hand in quite an affecting manner.

'Then I leave you, Miss Wick,' she said, 'to this lady—and to Providence.'

"'THEN I LEAVE YOU, MISS WICK,' SHE SAID, 'TO THIS LADY—AND TO PROVIDENCE'!"

'Between them,' I said, 'I ought to have a very good time.' Mrs. Portheris dropped my hand. 'I feel,' she said, 'that I have done my part toward you; but remember, if ever you want a home, Miss Purkiss will take you in. When in doubt——'

'Play trumps!' said Mrs. Torquilin from the window, where she stood with her back to all of us. 'I always do. Is that your carriage waiting outside, Mrs. Cummers Portheris?'

'It is,' said my relation, betrayed into asperity. 'I hope you have no objection to it!'

'Oh, none—not the least. But the horses seem very restive.'

'Come, Miss Purkiss!' said my relation.

'The wine and biscuits, dear love,' said Miss Purkiss, 'are just arriving.'

But Mrs. Portheris was bowing, with stately indefiniteness, to Mrs. Torquilin's back.

'Come, Miss Purkiss!' she commanded again. 'You can get a sandwich at the "A. B. C."'

And Miss Purkiss arose and followed my relation, which was the saddest thing of all.

As soon as they were well out of the room, Mrs. Torquilin turned round. 'I suppose you'll wonder about the why and wherefore of all this turn-up,' she said to me, her cheeks flushed and her eyes sparkling. 'It's a long story, and I'll tell you another time. But it comes to this in the end—that creature and I married into the same family. My husband and the late John Portheris, poor fellow, were step-brothers; and that old cat had the impudence—but there's no use going into it now. All I have to say is, she generally meets her match when she meets me. I'll put up with no hanky-panky work from Mrs. Cummers Portheris, my dear—and well she knows it!'

'It was certainly nice of you to help me out of the difficulty, Mrs. Torquilin,' I said, 'for I'd rather go anywhere than to Miss Purkiss's; but I'm sorry you had to——'

'Tell a tarradiddle? Not a bit of it, my dear—I meant it. Two are better than one, any day—I've plenty of room in my little flat, and if you like to share the expenses, I'll not object. At all events, we can but try it, and it will be showing very good feeling towards the Maffertons. I'm not a great hand for junketing, mind you, but we'll manage to amuse ourselves a little—a little giddy-goating does nobody any harm.'

Then I kissed Mrs. Torquilin, and she kissed me, and I told her how extremely obliged I was to her, and asked her if she had really considered it; and Mrs. Torquilin said, wasn't it enough that I should be left to 'that woman,' meaning my relation, and that I should come next day to see how we could best arrange matters. 'And while I think of it, child, here is my address,' my friend continued, taking out her card-case, and watching me very carefully, with a little smile about her mouth. I looked at it. I think my embarrassment gratified her a little, for the card read, '*Lady Torquilin*, 102 Cadogan Mansions, S.W.' I didn't know what to say. And I had been calling a lady of title 'Mrs.' all this time! Still, I reflected, she would hardly have been so nice to me if I had offended her very much, and if she had been particular about her title she could have mentioned it.

'It seems,' I said, 'that I have been making a mistake. I expected to make mistakes in this country; but I'm sorry I began with you.'

'Nonsense, child!' she returned. 'It was just my little joke—and I made Charlie Mafferton keep it. There's precious little in the handle I assure you—except an extra half-crown in one's bills!' And Lady Torquilin gave me her hand to say good-bye.

'Good-bye,' I said; 'I think handles are nice all the same.' And then—it is an uncomfortable thing to write, but it happened—I thought of something. I was determined to make no more mistakes if asking would prevent it.

'Please tell me,' I said, 'for you see I can't possibly know—am I to call you "your ladyship," or "my lady"?'

'Now don't talk rubbish!' said Lady Torquilin. 'You're to call me by my name. You are *too* quaint. Be a good child—and don't be late to-morrow.'

VIII

'IF I only had my own house in Portman Street,' Lady Torquilin remarked next day when we were having our tea in her flat, 'I could make you a great deal more comfy. Here we are just a bit cramped—"crowded," as you say in America. But you can't eat your cake and have it too.'

'Which have you done, Lady Torquilin,' I inquired, 'with your cake?'

'Let it,' said my friend—'twenty-five guineas a week, my dear, which is something to a poor woman. Last season it only brought twenty, and cost me a fortune to get it clean again after the pigs who lived in it. For the extra five I have to be thankful to the Duchess.'

'Did you really let it to a Duchess?' I asked, with deep interest. 'How lovely!'

'Indeed I did not! But the Duchess came to live round the corner, and rents went up in consequence. You don't know what it means to property-owners in London to have a duchess living round the corner, my child. It means *everything*. Not that I'm freehold in Portman Street—I've only a lease,' and Lady Torquilin sighed. This led us naturally into matters of finance, and we had a nice, sensible, practical discussion about our joint expenses. It doesn't matter to anybody what our arrangement was, but I must say that I found great occasion for protest against its liberality towards me. 'Nonsense!' said Lady Torquilin, invariably; 'don't be a foolish kitten! It's probably less than you would pay at a good private hotel—that's the advantage to you. Every time we take a hansom it will be only sixpence each instead of a shilling—that's the advantage to me; and no small advantage it is, for cabs are my ruin. And you'll save me plenty of steps, I'm sure, my dear! So there, say no more about it, but go and get your boxes.'

So I drove back to the Métropole finally, and as I locked my last trunk I noticed a fresh card on the mantelpiece. It was another of Mr. Charles Mafferton's; and on the back was written in pencil: '*I hope you are meeting with no difficulties. Should be glad to be of use in any way. Please let me know your permanent address as soon as possible, as the mother and sisters would like to call upon you.—G. M.*' This was nice and kind and friendly, and I tried in vain to reconcile it with what I had heard of English stiffness and exclusiveness and reserve. I would write to Mr. Mafferton, I thought, that very night. I supposed that by *the* mother he meant his own, but it struck me as a curious expression. In America we specify our parents, and a reference to 'the mother' there would probably be held to refer back to Eve. But in England you like all kinds of distinguishing articles, don't you?

Lady Torquilin's flat was a new one, of the regular American kind—not a second or third floor in an old-fashioned London house—and had a share, I am thankful to say, in a primitive elevator. The elevator was very small, but the man in the lower hall seemed to stand greatly in awe of it. 'To get them there boxes up in this 'ere lift, miss,' he said, when I and my trunks presented ourselves, 'she'll 'ave to make three trips at least'—and he looked at me rather reproachfully. 'Ware do you want 'em put out?' I said, 'Lady Torquilin's flat.' 'That's Number Four,' he commented, 'a good ways up. If you wouldn't mind a h'extra sixpence, miss, I could get a man off the street to 'elp me with 'em— they do be a size!' I said by all means, and presently my impedimenta were ascending with much deliberate circumstance, one piece at a time. The acoustic properties of Cadogan Mansions are remarkable. Standing at the foot of that elevator, encouraging its labours as it were, I could not possibly help overhearing Lady Torquilin's reception of my trunks, mingled with the more subdued voices of her housemaids. It was such a warm reception, expressed in such graphic terms, that I thought I ought to be present myself to acknowledge it; and the man put on two ordinary-sized valises next, to allow me to go up at the same time. 'We've got our orders, miss, to be pertickeler about wot she carries, miss,' he said, when I thought a trunk or two might accompany me. 'You see, if anything went wrong with 'er works, miss, there's no sayin' ware we'd be!'—and we solemnly began to rise. 'Ladies in the Mansions don't generally use the lift such a very great deal,' he remarked further, 'especially goin' down. They complain of the sinkin'.'

'I shall always go up and down in it,' I said. 'I don't mind the sinking. I'm used to it.'

'Very well, miss. You 'ave only to press the button and she'll come up; an' a great convenience you'll find 'er, miss,' he returned, resignedly, unlocking the grated door on Lady Torquilin's flat, where my hostess stood with her hands folded, and two maids respectfully behind her, regarding the first instalment of my baggage. After she had welcomed me: 'It's curiosity in its way,' said Lady Torquilin; 'but what's to be done with it, the dear only knows—unless we sublet it.' It required some strength of mind to tell her that there were two more coming up. The next one she called an abnormity, and the third she called a barn—simply. And I must say my trunks did look imposing in Lady Torquilin's flat. Finally, however, by the exercise of ingenuity on our parts and muscle on the maids', we got the whole of my baggage 'settled up,' as Lady Torquilin expressed it, and I was ready for my first approved and endorsed experience in your metropolis.

It came that afternoon. 'I am going to take you,' said Lady Torquilin at lunch, 'to Mrs. Fry Hamilton's "at home." She likes Americans, and her parties— "functions," as society idiots call it—disgusting word—are generally rather "swagger," as they say. I daresay you'll enjoy it. Make yourself as tidy as possible, mind. Put on your pretty grey; tuck in that "fringe" of yours a bit too, my dear; and be ready by five sharp.'

'Don't you like my bangs, Lady Torquilin?'

'Say your fringe, child; people don't "bang" in England—except doors and the piano. No, I can't say I'm fond of it. What were you given a forehead for, if you were not intended to show it? I fancy I see Sir Hector, when he was alive, allowing me to wear a fringe!' And Lady Torquilin pushed my hair up in that fond, cheerful, heavy-handed way people have, that makes you back away nervously and feel yourself a fright. I went to my room wondering whether my affection for Lady Torquilin would ever culminate in the sacrifice of my bangs. I could not say, seriously, that I felt equal to it then.

We went to Mrs. Fry Hamilton's in a hansom—not, as Lady Torquilin said, that she had the least objection to omnibuses, especially when they didn't drop one at the very door, but because there were no omnibuses very convenient to the part of Cromwell Road that Mrs. Fry Hamilton lived in. We inspected several before Lady Torquilin made a selection—rubber-tyred, yellow-wheeled, with a horse attached that would hardly stand still while we got in. I was acutely miserable, he went so fast; but Lady Torquilin liked it. 'He's perfectly fresh, poor darling!' she said. 'It breaks my heart to drive behind a wretched worn-out creature with its head down.' I said, Yes, I thought he was very fresh indeed, and asked Lady Torquilin if she noticed how he waggled his head. 'Dear beastie!' she replied, he's got a sore mouth. Suppose your mouth were perfectly raw, and you had a bit in it, and a man tugging at the reins——' But I couldn't stand it any longer; I put my parasol up through the door in the top.

'"MAKE HIM STOP WAGGLING," I CALLED TO THE DRIVER'

'Make him stop waggling!' I called to the driver. 'It's only a little 'abit of 'is, miss,' the driver said, and then, as the horse dropped his pace, he whipped him. Instantly Lady Torquilin's parasol admonished him. 'If you flog your horse,' she said emphatically, 'I get out.' I don't think I have ever driven in a hansom with Lady Torquilin since that our parasols have not both gone through the roof to point statements like these to the cabman, Lady Torquilin usually anguished on the dear horse's account, and I unhappy on my own. It enlivens the most monotonous drive, but it is a great strain on the nerves. I generally beg for a four-wheeler instead; but Lady Torquilin is contemptuous of four-wheelers, and declares she would just as soon drive in the British Museum. She says I will get used to it if I will only abstract my mind and talk about something else; and I am trying, but the process is a very painful one.

When we arrived at Mrs. Fry Hamilton's I rang the bell.

'Bless you, child!' said Lady Torquilin, 'that's not the way. They'll take you for a nursery governess, or a piano-tuner, or a bill! This is the proper thing for visitors.' And with that Lady Torquilin rapped sonorously and rang a peal—such a rap and peal as I had never heard in all my life before. In America we have only one kind of ring for everybody—from the mayor of the city to the man who sells plaster Cupids and will take old clothes on account. We approach each other's door-bells, as a nation, with much greater deference; and there is a certain humility in the way we introduce our personalities anywhere.

I felt uncomfortable on Mrs. Fry Hamilton's doorstep, as if I were not, individually, worth all that noise. Since then I have been obliged to rap and ring myself, because Lady Torquilin likes me to be as proper as I can; but there is always an incompleteness about the rap and an ineffectualness about the ring. I simply haven't the education to do it. And when the footman opens the door I feel that my face expresses deprecatingly, 'It's only me!' 'Rap and ring!' says Lady Torquilin, deridingly, 'it's a tap and tinkle!' Lady Torquilin is fond of alliteration.

Inside quite a few people were ascending and descending a narrow staircase that climbed against the wall, taking up as little room as it could; and a great many were in the room on the ground-floor, where refreshments were being dispensed. They were all beautifully dressed—if I have learned anything in England, it is not to judge the English by the clothes they wear in America—and they moved about with great precision, making, as a general thing, that pleasant rustle which we know to mean a silk foundation. The rustle was the only form of conversation that appeared to be general, but I noticed speaking going on in several groups of two or three. And I never saw better going up and down stairs—it was beautifully done, even by ladies weighing, I should think, quite two hundred pounds apiece, which you must reduce to "stun" for yourself. Lady Torquilin led the way with great simplicity and directness into the dining-room, and got tea for us both from one of the three white-capped modestly-expressionless maids behind the table—I cannot tell you what a dream of peace your servants are in this country—and asked me whether I would have sponge-cake, or a cress sandwich, or what. 'But,' I said, 'where is Mrs. Fry Hamilton?—I haven't been introduced.'

'All in good time,' said Lady Torquilin. 'It's just as well to take our tea when we can get it—we won't be able to turn round in here in half an hour!'—and Lady Torquilin took another sandwich with composure. 'Try the plum-cake,' she advised me in an aside. 'Buszard——I can tell at a glance! I have to deny myself.'

And I tried the plum-cake, but with a sense of guilty apprehension lest Mrs. Fry Hamilton should appear in the doorway and be naturally surprised at the consumption of her refreshments by an utter stranger. I noticed that almost everybody else did the same thing, and that nobody seemed at all nervous; but I occupied as much of Lady Torquilin's shadow as I could, all the same, and on the way up implored her, saying, '*Have* I any crumbs?' I felt that it would require more hardihood than I possessed to face Mrs. Fry Hamilton with shreds of her substance, acquired before I knew her, clinging to my person. But concealment was useless, and seemed to be unnecessary.

'Have you had any tea?' said Mrs. Fry Hamilton to Lady Torquilin, her question embracing us both, as we passed before her; and Lady Torquilin said, 'Yes, thanks,' as nonchalantly as possible.

Lady Torquilin had just time to say that I was an American.

'Really!' remarked Mrs. Fry Hamilton, looking at me again. 'How nice. The only one I have to-day, I think.' And we had to make room for somebody else. But it was then that the curious sensation of being attached to a string and led about, which I have felt more or less in London ever since, occurred to me first—in the statement that I was the only one Mrs. Fry Hamilton had to-day.

Lady Torquilin declared, as she looked round the room, that she didn't see a soul she knew; so we made our way to a corner and sat down, and began to talk in those uninterested spasms that always attack people who come with each other. Presently—'There is that nice little Mrs. Pastelle-Jones!' said Lady Torquilin, 'I must go and speak to her!'—and I was left alone, with the opportunity of admiring the china. I don't wonder at your fondness for it in London drawing-rooms. It seems to be the only thing that you can keep clean. So many people were filing in past Mrs. Fry Hamilton, however, that the china soon lost its interest for me. The people were chiefly ladies—an impressive number of old, stout, rosy, white-haired ladies in black, who gave me the idea of remarkable health at their age; more middle-aged ones, rather inclined to be pale and thin, with narrow cheek-bones, and high-arched noses, and sweet expressions, and a great deal of black lace and jet, much puffed on the shoulders; and young ones, who were, of course, the very first English young ladies I had ever seen in an English drawing-room. I suppose you are accustomed to them; you don't know what they were to me—you couldn't understand the intense interest and wonder and admiration they excited in me. I had never seen anything human so tall and strong and fine and fresh-coloured before, with such clear limpid eyes, such pretty red lips, and the outward showing of such excellent appetites. It seemed to me that everyone was an epitome of her early years of bread-and-butter and milk puddings and going to bed at half-past nine, and the epitomes had a charming similarity. The English young lady stood before me in Mrs. Fry Hamilton's drawing-room as an extraordinary product—in almost all cases five-eight, and in some quite six feet in height. Her little mamma was dwarfed beside her, and when she smiled down upon the occasional man who was introduced to her, in her tall, compassionate way, he looked quite insignificant, even if he carried the square, turned-back shoulders by which I have learned to tell military men in this country. We have nothing like it in America, on the same scale; although we have a great deal more air to breathe and vegetables to eat than you. I knew that I had always been considered 'a big girl,' but beside these firm-fleshed young women I felt myself rather a poor creature, without a muscular advantage to my name. They smiled a good deal, but I did not see them talk much—it seemed enough for them to be; and they had a considering air, as if things were new to them, and they had not quite made up their minds. And as they considered they blushed a good deal, in a way that was simply sweet. As I sat musing upon them I saw Lady Torquilin advancing toward me, with one of the tallest, pinkest, best-developed, and most tailor-made of all immediately behind her, following, with her chin outstretched a little, and her eyes downcast, and a pretty expression of doing what she was told.

'My dear,' said Lady Torquilin, 'this is Miss Gladys Fortescue. Gladys—Miss Wick, my young lady friend from Chicago. Miss Fortescue has a brother in America, so you will have something to chat about.'

'Howdj-do?' said Miss Fortescue. She said it very quickly, with a sweet smile, and an interesting little mechanical movement of the head, blushing at the same time; and we shook hands. That is, I think one of us did, though I can't say positively which one it was. As I remember the process, there were two shakes; but they were not shakes that ran into each other, and one of them— I think it was mine—failed to 'come off,' as you say in tennis. Mine was the shake that begins nowhere in particular, and ends without your knowing it— just the ordinary American shake arranged on the muscular system in common use with us. Miss Fortescue's was a rapid, convulsive movement, that sprang from her shoulder and culminated with a certain violence. There was a little push in it, too, and it exploded, as it were, high in air. At the same time I noticed the spectacles of a small man who stood near very much in peril from Miss Fortescue's elbow. Then I remembered and understood the sense of dislocation I had experienced after shaking hands with Mrs. Fry Hamilton, and which I had attributed, in the confusion of the moment, to being held up, so to speak, as an American.

'Do you know my brother?' said Miss Fortescue.

'I am afraid not,' I replied. 'Where does he live?'

'In the United States,' said Miss Fortescue. 'He went out there six months ago with a friend. Perhaps you know his friend—Mr. Colfax.'

I said I knew two or three Mr. Colfaxes, but none of them were English—had not been, at least, for some time back; and did Miss Fortescue know what particular part of the Union her brother and his friend had gone to? 'You know,' I said, 'we have an area of three million square miles,' I daresay I mentioned our area with a certain pardonable pride. It's a thing we generally make a point of in America.

I shouldn't have thought there was anything particularly humorous in an area, but Miss Fortescue laughed prettily. 'I remember learning that from my governess,' she said. 'My brother is out in the West—either in the town of Minneapolis and the State of Minnesota, or the town of Minnesota and the State of Minneapolis. I never know, without looking out his address, which comes first. But I daresay there are a good many people in the United States—you might easily miss him.'

'We have sixty millions, Miss Fortescue,' I said; and Miss Fortescue returned that in that case she didn't see how we could be expected to know anybody; and after that the conversation flagged for a few seconds, during which we both looked at the other people.

'I have never been to America,' Miss Fortescue said. 'I should like to go. Is it very cold?'

I did not mention the area again. 'In some places,' I said.

'I should not like that. But then, you have the toe-beganing—that must be nice.

"YOU HAVE THE TOE-GROANING—THAT MUST BE NICE"

I assented, though I did not in the least know, until Miss Fortescue spoke of skating, what she meant. Miss Fortescue thought the skating must be nice, too, and then, she supposed, though it was cold, we always went out *prepared* for it. And the conversation flagged again. Fortunately, a gentleman at the other end of the room, where the piano was, began at that moment to sing something very pleading and lamentable and uncomfortable, with a burden of 'I love thee so,' which generally rhymed with 'woe'—an address to somebody he called 'Dear-r-r Hear-r-r-t!' as high as he could reach, turning up his eyes a good deal, as if he were in pain. And for the time it was not necessary to talk.

When he had finished Miss Fortescue asked me if it was not delightful, and I said it was—did she know the gentleman's name? Miss Fortescue said she did not, but perhaps Lady Torquilin would. And then, just as Lady Torquilin came up, 'How do you like England?' asked Miss Fortescue.

'Well,' asked Lady Torquilin, as we drove home in another hansom, what did you and Gladys Fortescue find to say to each other?'

I said, quite truly, that I did not remember at the moment, but I admired Miss Fortescue—also with great sincerity—so enthusiastically, that I daresay Lady Torquilin thought we had got on splendidly together.

And what I wonder is, if Miss Fortescue had been asked about our conversation, what she would have said.

IX

'YOU are sure you know where you're going?' said Lady Torquilin, referring to the 'Army and Navy.' '*Victoria* omnibus, remember, at Sloane-square; a penny fare, and not more, mind. You must learn to look after your pennies. Now, what are you to do for me at the Stores?'

'A packet of light Silurian; your camphor and aconite pilules; to ask how long they intend to be over the valise, they're fixing for you——'

'Portmanteau they're re-covering. Yes, go on!'

'And what their charge is for cleaning red curtains.'

'*And* to complain about the candles,' added Lady Torquilin.'

'And to complain about the candles.'

'Yes. Don't forget about the candles, dear. See what they'll do. And I'm very sorry I can't go with you to Madame Tussaud's, but you know I've been trotting about the whole morning, and all those wax people, with their idiotic expressions, this afternoon would simply finish me off! I'll just lie down a bit, and go with you another day; I couldn't stand up much longer to talk to the Queen herself! You pop into the "Underground," you know, at St. James's Park, and out at Baker Street. Now, where do you pop in?—and out? That's quite right. Good-bye, child. I rang for the lift to come up a quarter of an hour ago; it's probably there now, and we mustn't keep it waiting. Off you go!' But the elevator-door was locked, and our descent had begun, when Lady Torquilin hurried along the passage, arrested, and kept it waiting on her own account. 'It's only to say, dear,' she called through the grating, 'that you are on no consideration whatever to get in or out of an Underground train while it is moving. *On no consideration what-*;' but the grating slowly disappeared, and the rest of Lady Torquilin's admonition came down on the top of the elevator.

I had done every one of the commissions. I had been magisterially raised and lowered from one floor to another, to find that everything I wanted was situated up and down so many staircases 'and turn to your right, madam,' that I concluded they kept an elevator at the Stores for pleasure. I had had an agreeable interview with a very blonde young druggist upon the pilules in the regions above, and had made it all right with a man in mutton-chop whiskers and an apron about the candles in the regions below. I had seen a thing I had never seen in my life before, a very curious thing, that interested me enormously—a husband and father buying his wife's and daughters' dry-goods—probably Lady Torquilin would tell me to say 'dress materials.' In America our husbands and fathers are too much occupied to make purchases for their families, for which it struck me that we had never been thankful enough 'I will not have you in stripes!' I heard him say, as I passed, full of commiseration for her. 'What arrogance!' I thought. 'In America they are glad to have us in anything.' And I rejoiced that it was so.

'"I WILL NOT HAVE YOU IN STRIPES," I HEARD HIM SAY.'

But, as I was saying, I had done all Lady Torquilin's commissions, and was making my last trip to the ground-floor with the old soldier in the elevator, when a gentleman got in at one of the stopping-places, and sat down opposite me. He had that look of deliberate indifference that I have noticed so many English gentlemen carry about with them—as if, although they are bodily present, their interest in life had been carefully put away at home—and he concentrated his attention upon the point of his umbrella, just as he used to do upon the salt-cellars crossing the Atlantic Ocean. And he looked up almost with astonishment when I said, 'How do you do, Mr. Mafferton?' rather as if he did not quite expect to be spoken to in an elevator by a young lady. Miss Wick!' he said, and we shook hands as the old soldier let us out. 'How very odd! I was on the point of looking you up at Lady Torquilin's. You see, I've found you out at last—no thanks to you—after looking all over the place.'

There was a very definite reproach in this, so I told Mr. Mafferton as we went down the steps that I was extremely sorry he had taken any trouble on my account; that I had fully intended to write to him in the course of a day or two, but he had no idea how much time it took up getting settled in a flat where the elevator ran only at stated intervals. 'But,' I said, with some curiosity, 'how *did* you find me out, Mr. Mafferton?' For if there is one interesting thing, it is to discover how an unexpected piece of information about yourself has been come by.

'Lady Torquilin dropped me a line,' replied Mr. Mafferton; 'that is, she mentioned it in—in a note yesterday. Lady Torquilin,' Mr. Mafferton went on, 'is a very old friend of mine—and an awfully good sort, as I daresay you are beginning to find out.'

By this time we had reached the pavement, and were standing in everybody's way, with the painful indetermination that attacks people who are not quite sure whether they ought to separate or not. "'Ansom cab, sir?" asked one of the porters. 'No!' said Mr. Mafferton. 'I was on the very point,' he went on to me, dodging a boy with a bandbox, 'of going to offer my services as cicerone this afternoon, if you and Lady Torquilin would be good enough to accept them.'

"'Ansom cab, sir?' asked another porter, as Mr. Mafferton, getting out of the way of a resplendent footman, upset a small child with a topheavy bonnet, belonging to the lady who belonged to the footman.

'UPSET A CHILD WITH A TOPHEAVY BONNET'

'*No!*' said Mr. Mafferton, in quite a temper. 'Shall we get out of this?' he asked me, appealingly; and we walked on in the direction of the Houses of Parliament. 'There's nothing on in particular, that I know of he continued;

'but there are always the stock shows, and Lady Torquilin is up to any amount of sight-seeing, I know.'

'She isn't today, Mr. Mafferton. She's lying down. I did my best to persuade her to come out with me, and she wouldn't. But I'm going sight-seeing this very minute, and if you would like to come too, I'm sure I shall be very glad.'

Mr. Mafferton looked a little uncomfortable. 'Where were you thinking of going?' he asked.

'To Madame Tussaud's,' I said. 'You go by the Underground Railway from here. Get in at St. James's Park Station, and out at Baker Street Station—about twenty-five minutes in the cars. And you are not,' I said, remembering what I had been told, 'under any consideration whatever, to get in or out of the train while it is moving.'

Mr. Mafferton laughed. 'Lady Torquilin has been coaching you,' he said: but he still looked uncomfortable, and thinking he felt, perhaps, like an intruder upon my plans, and wishing to put him at his ease, I said: 'It would really be very kind of you to come, Mr. Mafferton, for even at school I never could remember English history, and now I've probably got your dynasties worse mixed up than ever. It would be a great advantage to go with somebody who knows all the dates, and which kings usurped their thrones, and who they properly belonged to.'

Mr. Mafferton laughed again. 'I hope you don't expect all that of me,' he said. 'But if you are quite sure we couldn't rout Lady Torquilin out, I will take you to Madame Tussaud's with the greatest pleasure, Miss Wick.'

'I'm quite sure,' I told Mr. Mafferton, cheerfully. 'She said all those wax people, with their idiotic expressions, this afternoon would simply finish her up!'—and Mr. Mafferton said Lady Torquilin put things very quaintly, didn't she? And we went together into one of those great echoing caverns in the sides of the streets that led down flights of dirty steps, past the man who punches the tickets, and widen out into that border of desolation with a fierce star burning and brightening in the blackness of the farther end, which is a platform of the Underground Railway.

'This,' said I to Mr. Mafferton as we walked up and down waiting for our train, 'is one of the things I particularly wanted to see.'

'The penny weighing-machine?' asked Mr. Mafferton, for I had stopped to look at that.

'The whole thing,' said I—'the Underground system. But this is interesting in itself,' I added, putting a penny in, and stepping on the machine.

'"WHAT DO YOU THINK OF THE UNDERGROUND?"'

'Please hold my parasol, Mr. Mafferton, so that I may get the exact truth for my penny.' Mr. Mafferton took the parasol with a slightly clouded expression, which deepened when one of two gentlemen who had just come on the platform bowed to him. 'I think, if you don't mind, Miss Wick, we had better go farther along the platform—it will be easier to get the carriage,' he said, in a manner which quite dashed my amiable intention of telling him how even the truth was cheaper in this country than in America, for our weighing-machines wouldn't work for less than a nickel, which was twice and a-half as much as a penny. Just then, however, the train came whizzing in, we bundled ourselves into a compartment, the door banged after us with frightful explosiveness—the Underground bang is a thing which I should think the omnibus companies had great cause to be thankful for—and we went with a scream and a rush into the black unknown. It seemed to me in the first few minutes that life as I had been accustomed to it had lapsed, and that a sort of semi-conscious existence was filling up the gap between what had been before and what would be again. I can't say I found this phase of being agreeable. It occurred to me that my eyes and my ears and my lungs might just as well have been left at home. The only organ that found any occupation was my nose—all sense seemed concentrated in that sharp-edged, objectionable smell. 'What do you think of the Underground?' said Mr. Mafferton, leaning across, above the rattle.

I told him I hadn't had time to analyse my impressions, in a series of shrieks, and subsided to watch for the greyness of the next station. After that had passed, and I was convinced that there were places where you could escape to the light and air of the outside world again, I asked Mr. Mafferton a number of questions about the railway, and in answering them he said the first irritating thing I heard in England. 'I hope,' he remarked, 'that your interest in the Underground won't take you all the way round the Circle to see what it's like.'

'Why do you hope that, Mr. Mafferton?' I said. 'Is it dangerous?'

'Not in the least.' he returned, a little confusedly. 'Only—most Americans like to "make the entire circuit," I believe.'

'I've no doubt they want to see how bad it can be,' I said. 'We are a very fair nation, Mr. Mafferton. But though I can't understand your hope in the matter, I don't think it likely I shall travel by Underground any more than I can help.' Because, for the moment, I felt an annoyance. Why should Mr. Mafferton 'hope' about my conduct?—Mr. Mafferton was not my maiden aunt! But he very politely asked me how I thought it compared with the Elevated in New York, and I was obliged to tell him that I really didn't think it compared at all. The Elevated was ugly to look at, and some people found it giddy to ride on, but it took you through the best quality of air and sunlight the entire distance; and if anything happened, at all events you could see what it was. Mr. Mafferton replied that he thought he preferred the darkness to looking through other people's windows; and this preference of Mr. Mafferton's struck me later as being interestingly English. And after that we both lapsed into meditation, and I thought about old London, with its Abbey, and its Tower, and its Houses of Parliament, and its Bluecoat boys, and its monuments, and its ten thousand hansom cabs, lying just over my head; and an odd, pleasurable sensation of undermining the centuries and playing a trick with history almost superseded the Underground smell. The more I thought about it, and about what Mr. Mafferton said, the more I liked that feeling of taking an enormous liberty with London, and by the time we reached Baker Street Station I was able to say to Mr. Mafferton, with a clear conscience, in spite of my smuts and half-torpid state of mind, that on consideration I thought I *would* like to compass London by the Underground—to 'make the entire circuit.'

X

IT struck me, from the outside, as oddly imposing—Madame Tussaud's. Partly, I suppose, because it is always more or less treated jocosely, partly because of the homely little familiar name, and partly because a person's expectations of a waxwork show are naturally not very lofty. I was looking out for anything but a swelling dome and a flag, and the high brick walls of an Institution. There seemed a grotesqueness of dignity about it, which was emphasised by the solemn man at the turnstile who took the shillings and let us through, and by the spaciousness inside—emphasised so much that it disappeared, so to speak, and I found myself taking the place quite seriously—the gentleman in tin on the charger in the main hall below, and the wide marble stairs, and the urns in the corners, and the oil paintings on the landings, and everything. I began asking Mr. Mafferton questions immediately, quite in the subdued voice people use under impressive circumstances; but he wasn't certain who the architect was, and couldn't say where the marble came from, and really didn't know how many years the waxworks had been in existence, and hadn't the least idea what the gross receipts were per annum—did not, in fact, seem to think he ought to be expected to be acquainted with these matters. The only thing he could tell me definitely was that Madame Tussaud was dead—and I knew that myself. 'Upon my word, you know,' said Mr. Mafferton, 'I haven't been here since I was put into knickers!' I was surprised at this remark when I heard it, for Mr.

Mafferton was usually elegant to a degree in his choice of terms; but I should not be now. I have found nothing plainer in England than the language. Its simplicity and directness are a little startling at first, perhaps, to the foreign ear; but this soon wears off as you become accustomed to it, and I dare say the foreigner begins to talk the same way—in which case my speech will probably be a matter of grave consideration to me when I get back to Chicago. In America we usually put things in a manner somewhat more involved. Yes, I know you are thinking of the old story about Americans draping the legs of their pianos; but if I were you I would discount that story. For my own part, I never in my life saw it done.

The moment we were inside the main hall, where the orchestra was playing, before I had time to say more than 'How very interesting, Mr. Mafferton! Who is that? and why is *he* famous?' Mr. Mafferton bought one of the red and gilt and green catalogues from the young woman at the door, and put it into my hand almost impulsively.

'I fancy they're very complete—and reliable, Miss Wick,' he said. 'You—you really mustn't depend upon me. It's such an unconscionable time since I left school.'

I told Mr. Mafferton I was sure that was only his modest way of putting it, and that I knew he had reams of English history in his head if he would only just think of it; and he replied, 'No, really, upon my word, I have not!' But by that time I realised that I was in the immediate society of all the remarkable old kings and queens of England; and the emotions they inspired, standing round in that promiscuous touchable way, with their crowns on, occupied me so fully, that for at least ten minutes I found it quite interesting enough to look at them in silence. So I sat down on one of the seats in the middle of the hall, where people were listening to the orchestra's selections from 'The Gondoliers,' and gave myself up to the curious captivation of the impression. 'It's not bad,' said Mr. Mafferton, reflectively, a little way off. 'No,' I said, 'it's beautiful!' But I think he meant the selections, and I meant the kings and queens, to whom he was not paying the slightest attention. But I did not find fault with him for that—he had been, in a manner, brought up amongst these things; he lived in a country that always had a king or queen of some sort to rule over it; he was used to crowns and sceptres. He could not possibly have the same feelings as a person born in Chicago, and reared upon Republican principles. But to me those quaint groups of royalties in the robes and jewels of other times, and arrayed just as much in their characters as in their clothes—the characters everybody knows them by—were a source of pure and, while I sat there, increasing delight. I don't mind confessing that I like the kings and queens at Madame Tussaud's better than anything else I've seen in England, at the risk of being considered a person of low intelligence. I know that Mr. James Russell Lowell—whom poppa always used to say he was proud to claim as a fellow-countryman, until he went Mugwump when Cleveland was elected—said of them that they were 'much like any other English party'; but I should think from that that Mr. Lowell was perhaps a little prejudiced against waxworks, and intolerant of the form of art which they represent; or, possibly, when he said it he had just come to London, and had not attended many English parties. For it seems to me that the peculiar charm and interest of the ladies and gentlemen at Madame Tussaud's is the ingenuous earnestness with which they show you their temperaments and tastes and dispositions, which I have not found especially characteristic of other English ladies and gentlemen. As Lady Torquilin says, however, 'that's as it may be.' All I know is, that whatever Mr. Lowell, from his lofty Harvard standard of culture, may find to say in deprecation of all that is left of your early sovereigns, I, from my humble Chicago point of view, was immensely pleased with them. I could not get over the feeling—I have not got over it yet—that they were, or at any rate had once been, veritable kings and queens. I had a sentiment of respect; I could not think of them, as I told Mr. Mafferton, 'as wax'; and it never occurred to me that the crowns were brass and the jewels glass. Even now I find that an unpleasant reflection; and I would not go back to Madame Tussaud's on any account, for fear the brassiness of the crowns and the glassiness of the jewels might obtrude themselves the second time, and spoil the illusion. English history, with its moated castles, and knights in armour, and tyrant kings and virtuous queens, had always seemed more or less of a fairy tale to me—it is difficult to believe in mediæval romance in America—and there, about me, was the fairy tale realised: all the curious old people who died of a 'surfeit of lampreys,' or of a bad temper, or of decapitation, or in other ways which would be considered eccentric now, in all their dear old folds and fashions, red and blue and gold and ermine, with their crowns on! There was a sociability among them, too, that I thought interesting, and that struck me as a thing I shouldn't have expected, some of their characters being so very good, and some so very bad; but I suppose, being all kings and queens, any other distinction would be considered invidious. I looked up while I was thinking about them, and caught Mr. Mafferton yawning.

'Are you impressed?' he said, disguising it with a smile.

'Very much,' I answered him. 'In a way. Aren't you?' 'I think they're imbecile,' said Mr. Mafferton. 'Imbecile old Things! I have been wondering what they could possibly suggest to you.'

Mr. Mafferton certainly spoke in that way. I remember it distinctly. Because I depended upon it in taking, as we went round, a certain freedom of criticism—depended upon it, I had reason to believe afterwards, unwarrantably.

'Let us look at them individually,' I said, rising. 'Collectively, I find them lovable.'

'Well, now, I envy them!' replied Mr. Mafferton, with great coolness. This was surprisingly frivolous in Mr. Mafferton, who was usually quite what would be called a serious person, and just for a minute I did not quite know what to say. Then I laughed a little frivolously too. 'I suppose you intend that for a compliment, Mr. Mafferton,' I said. Privately, I thought it very clumsy. 'This is Number One, I think'—and we stopped before William the Conqueror asking Matilda of Flanders to sit down.

'I don't know that I did,' said Mr. Mafferton—which made the situation awkward for me; for if there is an uncomfortable thing, it is to appropriate a compliment which was not intended. An Englishman is a being absolutely devoid of tact.

'So this is William the Conqueror?' I said, by way of changing the subject.

"SO THIS IS WILLIAM THE CONQUEROR!"

'It may be a little like his clothes,' said Mr. Mafferton, indifferently.

'Oh! don't say that, Mr. Mafferton. I'm sure he looks every inch a William the Conqueror! See how polite he is to his wife, too—I suppose that's because he's French?'

Mr. Mafferton didn't say anything, and it occurred to me that perhaps I had not expressed myself well.

'Do you notice,' I went on, 'how he wears his crown—all tipped to one side? He reminds me just a little, Mr. Mafferton, with that type of face—enterprising, you know—and hair that length, only it ought to be dark, and if the crown were only a wide-brimmed, soft felt hat—he reminds mo *very much* of those Californian ranchers and miners Bret Harte and Joaquin Miller write about.'

'Do you mean cowboys?' asked Mr. Mafferton, in a way that told me he wasn't going to agree with me.

'Yes, that kind of person. I think William the Conqueror would make a beautiful cowboy—a regular "Terror of the Canyon."'

'Can't say I see it,' said Mr. Mafferton, fixing his eye upon the bass 'cello at the other end of the room.

'It isn't in that direction,' I said, and Mr. Mafferton became exceedingly red. Then it occurred to me that possibly over here that might be considered impertinent, so I did my best to make up for it. 'A very *nice* face, isn't it?' I went on. 'What is he particularly noted for, Mr. Mafferton, besides the Curfew, and the Doomsday Book, and introducing old families into England?'

Mr. Mafferton bit his moustache. I had never seen anybody bite his moustache before, though I had always understood from novels that it was done in England. Whether American gentlemen have better tempers, or whether they are afraid of injuring it, or why the habit is not a common one with us, I am unable to say.

'Really, Miss Wick,' Mr. Mafferton responded, with six degrees of frost, 'I—is there nothing about it in the catalogue? He established the only date which would ever stick in my memory—1066. But you mustn't think he brought all the old families in England over with him, Miss Wick—it is incorrect.'

'"I daresay," I said; 'people get such curious ideas about England in America, Mr. Mafferton.' But that did not seem to please Mr. Mafferton either. 'I think they ought to know,' he said, so seriously that I did not like to retaliate with any English misconceptions of American matters. And from what I know of Mr. Mafferton now, I do not think he would have seen the slightest parallel.

'How this brings it all back, I said, as we looked at William the Second, surnamed Rufus, in blue and yellow, with a plain front—'the marks in history at school, and the dates let in at the sides of the pages! "His dead body, with an arrow sticking in it, was found by Purkiss, a charcoal-burner, and carried in a cart to Winchester, where it was buried in the Cathedral." I remember I used to torment myself by wondering whether they pulled the arrow out, because in my history it didn't say they did.'

'It's a fact,' said Mr. Mafferton; 'one always does think of the old chap with the arrow sticking in him. Burne-Jones or one of those fellows ought to paint it—the forest, you know, twilight, and the charcoal-burner in a state of funk. Tremendously effective—though, I daresay, it's been done scores of times.'

'And sold to be lithographed in advertisements!' I added.

'Ah, Miss Wick, that is the utilitarian American way of looking at things!' Mr. Mafferton remarked, jocularly; and I don't think I could have been expected to refrain from telling him that I had in mind a certain soap not manufactured in America.

When we got as far as Henry the Second, Curtmantle, whom Madame Tussaud describes as a 'wise and good king,' and who certainly has an amiable, open countenance, I noticed that all the crowns were different, and asked Mr. Mafferton about it—whether at that time every king had his crown made to order, and trimmed according to his own ideas, or had to take whatever crown was going; and whether it was his to do as he liked with, or went with the throne; and if the majority of the kings had behaved properly about their crowns, and where they all were. But if Mr. Mafferton knew, he chose to be equivocal—he did not give me any answer that I feel I could rely upon sufficiently to put into print. Then we passed that nice brave crusading Richard the First, surnamed Coeur de Lion, in some domestic argument with his sweet Berengaria; and Mr. Mafferton, talking about her, used the expression, 'Fair flower of Navarre.' But at that time he was carrying the catalogue.

King John I thought delightful; I could not have believed it possible to put such a thoroughly bad temper into wax, and I said so to Mr. Mafferton, who agreed with me, though without enthusiasm. 'The worst king who ever sat on the English throne!' I repeated, meditatively, quoting from Madame Tussaud—'that's saying a great deal, isn't it, Mr. Mafferton?' My escort said No, he couldn't say he thought it represented such an acme of wickedness, and we walked on, past swarthy little sad Charles the Second, in armour and lace, who looks—and how could he help it?—as if he were always thinking of what happened to his sire—I suppose the expression 'poppa' is unknown among royalties. Mr. Mafferton would not agree to this either; he seemed to have made up his mind not to agree to anything further.

I should like to write a whole chapter about Henry the Eighth as he looked that day, though I daresay it is an habitual expression, and you may have seen it often yourself. He was standing in the midst of a group of ladies, including some of his wives, stepping forward in an impulsive, emotional way; listening, with grief in both his eyes, to the orchestra's rendition of

Bury! Bury! Let the grave close o'er.

as if deeply deprecating the painful necessity of again becoming a widower. It was beautiful to see the way the music worked upon his feelings. It will be impossible for me ever to think so badly of him again.

'What is your impression of *him?*' asked Mr. Mafferton.

I said I thought he was too funny for words.

'He was a monster!' my friend remarked, 'and you are quite the first person, I should say, who has ever discovered anything humorous in him.' And I gathered from Mr. Mafferton's tone that, while it was pardonable to think badly of an English monarch, it was improper to a degree to find him amusing.

Then I observed that they were all listening with Henry the Eighth—Philippa of Hainault with her pink nose, and the Black Prince in mail, and Catharine of Arragon embracing her monkey, and Cardinal Wolsey in red, and Caxton in black, and Chaucer in poet's grey, listening intently—you could tell even by their reflections in the glass—as the orchestra went on—

The days that have been, and never shall be more!

Personally, I felt sorry for them all, even for that old maid in armour, James the Second. Mr. Mafferton, by the way, could see nothing in the least old-maidish about this sovereign. They must have had, as a rule, such a very good time while it lasted—it must have been so thoroughly disagreeable to die! I wanted immensely to ask Mr. Mafferton—but somehow his manner did not encourage me to do it—whether in those very early times kings were able to wear their crowns every day without exciting comment, as Madame Tussaud distinctly gives you the idea that they did. And it seemed to me that in those days it must have been really worth while to be a king, and be different from other people, in both dress and deportment. I would not go through the other rooms, because I did not believe anything could be more beautiful than the remains of your early sovereigns, and, moreover, Mr. Mafferton was getting so very nearly sulky that I thought I had better not. But just through the door I caught a glimpse of one or two American Presidents in black, with white ties. They had intelligent faces, but beside your Plantagenets I don't mind confessing they didn't look anything!

XI

I HAD not the least expectation of being fortunate enough to see your Parliament open, having always heard that all the peeresses wanted to go on that occasion, and knowing how little sitting accommodation you had for anybody. Americans find nothing more impressive in England than the difficulty of getting a look at your system of government—our own is so very accessible to everyone who chooses to study it, and to come and sit in the general gallery of the House of Congress or the Senate without making a disturbance. The thing an American tells first, and with most pride, when he comes home after visiting England, is that he has attended a sitting of Parliament and seen Mr. Gladstone; if he has heard your veteran politician speak, he is prouder still. So I had cherished the hope of somehow getting into the House while Parliament was in session, and seeing all the people we read so much about at home in connection with the Irish Question—it was the thing, I believe, I had set my heart upon doing most; but tickets for the opening of Parliament from Mr. Mafferton, with a note informing Lady Torquilin that his cousin had promised to look after us on the occasion, represented more than my highest aspiration.

Lady Torquilin was pleased, too, though I don't think she intended to express her pleasure when she said, with an air of philosophical acceptance of whatever Fate might send, 'Providence only knows, my dear, how the old man will behave! He *may* be as agreeable as possible—as merry as a grig—and he may be in a temper like the———'; and Lady Torquilin compressed her lips and nodded her head in a way that told me how her remark would finish if she were not a member of the Church of England, rather low, and a benefactor to deep-sea fishermen and Dr. Barnardo, with a strong objection to tobacco in any form. 'We must avoid subjects that are likely to provoke him: local self-government for Ireland has given him apoplexy twice; I've heard of his getting awful tantrums about this last Licensing Bill; and marriage with a deceased wife's sister, I know, is a thing to avoid!'

Then it dawned upon me that this was Mr. Mafferton's cousin, who was a lord, and I had a very great private satisfaction that I should see what he was like.

'I remember,' I said. 'This is the cousin that you said was an old———'

'Brute!' Lady Torquilin finished for me, seeing that I didn't quite like to. 'So he is, when he's in a rage! I wouldn't be Lady Mafferton, poor dear, for something! An ordinary "K" and an ordinary temper for me!' I asked Lady Torquilin what she meant by 'an ordinary K'; and in the next half-hour I got a lesson on the various distinctions of the English aristocracy that interested me extremely. Lady Torquilin's 'K,' I may say, while I am talking about it, was the 'C.M.G.' kind, and not the 'K' sometimes conferred late in life upon illustrious butchers. Lady Torquilin didn't seem to think much of this kind of 'K,' but I was glad to hear of it. It must be a great encouragement to honesty and industry in the humbler walks of life, or, as you would say, among the masses; and though, I suppose, it wouldn't exactly accord with our theory of government, I am sorry we have nothing even remotely like it in America.

It was a nice day, a lovely day, an extraordinary day, the February day Lady Torquilin and I compromised upon a hansom and drove to the Parliament buildings. A person has such a vivid, distinct recollection of nice days in London! The drive knocked another of my preconceived ideas to pieces—the idea that Westminster was some distance off, and would have to be reached by train—not quite so far, perhaps, as Washington is from New York, for that would just as likely as not put it in the sea, but a considerable distance. I suppose you will think that inexcusable; but it is very difficult to be enough interested in foreign capitals to verify vague impressions about them, and Westminster is a large-sounding name, that suggests at least a mayor and a town council of its own. It was odd to find it about twenty minutes from anywhere in Loudon, and not to know exactly when you had arrived until the cab rolled under the shadow of the Abbey, and stopped in the crowd that waited to cheer the great politicians. Lady Torquilin immediately asked one of the policemen which way to go—I don't know anybody who appreciates what you might call the encyclopaedic value of the London police more that Lady Torquilin—and he waved us on. 'Straight ahead, madame, and turn in at the 'orseback statyou,' he said, genially, the distance being not more than two hundred yards from where we stood, and the turning-in point visible On the way, notwithstanding, Lady Torquilin asked two other policemen. My friend loves the peace of mind that follows absolute certainty. Presently we were following the rustling elegance of two or three tall ladies, whom I at once pronounced to be peeresses, through the broad, quiet, red corridor that leads to the House of Lords.

We were among the very first, and had our choice of the long, narrow seats that run along the wall in a terrace on each side of the Chamber. Fortunately, Lady Torquilin had attended other openings of Parliament, and knew that we must sit on the left; otherwise we might just as likely as not have taken our places on the other side, where there were only two or three old gentlemen with sticks and silk hats—which, I reflected afterwards, would have been awful. But, as it happened, we sat down very decorously in our proper places, and I tried to realise, as we looked at the crowded galleries and the long, narrow, solemn crimson room with the throne-chair at one end, that I was in the British House of Lords. Our Senate, just before the opening of Congress, is so very different. Most of the senators are grey-haired, and many of them are bald, but they all walk about quite nimbly, and talk before the proceedings begin with a certain vivacity; and there are pages running round with notes and documents, and a great many excited groups in the lobbies, and a general air of crisp business and alacrity everywhere. The only thing I could feel in the House of Lords that morning was a concentrated atmospheric essence of Importance. I was thinking of a thing Senator Ingalls said to me two years ago, which was what you would call 'comic,' when the idea struck me that it was almost time for Parliament to open, and not a single peer had arrived. So I asked Lady Torquilin when the lords might be expected to come in. Up to this time we had been discussing the millinery by which we were surrounded.

'I daresay there won't be many to-day,' said Lady Torquilin. 'Certainly very few so far!'

'Are there any here?' I asked her.

'Oh, yes—just opposite, don't you see, child! That wellset-up man with the nice, wholesome face, the third from the end in the second row from the bottom—that's Lord Rosebery; and next him is the great beer-man—I forget his title; and here is Lord Mafferton now—don't look—coming into the first row from the bottom, and leaning over to shake hands with Lord Rosebery.'

'Tell me when I can look,' I said, 'because I want to awfully. But, Lady Torquilin, are *those* peers? They look very respectable and nice, I'm sure, but I did expect more in the way of clothes. Where are their flowing mantles, and their chains and swords and things?'

'Only when the Queen opens Parliament in person,' said Lady Torquilin. 'Then there is a turn-out! Now you can look at Lord Mafferton—the rude old man! Fancy his having the impudence to sit there with his hat on!'

I looked at Lord Mafferton, who certainly had not removed his hat—the large, round, shiny silk hat worn by every gentleman in England, and every commercial traveller in America. Under the hat he was very pink and fat, with rather a snubby nose, and little twinkling blue eyes, and a suggestion of white whisker about the place where his chin and his cheek disappeared into his neck. He wore lavender-kid gloves, and was inclined to corpulency. I should not have trusted this description of a peer of your realm if it had come from any other American pen than my own—I should have set it down as a gross exaggeration, due to envy, from the fact that we can neither produce peers in our own country nor keep them there for any length of time; but I was obliged to believe my own eyes, and that is the way they reported Lord Mafferton from the other side of your Upper House. There were other gentlemen in the rows opposite—gentlemen all in black, and gentlemen in light waistcoats, bearded and clean-shaven, most of them elderly, but a few surprisingly middle-aged—for your natural expectation is to see a peer venerable—but I must say there was not one that I would have picked out to be a peer, for any particular reason, in the street. And it seemed to me that, since they are constitutional, as it were, there ought to be some way of knowing them. I reasoned again, however, that perhaps my lack of discrimination was due to my not being accustomed to seeing peers—that possibly the delicate distinctions and values that make up a peer would be perfectly evident to a person born, so to speak, under the shadow of the aristocracy. And in the meantime the proceedings began by everybody standing up. I don't know whether I actually expected a procession and a band, but when I discovered that we were all standing while four or five gentlemen in red gowns walked to the other end of the room and took chairs, my emotions were those of blank surprise. Presently I felt Lady Torquilin give an emphatic tug to my skirt. 'Sit down, child!' she said. 'Everybody else has! Do you want to make a speech?'—and I sat down quickly. Then I observed that a gentleman in black, also in fancy dress, was reading something indistinctly to the four or five red-gowned gentlemen, who looked very solemn and stately, but said nothing. It was so difficult for a stranger to understand, that I did not quite catch what was said to another gentleman in black with buckled shoes, but it must have been to the purport of 'Go and fetch it!' for he suddenly began to walk out backwards, stopping at every few steps to bow with great deference to them of the red gowns, which must have been very trying, for nobody returned the bows, and he never could tell who might have come in behind him. 'I suppose he has gone out for a minute to get something,' I said to Lady Torquilin; and then she told me what, of course, I ought to have known if I had refreshed myself with a little English history before starting—that he was the Usher of the Black Rod, and had been sent to bring the members of the other Parliament. And presently there was a great sound of footsteps in the corridors outside, and your House of Commons came hurrying to the 'bar,' I believe it is called, of your House of Lords. It was wonderfully interesting to look at, to a stranger, that crowd of members of your Lower House as it came, without ceremony, to the slender brass rod and stopped there, because it could come no farther—pressing against it, laying hands upon it, craning over it, and yet held back by the visible and invisible force of it. Compared with the well-fed and well-groomed old gentlemen who sat comfortably inside, these outsiders looked lean and unkempt; but there were so many of them, and they seemed so much more in earnest than the old gentlemen on the benches, that the power of the brass rod seemed to me extraordinary. I should not have been an American if I had not wondered at it, and whether the peers in mufti would not some day be obliged to make a habit of dressing up in their mantles and insignia on these occasions to impress the Commoners properly with a sense of difference and a reason for their staying outside.

Then, as soon as they were all ready to pay attention, the Vice-Chancellor read the Queen's letter, in which Her Majesty, so far as I could understand, regretted her inability to be present, told them all a good deal about what she had been doing since she wrote last, and closed by sending her kind regards and best wishes—a very pleasant letter, I thought, and well-written. Then we all stood up again while the gentlemen in red, the Lord Chancellor, and the others walked out; after which everybody dispersed, and I found myself shaking hands with Lord Mafferton in a pudgy, hearty way, as he and Lady Torquilin and I departed together.

LORD MAFFERTON.

'So this is our little Yankee!' said Lord Mafferton, with his fat round chin stretched out sideways, and his hands behind his back. Now I am quite five-feet eight, and I do not like being called names, but I found a difficulty in telling Lord Mafferton that I was not their little Yankee; so I smiled, and said nothing. 'Well, well! Come over the "duckpond"—isn't that what you call the Atlantic Ocean?—to see how fast old England is going to pieces, eh?'

'Oh!' said Lady Torquilin, 'I think Miss Wick is delighted with England, Lord Mafferton.'

'Yes,' I said, 'I am. Delighted with it! Why should anybody think it is going to pieces?'

'Oh, it's a popular fancy in some quarters,' said Lord

Mafferton. Being a lord, I don't suppose he winked at Lady Torquilin, but he did something very like it.

'I should call it a popular fallacy,' I declared; at which Lord Mafferton laughed, and said, 'It was all very well, it was all very well,' exactly like any old grandpapa. 'Miss Wick would like a look over the place, I suppose,' he said to Lady Torquilin. 'You think it would be safe, eh? No explosives concealed about her—she doesn't think of blowing us up?' And this very jocular old peer led the way through a labyrinth of chambers and corridors of which I can't possibly remember the locality or the purpose, because he went so fast.

'No doubt you've heard of Cromwell,' he said beside one door. I should have liked to know why he asked me, if there was no doubt of it; but I suppose a lord is not necessarily a logician. 'This is the room in which he signed the death-warrant of Charles the First.'

'Dear me,' I said. 'The one that he's holding a copy of on his lap at Madame Tussaud's?'

'I dare say! I dare say!' said Lord Maflerton. 'But not so fast, my dear young lady, not so fast! You mustn't go in, you know. That's not allowable!' and he whisked us away to the Library. 'Of course, Miss Wick understands,' he said to Lady Torquilin, 'that every word spoken here above a whisper means three days in a dungeon on bread and water!' By this time my ideas of peers had become so confused that I was entirely engaged in trying to straighten them out, and had very little to say of any sort; but Lord Mafferton chatted continually as we walked through the splendid rooms, only interrupting himself now and then to remind me of the dungeon and the penalty of talking. It was very difficult getting a first impression of the English House of Parliament and an English peer at the same time—they continually interrupted each other. It was in the Royal Banqueting Hall, for instance, where I was doing my best to meditate upon scenes of the past, that Lord Mafferton stated to Lady Torquilin his objection to the inside of an omnibus, and this in itself was distracting. It would never occur to anybody in America to think of a peer and an omnibus together. The vestibule of the House of Commons was full of gentlemen walking about and talking; but there was a great deliberateness about the way it was done—no excitement, and every man in his silently-expressive silk hat. They all seemed interested in each other in an observing way, too, and whether to bow or not to bow; and when Lord Mafferton recognised any of them, he was usually recognised back with great cordiality. You don't see so much of that when Congress opens. The members in the lobby are usually a great deal too much wrapped up in business to take much notice of each other. I observed, too, that the British Government does not provide cuspidores for its legislators, which struck me as reflecting very favourably upon the legislative sense of propriety here, especially as there seemed to be no obvious demand for such a thing.

'Bless you, my dear young lady, you mustn't go in *there!*' exclaimed Lord Mafferton at the door of the House, as I stepped in to take a perfectly inoffensive look at it. 'Out with you quick, or they'll have you off to the Tower before you can say George Washington!'

'But why?' I asked, quite breathless with my sudden exit.

'Young people should never ask "why?"' said Lord Mafferton, serio-comically. 'Thank your American stars that Salisbury or any of those fellows were not about!'

This peer evidently thought I was very, very young—about twelve; but I have noticed since that not only peers, but all agreeable old gentlemen in England, have a habit of dating you back in this way. It is a kindly, well-meant attitude, but it leaves you without very much to say.

I thought feminine privileges in your House of Commons very limited indeed then, but considerably more so when I attended a sitting with Lady Torquilin a week later, and disarranged my features for life trying to look through the diamonds of the iron grating with which Parliament tries to screen itself from the criticism of its lady relations.

'DISARRANGED MY FEATURES FOR LIFE.'

Lord Mafferton came up that day with us, and explained that the grating was to prevent the ladies from throwing themselves at the heads of the unmarried members—a singular precaution. The only other reason I could hear why it should not be taken down was that nobody had done it since it was put up—a remarkably British reason, and calculated, as most things seem to be in this country, to last.

And I saw your Prince that afternoon. He came into the Peers' Gallery in a light overcoat, and sat down with two or three friends to watch his people governing their country below. He seemed thoroughly interested, and at times, when Mr. O'Brien or Mr. O'Connor said something that looked toward the dismemberment of his empire, amused. And it was an instructive sight to see your future king pleased and edified, and unencumbered by any disagreeable responsibilities, looking on.

XII

ITOLD Lady Torquilin that the expression struck me as profane.

'How ridiculous you are, child! It's a good old English word. *Nobody* will understand you if you talk about your "rubbers" in this country. "Goloshes," certainly. G-o-l-o-s-h-e-s, "goloshes." Now, go directly and put them on, and don't be impertinent about the English language in England, whatever you may be out of it!'

I went away murmuring, '"G-o-l-o-s-h-e-s, goloshes"! What a perfectly awful—literally unutterable word! No, I love Lady Torquilin, and I like her England, but I'll never, never, *never* say "goloshes"! I'd almost rather swear!' And as I slipped on the light, thin, flexible articles manufactured, I believe, in Rochester, N.Y., and privately compared them with the remarkable objects worn by the British nation for the purpose of keeping its feet dry, the difference in the descriptive terms gave me a certain satisfaction.

Lady Torquilin and I were going shopping. I had been longing to shop in London ever since I arrived, but, as Lady Torquilin remarked, my trunks seemed to make it almost unreasonable. So up to this time I had been obliged to content myself with looking at the things in the windows, until Lady Torquilin said she really couldn't spend so much time in front of shop-windows—we had better go inside. Besides, she argued, of course there was this to be said—if you bought a good thing, there it was—always a good thing! I And it isn't as if you were obliged to pinch, my dear. I would be the last one to counsel extravagance,' said Lady Torquilin. 'Therefore we'll go to the cheapest place first'—and we got an omnibus. It seemed full of people who were all going to the cheapest place, and had already come, some of them a long way, to go to it, judging by their fares. They were not poor people, nor respectably-darned people, nor shabby-genteel people. Some of them looked like people with incomes that would have enabled them to avoid the cheapest place, and some gave you the idea that, if it were not for the cheapest place, they would not look so well. But they had an invariable expression of content with the cheapest place, or appreciation of it, that made me quite certain they would all get out when we stopped there; and they did.

We went in with a throng that divided and hurried hither and thither through long 'departments,' upstairs and down, past counters heaped with cheapnesses, and under billowing clouds and streaming banners of various colours, marked 1s. 1d. and 11d. in very black letters on a very white ground. The whole place spoke of its cheapness, invited you to approach and have your every want supplied at the lowest possible scale of profit—for cash. Even the clerks—as we say in America, incorrectly, I believe—the people behind the counter suggested the sweet reasonableness of the tariff; not that

I mean anything invidious, but they seemed to be drawn from an unpretending, inexpensive class of humanity. The tickets claimed your attention everywhere, and held it, the prices on them were so remarkably low; and it was to me at first a matter of regret that they were all attached to articles I could not want under any circumstances. For, the moment I went in. I succumbed to the cheapest place; I desired to avail myself of it to any extent—to get the benefit of those fascinating figures personally and immediately. I followed Lady Torquilin with eagerness, exclaiming: but nothing would induce her to stop anywhere; she went straight for the trifles she wanted, and I perforce after her. 'There are some things, my dear,' she said, when we reached the right counter, 'that one *must* come here for, but beyond those few odds and ends—well, I leave you to judge for yourself.'

'THE WHOLE PLACE SPOKE OF ITS CHEAPNESS'

This was calculated to dash a person's enthusiasm, and mine was dashed at once. There is nothing, in shopping, like a friend's firm and outspoken opinion, to change your views. I began to think unfavourably of the cheapest place immediately, and during the twenty-five minutes of valuable time which Lady Torquilin spent, in addition to some small silver, upon a box of pink paper trimmings for pudding-dishes, I had arrived at a state of objection to the cheapest place, which intensified as we climbed more stairs, shared more air with the British Public of the cheapest place, and were jostled at more counters. 'For,' Lady Torquilin said, 'now that we *are* here, though I loathe coming, except that it's something you ought to do, we really might as well see what there is!'—and she found that there were quite a number of little things at about a shilling and a ha'penny that she absolutely needed, and would have to pay 'just double for, my dear, anywhere else.' By that time my objection became active, and embraced the cheapest place and everything connected with it, quite unreasonably. For there was no doubt about the genuineness of the values offered all over its counters, or about the fact that the clerks were doing the best they could to sell seven separate shillings'-worth at the same moment to different individuals, or of the respectability of the seven people who were spending the seven shillings. It would have been a relief, indeed, to have detected something fraudulent among the bargains, or some very great adventuress among the customers. It was the deadly monotony of goodishness and cheapishness in everything and everybody that oppressed you. There were no heights of excellence and no contrasting depths—all one level of quality wherever you looked—so that the things they sold at the cheapest place—sold with mechanical respect, and as fast as they could tie them up—seemed to lack all individuality, and to have no reason for being, except to become parcels. There was none of the exultation of bargain-getting; the bargains were on a regular system of fixed laws—the poetic delight of an unexpected 'reduction' was wholly absent. The cheapest place resolved itself into a vast, well-organised Opportunity, and inside you saw the British Public and the Opportunity together.

'Ere is your chainge, madam,' said the hollow-eyed young woman who had been waiting upon Lady Torquilin in the matter of a letter-weight and a Japanese umbrella. 'Thank you,' said Lady Torquilin. 'I'm afraid you get very tired, don't you, before the day is over?' my friend asked the young woman, with as sweet a smile as she could have given anybody. The young woman smiled back again, and said, 'Very, madame'; but that was all, for three other people wanted her. I put this in because it is one of the little things she often says that show the niceness of Lady Torquilin.

'Now, what do you think of the cheapest place?' asked Lady Torquilin as we walked together in the Edgware Road. I told her as I have told you. 'H'mph!' said she. 'It's not a shop I like myself, but that's what I call being *too* picksome! You get what you want, and if you don't want it you leave it, and why should you care! Now, by way of variety, we'll go to the dearest place;' and the omnibus we got into rattled off in the direction of Bond Street. It struck me then, and often since, how oddly different London is from an American city to go shopping in. At home the large, important stores are pretty much together, in the business part of the city, and anybody can tell from the mere buildings what to expect in the way of style and price. In London you can't tell at all, and the well-known shops are scattered over square miles of streets, by twos and threes, in little individual towns, each with its own congregation of smaller shops, and its own butchers and bakers and newsstands, and post-office and squares and 'places,' and blind alleys and strolling cats and hand organs; and to get from one to another of the little towns it is necessary to make a journey in an omnibus. Of course, I know there are a few places preeminent in reputation and 'form' and price—above all in price—which gather in a few well-known streets; but life in all these little centres which make up London would be quite complete without them. They seem to exist for the benefit of that extravagant element here that has nothing to do with the small respectable houses and the little domestic squares, but hovers over the city during the time of year when the sun shines and the fogs are not, living during that time in notable localities, under the special inspection of the 'Morning Post.' The people who really live in London—the people of the little centres—can quite well ignore these places; they have their special shop in Uxbridge Road or St. Paul's Churchyard, and if they tire of their own particular local cut, they can make morning trips from Uxbridge Road to the High Street, Kensington, or from either to Westbourne Grove. To Americans this is very novel and amusing, and we get a great deal of extra pleasure out of shopping in London in sampling, so to speak, the different submunicipalities.

While I was thinking these things, Lady Torquilin poked me with her parasol from the other end of the omnibus. 'Tell him to stop!' she said, and I did; at least, the gentleman in the corner made the request for me. That gentleman in the corner is a feature of your omnibus system, I think. His arm, or his stick, or his umbrella, is always at the service of any lady who wants the bell rung. It seems to be a duty that goes with the corner seat, cheerfully accepted by every man that sits there.

'THAT GENTLEMAN IN THE CORNER IS A FEATURE OF YOUR OMNIBUS SYSTEM, I THINK.'

We had arrived in Bond Street, at the dearest place. From what Lady Torquilin told me, I gathered that Bond Street was a regular haunt for dearest places; but it would be impossible for any stranger to suppose so from walking through it—it is so narrow and crooked and irregular, and the shops are so comparatively insignificant after the grand sweep of Regent Street and the wide variety of the circuses. For one, I should have thought circuses would be the best possible places for business in London, not only because the address is so easily remembered, but because once you get into them they are so extremely difficult to get out of. However, a stranger never can tell.

Inside, the dearest place was a stronger contrast to the cheapest place than I could describe by any antithesis. There was an exclusive emptiness about it that seemed to suggest a certain temerity in coming in, and explained, considered commercially, why the rare visitors should have such an expensive time of it. One or two tailor-made ladies discussed something in low tones with an assistant, and beside these there was nobody but a couple of serious-minded shopwalkers, some very elegant young ladies-in-waiting, and the dummies that called your attention to the fashions they were exhibiting. The dummies were headless, but probably by the variety of their clothes they struck you as being really the only personalities in the shop. We looked at some of them before advancing far into the august precincts of the dearest place, and Lady Torquilin had a sweeping opinion of them. '*Hideous!* I call them,' she said; but she said it in rather a hushed tone, quite different from the one she would have used in the cheapest place, and I am sure the shopwalker did not overhear. 'Bulgarian atrocities! How in the world people imagine such things! And as to setting to work to *make* them——'

I can't say I agreed with Lady Torquilin, for there was a distinct idea in all the dresses, and a person always respects an idea, whether it is pretty or not; but neither can I profess an admiration for the fashions of the dearest place. They were rather hard and unsympathetic; they seemed to sacrifice everything to be in some degree striking; their motto seemed to be, 'Let us achieve a difference'—presumably from the fashions of places that were only dear in the comparative degree. While we were looking at them, one of the pale young women strolled languidly up and remarked, with an absent expression, that one of them was 'considered a smart little gown, moddam!' 'Smart enough, I daresay,' said Lady Torquilin, with a slightly invidious emphasis on the adjective; whereat the young woman said nothing, but looked volumes of repressed astonishment at the ignorance implied. Lady Torquilin went on to describe the kind of dress I thought of buying.

'THE YOUNG WOMAN CRAWLED AWAY WITH THE NEGLIGENCE THAT BECAME THE DEAREST PLACE'

'Certainly, moddam! Will you take a seat, moddam? Something *quite* simple I think you said, moddam, and in muslin. I'll be with you in one moment, moddam.' And the young woman crawled away with the negligence that became the dearest place. After an appreciable time she returned with her arms full of what they used to call, so very correctly, 'furbelows,' in spotted and flowered muslins.

'Dearie me!' said Lady Torquilin. 'That's precisely what I wore when I was a girl!'

'Yes, moddam!' said the young woman, condescending to the ghost of a smile. 'The old styles are all comin' in again'—at which burst of responsiveness she suddenly brought herself up sharply, and assumed a manner which forbade you to presume upon it.

I picked up one of the garlanded muslins and asked the price of it. It had three frills round the bottom and various irrelevant ribbon-bows.

'Certainly, moddam! One moment, moddam!' as she looked at the ticket attached.

'This one is seventeen guineas, moddam. Silk foundation. A Paris model, moddam, but I dare say we could copy it for you for less.'

Lady Torquilin and I made a simultaneous movement, and looked at each other in the expressive way that all ladies understand who go shopping with each other.

'Thanks!' I said. 'It is much too expensive for me.'

'We have nothing of this style under fifteen guineas, moddam,' replied the young woman, with a climax of weary frigidity. 'Then, shall we go?'

I asked Lady Torquilin—and we went.

'*What* a price!' said Lady Torquilin, as we left the dearest place behind us.

I said I thought it was an insult—eighty-five dollars for a ready-made sprigged muslin dress!—to the intelligence of the people who were expected to buy it. That, for my part, I should feel a distinct loss of self-respect in buying anything at the dearest place. What would I be paying for?

'For being able to say that it came from the dearest place,' said Lady Torquilin. 'But I thought you Americans didn't mind what anything cost.'

That misconception of Lady Torquilin's is a popular one, and I was at some pains to rectify it. 'We don't,' I said, 'if we recognise the fairness of it; but nobody resents being imposed upon more than an American, Lady Torquilin. We have our idiots, like other nations, and I daresay a good many of them come to London every year and deal exclusively at the dearest place; but as a nation, though we don't scrimp we do like the feeling that we are paying for value received.'

'Well,' said Lady Torquilin, 'I believe that is the case. I know Americans talk a great deal about the price of things—more, I consider, than is entertaining sometimes.' I said I knew they did—it was a national fault—and what did Lady Torquilin think the dress I had on cost, just to compare it with that muslin, and Chicago was by no means a cheap place for anything. Lady Torquilin said she hadn't an idea—our dollars were so difficult to reckon in; but what did I think hers came to—and not a scrap of silk lining about it. And so the time slipped away until we arrived in the neighbourhood of Cavendish Square, at what Lady Torquilin called 'the happy medium,' where the windows were tempting, and the shopwalker smiled, and the lady-in-waiting was a person of great dignity, in high, black sleeves, with a delightful French accent when she talked, which she very seldom forgot, and only contradicted when she said "Ow' and "elliotrope,' and where things cost just about what they did in America.

'A PERSON OF GREAT DIGNITY IN HIGH, BLACK SLEEVES'

I have gone very patiently ever since to the happy medium, partly to acquire the beautiful composure of the lady-in-waiting, partly to enjoy the respect which all Americans like so much in a well-conducted English shop, and partly because at the happy medium they understand how to turn shopping into the pleasant artistic pastime it ought to be, which everybody in America is in far too much of a hurry to make a fortune and retire to do for his customers. I am on the most agreeable footing with the lady in the sleeves now, and I have observed that, as our acquaintance progresses, her command of English consonantal sounds remarkably increases. But I have never been able to reconcile myself, even theoretically, either to the cheapest place, in the Edgware Road, or the dearest place, in Bond Street.

XIII

'AS a nation I can't bear 'em—individually, I like 'em *fairly* well,' read out Lady Torquilin from a letter at breakfast. 'Bless me!' my friend went on, 'she's talking about Americans, and she's coming to see "your specimen"—meaning you, child—this very afternoon.'

So she did. She came to see me that very afternoon—the lady who couldn't bear us as a nation, but individually liked us fairly well. Her name was Corke, and she belonged, Lady Torquilin said, to *the* Corkes. I heard all about her before she came. She was a lady of moderate income, unmarried, about ten years older than I was. She knew all about everything.

'You never saw such a reader, my dear! I won't say it happens often, for that it does not, but Peter Corke has made me feel like a perfect ignoramus.'

'*Peter* Corke?' I said, with some surprise.

'Too ridiculous, I call it! Her proper name is Catharine Clarissa, but she hates her proper name—sensible girl as she is in every other way—prefers Peter! And if she happens to take a fancy to you, she will tell you all manner of interesting things. For old holes and corners, I always say, go to Peter Corke.'

'I'm glad,' I said, 'that she likes us, individually, fairly well—it's the only way in which I would have any chance! But she won't like my accent.'

'If she doesn't,' Lady Torquilin said, 'I promise you she'll tell you. And you won't mind a bit.'

When Miss Corke arrived I forgot entirely about the doubtfulness of her liking me—I was too much absorbed in liking her. She was rather a small person, with a great deal of dignity in her shoulders and a great deal of humour in her face—the most charming face I have seen in England, and I can't even make an exception in favour of the Princess of Wales. I may tell you that she had delightful twinkling brown eyes, and hair a shade darker, and the colour and health and energy that only an English woman possesses at thirty, without being in the least afraid that you could pick her out in the street, or anywhere—she would not like that—and being put in print, so that people would know her, at all; it's a thing I wouldn't do on any account, knowing her feelings. It is only because I am so well convinced that I can't tell you what she was like that I try, which you may consider a feminine reason, if you want to. Miss Peter Corke's personality made you think at once of Santa Claus and a profound philosopher—could you have a more difficult combination to describe than that? While you listened to a valuable piece of advice from her lips you might be quite certain that she had an orange for you in the hand behind her back; and however you might behave, you would get the orange. Part of her charm was the atmosphere of gay beneficence she carried about with her, that made you want to edge your chair closer to wherever she was sitting; and part of it was the remarkable interest she had in everything that concerned you—a sort of interest that made you feel as if such information as you could give about yourself was a direct and valuable contribution to the sum of her knowledge of humanity; and part of it was the salutary sincerity of everything she had to say in comment, though I ought not to forget her smile, which was a great deal of it. I am sure I don't know why I speak of Miss Peter Corke in the past tense, however. She is not dead—or even married; I cannot imagine a greater misfortune to her large circle of friends in London.

'*Two* lumps, please,' begged Miss Corke of me in the midst of a succession of inquiries about Lady Torquilin's cough, whether it could possibly be gout, or if she had been indulging in salmon and cucumber lately, in which case it served her perfectly right. 'What a disappointment you are! Why don't you ask me if I like it with all the trimmings?'

'The trimmings?' I repeated.

'Certainly! the sugar and milk! Fancy being obliged to explain Americanisms to an American!' said Miss Corke to Lady Torquilin.

'Is trimmings an Americanism?' I asked. 'I never heard it before. But I dare say it is an expression peculiar to Boston, perhaps.'

'You had better not have any doubt,' said Miss Corke, with mock ferocity, 'of anything you hear in England.'

'I've heard fixings often at home,' I declared, 'but never trimmings.'

'Oh!' remarked Miss Corke, genially; 'then fixings is the correct expression.'

'I don't know,' I said, 'about its being the correct expression. Our washerwoman uses it a good deal.'

'Oh!' said Miss Corke, with an indescribable inflection of amusement; and then she looked at me over the top of her teacup, as much as to say, 'you had better not go too far!'

'Are your father and mother living?' she asked; and just then I noticed that it was twenty minutes past four by the clock. I answered Miss Corke in the affirmative, and naturally I was glad to be able to; but I have often wondered since why that invariable interest in the existence or non-existence of a person's parents should prevail in England as it does. I have seldom been approached by any one in a spirit of kindly curiosity with a different formula. 'Any brothers and sisters?' Miss Corke went on. 'When did you come? Where did you go first? How long do you mean to stay? What have you seen? Did you expect us to be as we are, or do we exceed your expectations? Have you ever travelled alone before? Are you quite sure you like the feeling of being absolutely independent? Don't you love our nice old manners and customs? and won't you wish when you get back that you could put your President on a golden throne, with an ermine robe, and a sceptre in his right hand?'

Miss Corke gave me space between these questions for brief answers, but by the time I looked at the clock again, and saw that it was twenty-five minutes past four, to the best of my recollection, she had asked me twelve. I liked it immensely—it made conversation so easy; but I could not help thinking, in connection with it, of the capacity for interrogation, which I had always heard credited exclusively to Americans.

'Peter,' said Lady Torquilin at last, a little tired of it, 'ask something about me; I haven't seen you for weeks.'

'Dear lady,' said Peter, 'of course I will. But this is something new, you see, so one takes an ephemeral—very ephemeral!—interest in it.'

Lady Torquilin laughed. 'Well!' said she, 'there's nothing more wonderful than the way it gets about alone.'

Then I laughed too. I did not find anything in the least objectionable in being called an 'it' by Miss Corke.

'So you've been in England a whole month!' said she. 'And what do you think you have observed about us? Basing your opinion,' said Miss Corke, with serio-comicality, 'upon the fact that we are for your admiration, and *not* for your criticism, how do you like us?'

I couldn't help it. 'Individually,' I said, 'I like you *fairly* well—as a nation, I can't——'

'Oh!' cried Miss Corke, in a little funny squeal, rushing at Lady Torquilin, 'you've gone and told her—you wicked woman!'—and she shook Lady Torquilin, a thing I didn't see how she dared to do. 'I can't bear it, and I won't! Private correspondence—I wonder you're not ashamed!'—and Miss Corke sank into a chair, and covered her face with her hands and her handkerchief, and squealed again, more comically than before.

'"YOU WICKED WOMAN"'

By the time I had been acquainted with Miss Corke a fortnight I had learned to look for that squeal, and to love it. She probably will not know until she reads this chapter how painfully I have tried to copy it, and how vainly, doubtless owing to the American nature of my larynx. But Miss Corke had a way of railing at you that made you feel rather pleased that you had misbehaved. I could see that it had that effect upon Lady Torquilin, though all she did was to smile broadly, and say to Miss Peter, 'Hoity-toity! Have another cup of tea.' In the course of further conversation, Miss Corke said that she saw my mind must be improved immediately if she had to do it herself; and where would I like to begin. I said almost anywhere, I didn't think it much mattered; and Miss Corke said, Well, that was candid on my part, and augured favourably, and was I architectururally inclined? I said I thought I was, some; and out came Miss Peter Corke's little shriek again. 'Tell her,' she said, prodding Lady Torquilin, 'that we say "rather" over here in that connection; I don't know her well enough.' And I was obliged to beg Lady Torquilin to tell *her* that we said 'some' over there in that connection, though not in books, or university lectures, or serious-minded magazines.'

'Oh, come!' said Miss Corke, 'do you mean to say you've got any serious-minded magazines?'

'I'll come anywhere you like,' I responded. 'Have you got any light-minded ones?'

Whereat Miss Corke turned again to Lady Torquilin, and confided to her that I was a flippant young woman to live in the same house with, and Lady Torquilin assured her that there wasn't really any harm in me—it was only my way.

'H'm!' remarked Miss Peter, perking up her chin in a manner that made me long to be on kissing terms with her—'the American way!' As I write that it looks disagreeable; as Peter Corke said it, it was the very nectar and ambrosia of prejudiced and favourable criticism. And I soon found out that whatever she might say, her words never conveyed anything but herself—never had any significance, I mean, that your knowledge of her delightful nature did not endorse.

'I suppose we'd better begin with the churches, don't you think?' said Miss Corke to Lady Torquilin. 'Poor dear! I dare say she's never seen a proper church!'

'Oh, yes!' I said, 'you have never been in Chicago, Miss Corke, or you wouldn't talk like that. We have several of the finest in America in our city; and we ourselves attend a very large one, erected last year, the Congregational—though momma has taken up Theosophy considerably lately. It's built in amphitheatre style, with all the latest improvements—electric light, and heated with hot water all through. It will seat five thousand people on spring-edged cushions, and has a lovely kitchen attached for socials!' 'Built in the amphitheatre style! repeated Miss Corke. 'To seat five thousand people on spring-edged cushions—with a kitchen attached! And now, will you tell me immediately what a "social" is?'

'There are different kinds, you know,' I replied. 'Ice-cream socials, and oyster socials, and ordinary tea-meetings; but they nearly always have something to eat in them—a dry social with only a collection never amounts to much. And they're generally held in the basement of the church, and the young ladies of the congregation wait.'

Miss Corke looked at me, amused and aghast. 'You see, I was quite right,' she said to Lady Torquilin. 'She never has! But I think this really ought to be reported to the Foreign Missions Society! I'll take you to the Abbey tomorrow,' she went on. 'You like "deaders," don't you? The time between might be profitably spent in fasting and meditation! Good-bye, dear love!'— to Lady Torquilin. 'No, you will *not* come down, either of you! Remember, young lady, three-thirty, *sharp*, at the entrance everybody uses, opposite Dizzy's statue—the same which you are never on any account to call Dizzy, but always Lord Disraeli, with the respect that becomes a foreigner! *Good-bye!*'

"REMEMBER, YOUNG LADY, THREE-THIRTY—*Sharp*."

XIV

WHAT do you mean?' asked Miss Corke, indicating the Parliament House clock with a reproachful parasol, as I joined her a week from the following afternoon outside the south cloister of the Abbey. We had seen a good deal of her in the meantime, but the Abbey visit had been postponed. Her tone was portentous, and I looked at the clock, which said ten minutes to four. I didn't quite understand, for I thought I was in pretty good time. 'Didn't you say I was to come about now?' I inquired. Miss Corke made an inarticulate exclamation of wrath.

'Half-past three may be "about now" in America!' she said, 'but it isn't here, as you may see by the clock. Fancy my having made an appointment with a young person who had an idea of keeping it "about" the time I had condescended to fix!'—and Miss Corke put down her parasol as we entered the cloisters, and attempted to wither me with a glance. If the glance had not had the very jolliest smile of good-fellowship inside it I don't know what I should have done, but as it was I didn't wither; though I regretted to hear that I had missed the Jerusalem Chamber by being late, where King Henry died—because he always knew he should expire in a place of that name, and so fulfilled prophecy, poor dear, by coming to kneel on the cold stone at St. Edward's shrine, where he would always say his prayers, and nowhere else, immediately after a number of extraordinary Christmas dinners—and Miss Corke was not in the least sorry for me, though it was a thing I ought to see, and we positively must come another day to see it.

We walked up past the little green square that you see in wide spaces through the side pillars, where the very oldest old monks lie nameless and forgotten, whose lives gathered about the foundations of the Abbey—the grey foundations in the grey past—and sank silently into its history just as their bodily selves have disappeared long ago in the mosses and grasses that cover them. 'No, Miss Mamie Wick, of Chicago, I will not hurry!' said Miss Corke, 'and neither shall you! It is a sacrilege that I will allow no young person in my company to commit—to go through these precincts as if there were anything in the world as well worth looking at outside of them.'

I said I didn't want to hurry in the very least.

'Are you sure you don't—inside of you?' she demanded. Certain you have no lurking private ambition to do the Abbey in two hours and get it over? Oh, I know you! I've brought lots of you here before.'

'I know,' I said, I as a nation we do like to get a good deal for our time.'

'It's promising when you acknowledge it'—Miss Corke laughed. 'All the old abbots used to be buried here up to the time of Henry III.; that's probably one of 'em'—and Miss Corke's parasol indicated a long, thick, bluish stone thing lying on its back, with a round lump at one end and an imitation of features cut on the lump. It lay there very solidly along the wall, and I tried in vain to get a point of view from which it was expressive of anything whatever. 'One of the early abbots?' said I, because it seemed necessary to say something.

'Probably,' said Miss Corke.

'Which particular abbot should you say?' I asked, deferentially, for I felt that I was in the presence of something very early English indeed, and that it became me to be impressed, whether I was or not.

'Oh, I don't know,' Miss Peter Corke replied. 'Postard, perhaps, or Crispin, or maybe Vitalis; nobody knows.'

'I suppose it would have been easier to tell a while ago,' I said. 'There is something so worn about his face, I should think even the other early abbots would find a difficulty in recognising him now. Nothing Druidical, I suppose?'

'Certainly not. If you are going to be disrespectful,' said Miss Corke, 'I shall take you home at once.' Whereat I protested that I did not dream disrespect—that he looked to me quite as much like a Druid as anything else. I even ventured to say that, if she had not told me he was an early abbot, I might have taken him for something purely and entirely geological. The whole of this discussion took place at what stood for the early abbot's feet, and occupied some little time; so that, finally, Miss Corke was obliged to tell me that, if there was one thing she couldn't bear, it was dawdling, and would I be pleased to look at the monumental tablet to Mr. Thomas Thynne, of which she would relate to me the history. So we paused in front of it, while Miss Corke told me how the gentleman in the basrelief chariot was Mr. Thomas Thynne, and the gentleman on horseback, shooting at him with a blunderbuss, was Kônigsmark, accompanied by his brother; and Kônigsmark was in the act of killing Mr. Thomas Thynne, with the horses getting unmanageable, and the two powdered footmen behind in a state of great agitation, because both Mr. Thomas Thynne and Kônigsmark were attached to the same lady—a young widow lady with a great deal of money—and she liked Mr. Thomas Thynne best, which was more than Mr. Kônigsmark could bear. So Mr. Kônigsmark first swore properly that he would do it, and then did it—all in Pall Mall, when Mr. Thomas was in the very act of driving home from paying a visit to the widow. It was a most affecting story, as Peter Corke told it, especially in the presence of the memorial with a white marble Cupid pointing to it, erected by Mr. Thynne's bereaved relatives; and I was glad to hear that the widow had nothing to do with Mr. Kônigsmark afterwards, in spite of the simplicity and skill of his tactics with regard to his rival. I thought the history of the event quite interesting enough in itself, but Miss Corke insisted that the point about it really worthy of attention was the fact that the younger Mr. Kônigsmark was the gentleman who afterwards went back to Hanover, and there flirted so disgracefully with Sophia Dorothea of Zell that King George said he wouldn't have it, and shut her up in Ahlden Tower for thirty-two years. Miss Corke explained it all in a delightful kindergarten way, mentioning volumes for my reference if I wanted to know more about the incident. 'Although this,' she said, 'is the sort of thing you ought to have been improving your mind with ever since you learned to read. I don't know what you mean by it, coming over here with a vast unbroken field of ignorance about our celebrities. Do you think time began in 1776?' At which I retaliated, and said that far from being an improving incident, I wasn't sure that it was altogether respectable, and I didn't know of a single church in Chicago that would admit a bas-relief of it, with or without a mourning Cupid. In return to which Miss Corke could find nothing better to say than 'Lawks!'

'Don't tell me you've read the "Spectator!"' she remarked a little farther on, 'because I know you haven't—you've read nothing but W. D. Howells and the "New York World!" Oh, you have? Several essays! When, pray? At school—I thought so! When you couldn't help it! Well, I know you've forgotten Sir Roger de Coverley, in the Abbey, stopping Addison here, to tell him that man thrashed his grandfather! His own grandfather, you know, not Addison's!' And we contemplated the studious effigy of Dr. Busby until I told Miss Corke that I wanted to be taken to the Poets' Corner.

'Of course you do,' said she; 'there are rows of Americans there now, sitting looking mournful and thinking up quotations. If I wanted to find an American in London, I should take up my position in the Poets' Corner until he arrived. You needn't apologise—it's nothing to your discredit,' remarked Miss Corke, as we turned in among your wonderful crumbling old names, past the bust of George Grote, historian of Greece. 'Of course, you have heard of his lady-wife,' she said, nodding at Mr. Grote. I ventured the statement that she was a very remarkable person.

'Well, she was!' returned Miss Corke, 'though that's a shot in the dark, and you might as well confess it. One of *the* most remarkable women of her time. All the biographers of the day wrote about her—as you ought to know, *intimately*. I have the honour of the acquaintance of a niece of hers, who told me the other day that she wasn't particularly fond of her. Great independence of character!'

'Where is Chaucer?' I asked, wishing to begin at the beginning.

'Just like every one of you that I've ever brought here!' Miss Corke exclaimed, leading the way to the curious old rectangular grey tomb in the wall. 'The very best—the very oldest—immediately! Such impatience I never saw!

There now—make out that early English lettering, if you can, and be properly sorry that you've renounced your claim to be proud of it!'

'I can't make it out, so I'll think about being sorry later,' I said. 'It is certainly very remarkable; he might almost have written it himself. Now, where is Shakespeare?'

'Oh, certainly!' exclaimed Miss Corke. 'This way. And after that you'll declare you've seen them all. But you might just take time to understand that you're walking over "O rare Ben Jonson!" who is standing up in his old bones down there as straight as you or I. Insisted—as you probably are *not* aware—on being buried that way, so as to be ready when Gabriel blows his trumpet in the morning. I won't say that he hasn't got his coat and hat on. Yes, that's Samuel—I'm glad you didn't say Ben was the lexicographer. Milton—certainly—it's kind of you to notice him. Blind, you remember. The author of several works of some reputation—in England.'

'I knew he was blind,' I said, 'and used to dictate to his daughters. We have a picture of it at home.' I made this remark very innocently, and Miss Corke looked at me with a comical smile. 'Bless it and save it!' she said, and then, with an attempt at a reproach, 'What a humbug it is!'

'WE LOOKED AT SHAKESPEARE, SUPREME AMONG THEM'

We looked at Shakespeare, supreme among them, predicting solemn dissolution out of 'The Tempest,' and turned from him to Gay, whose final reckless word I read with as much astonishment as if I had never heard of it before.

Life's a jest, and all things show it;

I thought so once, and now I know it,

has no significance at all read in an American school-book two thousand miles, and a hundred and fifty years from the writer of it, compared with the grim shock it gives you when you see it actually cut deep in the stone, to be a memorial always of a dead man somewhere not far away.

' " LIFE'S A JEST, AND ALL THINGS SHOW IT;
I THOUGHT SO ONCE, AND NOW I KNOW IT " '

'That you should have heard of Nicholas Rowe,' said Miss Corke, 'is altogether too much to expect. Dear me! it would be considerably easier to improve your mind if it had ever been tried before. But he was poet-laureate for George the First—you understand the term?'

'I think so,' I said. 'They contract to supply the Royal Family with poetry, by the year, at a salary. We have nothing of the kind in America. You see our

Presidents differ so. They might not all like poetry. And in that case it would be wasted, for there isn't a magazine in the country that would take it second-hand.'

'Besides having no poets who could do it properly, poor things!' said Miss Corke—to which I acceded without difficulty.

'Well, Mr. Rowe was a poet-laureate, though that has nothing whatever to do with it. But he had a great friend in Mr. Pope—Pope, you know him—by reputation—and when he and his daughter died, Mr. Pope and Mrs. Rowe felt so bad about it that he wrote those mournful lines, and she had 'em put up.

Now listen!—

To those so mourned in death, so lov'd in life,

The childless parent and the widowed wife—

meaning the same lady; it was only a neat way they had of doubling up a sentiment in those days!—

With tears inscribes this monumental stone,

That holds their ashes and expects her own!

and everybody, including Mr. Pope, thought it perfectly sweet at the time. Then what does this degenerate widow do, after giving Mr. Pope every reason to believe that she would fulfil his poetry?'

'She marries again,' I said.

'Quite right; she marries again. But you needn't try to impose upon me, miss! To come to that conclusion you didn't require any previous information whatever! She marries again, and you can't think how it vexed Mr. Pope.'

'I know,' I said, 'he declared that was the last of his lending the use of his genius to widows'—for I had to assume some knowledge of the subject.

Miss Corke looked at me. 'You idjit!' she said. 'He did nothing of the sort.'

'Michael Drayton!' I read amongst other names which surprised me by their unfamiliarity; for in America, whatever Peter Corke may say, if we have a strong point, it is names—'who was Michael Drayton? and why was *he* entitled to a bust?'

'He wrote the "Polyolbion,"' said Miss Corke, as if that were all there was to say about it.

'Do you know,' I said—'I am ashamed to confess it, but even of so well-known and interesting a work of genius as the "Polyolbion" I have committed very few pages to memory!'

'Oh!' returned Miss Peter, 'you're getting unbearable! There's a lovely epitaph for you, of Edmund Spenser's, "whose divine spirit needs noe othir witnesse than the workes which he left behind him." You will kindly make no ribald remarks about the spelling, as I perceive you are thinking of doing. Try and remember that we taught you to spell over there. And when Edmund Spenser was buried, dear damsel, there came a company of poets to the funeral—Shakespeare, doubtless, among them—and cast into his grave all manner of elegies.'

'Of their own composition?' I inquired.

'Stupid!—certainly! And the pens that wrote them!'

I said I thought it a most beautiful and poetic thing to have done, if they kept no copies of the poems, and asked Miss Corke if she believed anything of the kind would be possible now.

'Bless you!' she replied. 'In the first place, there aren't the poets; in the second place, there isn't the hero-worship; in the third place, the conditions of the poetry-market are different nowadays—it's more expensive than it used to be; the poets would prefer to send wreaths from the florist's—you can get quite a nice one for twelve-and-six;' and Peter Corke made a little grimace expressive of disgust with the times. 'We used to have all poets and no public, now we have all public and no poets!' she declared, 'now that *he* is gone—and Tennyson can't live for ever.' Miss Corke pointed with her parasol to a name in the stone close to my right foot. I had been looking about me, and above me, and everywhere but there. As I read it I took my foot away quickly, and went two or three paces off. It was so unlooked-for, that name, so new to its association with death, that I stood aside, held by a sudden sense of intrusion. He had always been so high and so far off in the privacy of his genius, so revered in his solitudes, so unapproachable, that it took one's breath away for the moment to have walked unthinkingly over the grave of Robert Browning. It seemed like taking an advantage one would rather not have taken—even to stand aside and read the plain, strong name in the floor, and know that he, having done with life, had been brought there, and left where there could be no longer about him any wonderings or any surmises. Miss Corke told me that she knew him, 'as one can say one knows such a man,' and how kindly his interest was in all that the ordinary people of his acquaintance like herself were thinking and doing; but the little, homely stories she related to me from her personal knowledge of him seemed curiously without relevance then. Nothing mattered, except that he who had epitomised greatness in his art for the century lay there beneath his name in the place of greatness. And then, immediately, from this grave of yesterday, there came to me light and definition for all the graves of the day before. It stole among the quaint lettering of the inscriptions, and into the dusty corners of the bas-reliefs, and behind all the sculptured scrolls and laurels, and showed me what I had somehow missed seeing sooner—all that shrined honour means in England; and just in that one little corner how great her possessions are! Miss Corke said something about the royal tombs and the coronation chair, and the wax effigies in the chamber above the Islip Chapel, and getting on; but, I if you don't mind,' I said, 'I should like to sit down here for a while with the other Americans and think.'

XV

It is said that there are four hundred people in New York who are exclusive, and there are a few more on Beacon Hill in Boston, and in Philadelphia. But most Americans are opposed to exclusiveness. I know that nothing of the sort flourishes in Chicago. Generally and individually, Americans believe that every man is as good as his neighbour; and we take pains to proclaim our belief whenever the subject of class distinction, is under discussion. Poppa's views, however—representing those of the majority in an individual, as we hope they soon may do in a senator—are strongly against any theory of exclusiveness whatever. And I will say for poppa, that his principles are carried out in his practice; for, to my knowledge, neither his retirement from business and purchase of a suburban lakeside residence, nor even his nomination for the Senate, has made the slightest difference in his treatment of any human being. And yet Americans coming over here with all their social theories in their trunks, so to speak, very carefully packed to be ready at a moment's notice, very seldom seem to find a use for them in England. I was brought up, you might say, on poppa's, and momma agreed with him on most points, with the one qualification that, if you couldn't have nice society, it was much better to go without any—'Scarce company, welcome trumpery!' momma always declared would never be her motto. Yet since I have been in England I have hardly had occasion to refer to them at all. I listened to an American author about it a while ago, before I had any intention of writing my own English experiences, and he said the reason Americans liked the exclusiveness over here was because its operation gave them such perfect types to study, each of its own little circle; while at home we are a great indeterminate, shifting mass, and a person who wanted to know us as a nation must know us very largely as individuals first. I thought that might be a very good reason for an author, especially for an author who liked an occasional cup of tea with a duchess; but I was not sure that it could be claimed by a person like myself, only over on a visit, and not for any special purpose of biological research. So I went on liking the way you shut some people out and let other people in, without inquiring further as to why I did—it did not seem profitable, especially when I reflected that my point of view was generally from the inside. My democratic principles are just the same as ever, though—a person needn't always approve what she likes. I shall take them back quite unimpaired to a country where they are indispensable—where you really want them, if you are going to be comfortable, every day of your life.

Nevertheless, I know it was the 'private' part of the 'Private View' that made me so anxious to go to the Academy on the first day of May this year. The pictures would be there the second day, and the day following, and days indefinitely after that, and for a quarter of a dollar I could choose my own time and circumstances of going to see them. I might, weather permitting, have taken my 'view' of the Academy in the publicity of five or six other people who, like me, would have paid a shilling a-piece to get in; but I found myself preferring the privacy of the five or six hundred who did not pay—preferring it immensely. Besides, I had heard all my life of the 'Private View.' Every year there are special cablegrams about it in our newspapers—who were there, and what they wore—generally to the extent of at least a column and a half. Our special correspondents in London glory in it, and rival each other, adjectivally, in describing it. Lady Torquilin had been talking about it a good deal, too. She said it was 'a thing to see,' and she meant to try to get me an invitation. Lady Torquilin went every year.

'OUR SPECIAL CORRESPONDENTS GLORY IN IT'

But when the thirtieth day of April came, Lady Torquilin told me in the evening, after dinner, that she hadn't been able to manage it, and showed me the card upon which the 'President and Members of the Royal Academy of Arts "requested" the pleasure of the company of Lady Torquilin,' only, 'Not transferable.'

'It's very tiresome of them,' said Lady Torquilin, 'to put that on. It means that you positively must not give it to anybody. Otherwise I would have handed it over to you, child, with the greatest pleasure—I don't care a pin's point about going, and you could have gone with the Pastelle-Browns. But there it is!'

Of course, nothing would have induced me to take Lady Torquilin's invitation, and deprive her of the pleasure of going; but I pinned her veil at the back, and saw her off down the elevator, next day at two, with an intensity of regret which cannot come often in the course of an ordinary lifetime. I was describing my feelings in a letter, addressed, I think, to Mr. Winterhazel, when, about an hour later, Lady Torquilin appeared again, flushed with exertion, and sank panting into a chair.

'Get ready, child!' said she. 'I'd wear your tailor-made; those stairs will kill me, but there was—no time—to waste on the lift. I can get you in—hurry up your cakes!'

'But am I invited?' I asked.

'Certainly you are—by a Royal Academician in person—so *fly!*'

I flew, and in twenty minutes Lady Torquilin and I were engaged in our usual altercation with a cabman on the way to Burlington House. When he had got his cab and animal well into a block in Bond Street, and nothing of any sort could possibly happen without the sanction of a Jove-like policeman at the crossing, Lady Torquilin took the opportunity of telling me how it was that she was able to come for me. 'You see,' she said, 'the very first person I had the good luck to meet when I went in was Sir Bellamy Bellamy—you remember Sir Bellamy Bellamy at the Mintherringtons? I tell you frankly that I wouldn't have mentioned it, my dear, unless he had first, though I knew perfectly well that what Sir Bellamy Bellamy can't do in that Academy simply can't be done, for you know I'm the last one to push; but he did. "Where is your young friend?" said he. Then I took my chance, and told him how I'd asked that old screw of a Monkhouse Diddlington for two, and only got one, and how I couldn't possibly give it to you because it was printed "Not transferable," and how disappointed you were; and he was nice about it. "My dear Lady Torquilin," he said, "we were children together, and you never came to me. I should have been *delighted!*"

'"Well," I said, "Sir Bellamy, can't we do anything about it now?" "It's rather late in the day," said he. "It *is* late in the day," said I. "Oh, I say!" said he, "she must come if she wants to—any friend of yours, Lady Torquilin"—such a humbug as the man is! "It's a bit irregular," he went on, "and we won't say anything about it, but if you like to go and get her, and see that she carries this in with her" (here Lady Torquilin produced a fat, pale-blue catalogue book), "there won't be any difficulty. I fancy." So there you are, Miss Wick, provided with Sir Bellamy Bellamy's own catalogue to admit you—if *that's* not a compliment, I don't know what is!'

'I don't feel as if I had been properly invited,' I said; 'I'm afraid I oughtn't to go, Lady Torquilin.'

'Rubbish, child!' said she. 'Do you want them to send a deputation for you?' And after that, what could I say?

'Hold up your head, and look perfectly indifferent,' advised Lady Torquilin, as our hansom deposited us in the courtyard before the outer steps. 'Don't grasp that catalogue as if it were a banner; carry it carelessly. Now follow me.' And Lady Torquilin, with great dignity, a sense of rectitude, and a catalogue to which she was properly entitled, followed by me with vague apprehensions, a bad conscience, and a catalogue that didn't belong to me, walked into the Private View. Nobody said anything, though I fancied one of the two old gentlemen in crimson and black by the door looked knowingly at the other when I passed, as much as to say: 'About that tailor-made there is something fraudulent.' I say I 'fancied,' though at the time I was certain they did, because my imagination, of course, may have had something to do with it. I know I was very glad of the shelter of Lady Torquilin's unimpeachable respectability in front. 'There now,' she said, when we were well into the crowd, 'we're both here, and it's much nicer, isn't it, dear? than for you to come with strangers, even if I could have made up my mind that it was right for you to be admitted on a ticket plainly marked "not transferable"—which I really don't think, dear. I should have been able to do.'

We moved aimlessly with the throng, and were immediately overtaken and possessed by the spirit that seemed to be abroad—a spirit of wonder and criticism and speculation and searching, that first embraced our nearest neighbours, went off at random to a curiously-dressed person in perspective, focussed upon a celebrity in a corner, and spent itself in the shifting crowd. Lady Torquilin bade me consider whether in all my life before I had ever seen such remarkable gowns, and I was obliged to confess that I had not. Some of them were beautiful, and some were not; many were what you so very properly and aptly call 'smart,' and a few were artistic. All of them, pretty and ugly, I might have encountered at home, but there was one species of 'frock' which no American, I think, could achieve with impunity. It was a protest against conventionalism, very much gathered, and usually presented itself in colours unattainable out of a London fog. It almost always went with a rather discouraged-looking lady having a bad complexion, and hair badly done up; and, invariably, it dragged a little on one side. I don't know exactly why that kind of dress would be an impossible adjunct to the person of an American woman, but I am disposed to believe there is a climatic reason. We have so much sun and oxygen in the United States that I think they get into our ideas of clothes; and a person upholstered in the way I have mentioned would very likely find herself specially and disrespectfully described in the newspapers. But I do not wish to be thought impertinent about the development of this particular English dress ideal. It has undoubted points of interest. I had a better opportunity of observing it at the Academy Soirée in June, when it shed abroad the suggestion of a Tennysonian idyll left out all night.

Lady Torquilin had just pointed out to me two duchesses: one large and round, who was certainly a duchess by mistake, and the other tall and beautiful, with just such a curved upper lip as a duchess ought to have, and a coronet easily imaginable under her bonnet, and we were talking about them, when I saw somebody I knew. He was a middle-aged gentleman, and I had a very interesting association with his face, though I couldn't for the moment remember his name or where I had met him. I told Lady Torquilin about it, with the excited eagerness that a person always feels at the sight of a familiar face in a foreign land. 'Some friend of poppa's, I am certain,' I said; and although I had only had a glimpse of him, and immediately lost him in the crowd, we decided to walk on in that direction in the hope of seeing him again. He reappeared at a distance, and again we lost him; but we kept on, and while Lady Torquilin stopped to chat with her numerous acquaintances I looked out carefully for my father's friend. I knew that as soon as he saw me he would probably come up at once and shake hands, and then the name would come back to me; and I yearned to ask a thousand things of Chicago. We came face to face with him unexpectedly, and as his eye caught mine carelessly it dawned upon me that the last time I had seen him it was *not* in a long grey overcoat and a silk hat—there was something incongruous in that. Also, I remembered an insolent grizzled chin and great duplicity. 'Oh!' I said to Lady Torquilin, 'I don't know him at all! It's——'

'It's Mr. Bancroft!' said Lady Torquilin.

'Who is Mr. Bancroft?' said I. 'It's the Abbé Latour!'

I had enjoyed 'The Dead Heart' so much a fortnight before, but I was glad I did not bow before I recognised that it was a gentleman with whom I had the honour of possessing only ten-and-sixpence worth of acquaintance.

I saw the various scandals of the year as well. Lady Torquilin mentioned them, just to call my attention to their dresses, generally giving her opinion that there had been altogether too much said about the matter. Lady Torquilin did not know many of the literary people who were present, but she indicated Mr. Anstey and Mr. William Black, whose works are extremely popular with us, and it was a particular pleasure to be able to describe them when I wrote home next day. I wanted to see Mr. Oscar Wilde very especially, but somebody told Lady Torquilin he was at the Grosvenor—'and small loss, I consider!' said she; 'he's just like any other man, dear child, only with more nonsense in his head than most of them!' But it was not in the nature of things or people that Lady Torquilin should like Mr. Oscar Wilde. Before we went she showed me two or three lady-journalists busy taking notes.

'There's that nice Miss Jay Penne,' said Lady Torquilin. 'I know all the Jay Pennes—such a literary family! And Miss Jay Penne always wants to know what I've got on. I think I must just speak to her, dear, if you don't mind waiting one moment; and then we'll go.

'She asked about you, too, dear,' said my friend when she rejoined me, with a little nudge of congratulation.

I should, perhaps, have stated before that there were a number of artists walking around trying to keep away from their own pictures; but this I gathered of myself, for, with the exception of Sir Bellamy Bellamy, who had gone away, Lady Torquilin did not know any of them. I noticed, too, that the walls of the rooms we were in were covered with pictures, but they did not seem to have anything to do with the Private View.

XVI

LADY POWDERBY'S ball was the first I attended in London, and therefore, I suppose, made the strongest impression upon me. It was quite different from a Chicago ball, though the differences were so intangible—not consisting at all in the supper, or the music, or the dresses, or the decorations—that I am by no means sure that I can explain them; so I beg that you will not be disappointed if you fail to learn from my idea of a London ball what a Chicago ball is like. It is very easy for you to find out personally, if you happen to be in Chicago.

We went in a four-wheeler at about eleven o'clock, and as the driver drew up before the strip of carpet that led to the door, the first thing that struck me was the little crowd of people standing waiting on either side to watch the guests go in. I never saw that in Chicago—that patience and self-abnegation. I don't think the freeborn American citizen would find it consistent with his dignity to hang about the portals of a party to which he had not been invited. He would take pains, on the contrary, to shun all appearance of wanting to go.

Inside I expected to find a crowd—I think balls are generally crowded wherever they are given; but I also expected to be able to get through it, in which for quite twenty minutes I was disappointed. Both Lady Torquilin and I made up our minds, at one time, to spend the rest of the evening in our wraps; but just as we had abandoned ourselves to this there came a breaking and a parting among the people, and a surge in one direction, which Lady Torquilin explained, as we took advantage of it, by the statement that the supper-room had been opened.

In the cloak-room several ladies were already preparing for departure. 'Do you suppose they are ill?' I asked Lady Torquilin, as we stood together, while two of the maids repaired our damages as far as they were able. 'Why do they go home so early?'

'Home, child!' said Lady Torquilin, with a withering emphasis. 'They're going *on*; I daresay they've got a couple more dances a-piece to put in an appearance at to night.' Lady Torquilin did not approve of what she called 'excessive riot,' and never accepted more than one invitation an evening; so I was unfamiliar with London ways in this respect. Presently I had another object-lesson in the person of a lady who came in and gave her cloak to the attendant, saying, 'Put it where you can get it easily, please. I'll want it again in a quarter of an hour.' I thought as I looked at her that social pleasures must be to such an one simply a series of topographical experiments. I also thought I should have something to say when next I heard of the hurry and high pressure in which Americans lived.

'It's of no use,' said Lady Torquilin, looking at the stairs; 'we can never get up; we might as well go with the rest and———'

'Have some supper,' added somebody close behind us; and Lady Torquilin said: 'Oh, Charlie Mafferton!' though why she should have been surprised was more than I could imagine, for Charlie Mafferton was nearly always at hand. Wherever we went to—at homes, or concerts, or the theatre, or sight-seeing, in any direction, Mr. Mafferton turned up, either expectedly or unexpectedly, with great precision, and his manner toward Lady Torquilin was always as devoted as it could be. I have not mentioned him often before in describing my experiences, and shall probably not mention him often again, because after a time I began to take him for granted as a detail of almost everything we did. Lady Torquilin seemed to like it, so I, of course, had no right to object; and, indeed, I did not particularly mind, because Mr. Mafferton was always nice in his manner to me, and often very interesting in his remarks. But if Lady Torquilin had not told me that she had known him in short clothes, and if I had not been perfectly certain she was far too sensible to give her affections to a person so much younger than herself, I don't know what I would have thought.

So we went with the rest and had some supper, and, in the anxious interval during which Lady Torquilin and I occupied a position in the doorway, and Mr. Mafferton reconnoitred for one of the little round tables, I discovered what had been puzzling me so about the house ever since I had come into it. Except for the people, and the flower decorations, and a few chairs, it was absolutely empty. The people furnished it, so to speak, moving about in the brilliancy of their dresses and diamonds, and the variety of their manners, to such an extent that I had not been able to particularise before what I felt was lacking to this ball. It was a very curious lack—all the crewel-work, and Japanese bric-à-brac, and flower lamp-shades, that go to make up a home; and the substitute for it in the gay lights and flowers, and exuberant supper-table, and dense mass of people, gave me the feeling of having been permitted to avail myself of a brilliant opportunity, rather than of being invited to share the hospitality of Lady Torquilin's friends.

'Has Lady Powderby just moved in?' I asked, as we sat down around two bottles of champagne, a lot of things *glacées*, a triple arrangement of knives and forks, and a pyramid of apoplectic strawberries.

'Lady Powderby doesn't live here,' Lady Torquilin said. 'No, Charlie, thank you—sweets for you young people if you like—savouries for me!' and my friend explained to me that Lady Powderby was 'at home' at this particular address only for this particular evening, and had probably paid a good many guineas house-rent for the night; after which I tried in vain to feel a sense of personal gratitude for my strawberries, which I was not privileged even to eat with my hostess's fork—though, of course, I knew that this was mere sentiment, and that practically I was as much indebted to Lady Powderby for her strawberries as if she had grown them herself. And, on general grounds, I was really glad to have had the chance of attending this kind of ball, which had not come within my experience before. I don't think it would occur to anybody in Chicago to hire an empty house to give an entertainment in; and though, now that I think of it, Palmer's Hotel is certainly often utilised for this purpose, it is generally the charity or benevolent society hop that is given there.

During supper, while Lady Torquilin was telling Mr. Mafferton how much we had enjoyed the 'Opening,' and how kind his cousin had been, I looked round. I don't know whether it is proper to look round at a ball in England—it's a thing I never should have thought of doing in Chicago, where I knew exactly what I should see if I did look round—but the impersonal nature of Lady Powderby's ball gave me a sense of irresponsibility to anybody, and the usual code of manners seemed a vague law, without any particular applicability to present circumstances. And I was struck, much struck, with the thorough business-like concentration and singleness of purpose that I saw about me. The people did not seem much acquainted, except by twos and threes, and ignored each other, for the most part, in a calm, high-level way, that was really educating to see. But they were not without a common sentiment and a common aim—they had all come to a ball, where it devolved upon them to dance and sup, and dance again—to dance and sup as often as possible, and to the greatest possible advantage. This involved a measuring-up of what there was, which seemed to be a popular train of thought. There was no undue levity. If a joke had been made in that supper-room it would have exploded more violently than the champagne-bottles. Indeed, there was as great and serious decorum as was possible among so many human beings who all required to be fed at once, with several changes of plates. I observed a great deal of behaviour and a great similarity of it—the gentlemen were alike, and the ladies were alike, except that some of the ladies were a little like the gentlemen, and some of the gentlemen were a little like the ladies. This homogeneity was remarkable to me, considering how few of them seemed to have even a bowing acquaintance with each other. But the impressive thing was the solid unity of interest and action as regarded the supper.

We struggled upstairs, and on the first landing met a lady-relation of our hostess, with whom Lady Torquilin shook hands.

'You'll never find her,' said this relation, referring to Lady Powderby. 'The Dyngeleys, and the Porterhouses, and the Bangley Coffins have all come and gone without seeing her.' But I may just state here that we did find her, towards morning, in time to say good-bye.

When I say that the floor of Lady Powderby's (temporary) ball-room was full, I do not adequately express the fact. It was replete—it ran over, if that is not too impulsive an expression for the movement of the ladies and gentlemen who were twirling round each other upon the floor, all in one direction, to the music. With the exception of two or three couples, whose excited gyration seemed quite tipsy by contrast, the ball upstairs was going on with the same profound and determined action as the ball downstairs. I noticed the same universal look of concentration, the same firm or nervous intention of properly discharging the responsibilities of the evening and the numbers of the programme, on the face of the sweet, fresh *debutante*, steadily getting pinker; of the middle-aged, military man, dancing like a disjointed foot-rule; of the stout old lady in crimson silk, very low in the neck, who sat against the wall. The popular theory seemed to be that the dancing was something to be Done—the consideration of enjoyment brought it to a lower plane. And it was an improving sight, though sad.

'DANCING LIKE A DISJOINTED FOOT RULE'

Mr. Mafferton asked me for Numbers seven, and nine, and eleven—all waltzes. I knew he would be obliged to, out of politeness to Lady Torquilin, who had got past dancing herself; but I had been dreading it all the time I spent in watching the other men go round, while Mr. Mafferton sought for a chair for her. So I suggested that we should try Number seven, and see how we got on, ignoring the others, and saying something weakly about my not having danced for so long, and feeling absolutely certain that I should not be able to acquit myself with the erectness—to speak of nothing else—that seemed to be imperative at Lady Powderby's ball. 'Oh! I am sure we shall do very well,' said Mr. Mafferton. And we started.

I admire English dancing. I am accustomed to it now, and can look at a roomful of people engaged in it without a sympathetic attack of vertigo or a crick in my neck. I think it is, perhaps, as good an exposition of the unbending, unswerving quality in your national character as could be found anywhere, in a small way but I do not think an American ought to tamper with it without preliminary training.

Mr. Mafferton and I started—he with confidence, I with indecision. You can make the same step with a pair of scissors as Mr. Mafferton made; I did it afterwards, when I explained to Lady Torquilin how impossible it was that I should have danced nine and eleven with him, Compared with it I felt that mine was a caper, and the height of impropriety. You will argue from this that they do not go together well; and that is quite correct. We inserted ourselves into the moving mass, and I went hopelessly round the May pole that Mr. Mafferton seemed to have turned into, several times. Then the room began to reel. 'Don't you think we had better reverse?' I asked; 'I am getting dizzy, I'm afraid.' Mr. Mafferton stopped instantly, and the room came right again.

'Reverse?' he said; 'I don't think I ever heard of it. I thought we were getting on capitally!' And when I explained to him that reversing meant turning round, and going the other way, he declared that it was quite impracticable—that we would knock everybody else over, and that he had never seen it done. After the last argument I did not press the matter. It took very little acquaintance with Mr. Mafferton to know that, if he had never seen it done, he never would do it. 'We will try going back a bit,' he proposed instead; with the result that after the next four or five turns he began to stalk away from me, going I knew not whither. About four minutes later we went back, at my urgent request, to Lady Torquilin, and Mr. Mafferton told her that we had 'hit it off admirably.' I think he must have thought we did, because he said something about not having 'been quite able to catch my step at first,' in a way that showed entire satisfaction with his later performance; which was quite natural, for Mr. Mafferton was the kind of person who, so long as he was doing his best himself, would hardly be aware whether anybody else was or not.

I made several other attempts with friends of Lady Torquilin and Mr. Mafferton, and a few of them were partially successful, though I generally found it advisable to sit out the latter parts of them. This, when room could be found, was very amusing; and I noticed that it was done all the way up two flights of stairs, and in every other conceivable place that offered two seats contiguously. I was interested to a degree in one person with whom I sat out two or three dances running. He was quite a young man, not over twenty-four or five, I should think—a nephew of Lady Torquilin, and an officer in the Army, living at Aldershot, very handsome, and wore an eyeglass, which was, however, quite a common distinction. I must tell you more about him again in connection with the day Lady Torquilin and I spent at Aldershot at his invitation, because he really deserves a chapter to himself. But it was he who told me, at Lady Powderby's ball, referring to the solid mass of humanity that packed itself between us and the door, that it was with the greatest difficulty that he finally gained the ball-room. 'Couldn't get in at all at first,' said he, 'and while I was standin' on the outside edge of the pavement, a bobby has the confounded impudence to tell me to move along. '"Can't,"' says I—"I'm at the party."'

I have always been grateful to the Aldershot officer for giving me that story to remember in connection with Lady Powderby's ball, although Mr. Mafferton, when I retailed it, couldn't see that it was in the least amusing. 'Besides,' he said, 'it's as old as "Punch."' But at the end of the third dance Mr. Mafferton had been sent by Lady Torquilin to look for me, and was annoyed, I have no doubt, by the trouble he had to take to find me. And Mr. Mafferton's sense of humour could never be considered his strong point.

XVII

A GREAT many other people *were* going to Aldershot the day we went there—so many that the train, which we were almost too late for, had nowhere two spare seats together. Just at the last minute, after Lady Torquilin had decided that we must travel separately, the guard unlocked the door of a first-class carriage occupied by three gentlemen alone. It afforded much more comfortable accommodation than the carriage Lady Torquilin was crowded into, but there was no time to tell her, so I got in by myself, and sat down in the left-hand corner going backward, and prepared to enjoy the landscape. The gentlemen were so much more interesting, however, that I am afraid, though I ostensibly looked at the landscape, I paid much more attention to them, which I hope was comparatively proper, since they were not aware of it.

'I OSTENSIBLY LOOKED AT THE LANDSCAPE'

They were all rather past middle age, all very trim, and all dressed to ride. There the similarity among them ended; and besides being different from one another, they were all different from any American gentlemen I had ever met. That is the reason they were so deeply interesting.

'THEY WERE ALL DIFFERENT FROM ANY AMERICAN GENTLEMEN'

One, who sat opposite me, was fair, with large blue eyes and an aquiline nose, and a well-defined, clean-shaven face, all but his graceful moustache. He was broad-shouldered and tall, and muscular and lean, and he lounged, illuminating his conversation with a sweet and easy smile. He looked very clever, and I think he must have been told all his life that he resembled the Duke of Wellington. The one in the other corner, opposite, was rosy and round-faced, with twinkling blue eyes and a grey moustache, and he made a comfortable angle with his rotund person and the wall, crossing his excellent legs.

The one on my side, of whom I had necessarily an imperfect view, was very grey, and had a straight nose and a pair of level eyes, rather pink about the edges, and carefully-cut whiskers and sloping shoulders. He did not lounge at all, or even cross his legs, but sat bolt upright and read the paper. He looked like a person of extreme views upon propriety, and a rather bad temper. The first man had the 'Times,' the second the 'Standard,' and the third the 'Morning Post.' I think they all belonged to the upper classes.

They began to talk, especially the two opposite, the lean man throwing his remarks and his easy smiles indolently across the valises on the seat between them. He spoke of the traffic in Piccadilly, where 'a brute of an omnibus' had taken off a carriage-wheel for him the day before. He was of opinion that too many omnibuses were allowed to run through Piccadilly—'a considerable lot' too many. He also found the condition of one or two streets in that neighbourhood 'disgustin,' and was 'goin' to call attention to it.' All in cool, high, pleasant, indolent tones.

'Write a letter to the "Times,"' said the other, with a broad smile, as if it were an excellent joke. 'I don't mind reading it.'

The first smiled gently and thoughtfully down upon his boot. 'Will you guarantee that anybody else does?' said he. And they chaffed. My neighbour turned his paper impatiently, and said nothing.

'What'r'you goin' to ride to-day?' asked the first. His voice was delightfully refined.

'Haven't a notion. Believe they've got something for me down there. Expect the worst'—which also, for some unknown reason, seemed to amuse them very much.

'You've heard 'bout Puhbelow, down heah year befoh last—old Puhbelow, used to c'mand 25th Wangers? A.D.C. wides up t' Puhbelow an' tells him he's wanted at headquahtehs immediately. "That case," says Puhbelow, "I'd better *walk!*" An' he *did*,' said my *vis-à-vis*.

'Lord!' returned the other, 'I hope it won't come to that.'

'It's the last day I shall be able to turn out,' he went on, ruefully.

'For w'y?'

'Can't get inside my uniform another year.'

'Supuhfluous adipose tissue?'

'Rather! Attended the Levée last week, an' came away black in the face! At my time o' life a man's got to consider his buttons. 'Pon my word, I envy you lean dogs.' He addressed both his neighbour and the pink-eyed man, who took no notice of the pleasantry, but folded his paper the other way, and said, without looking up, that that had been a very disastrous flood in the United States.

'They do everything on a big scale over thayah,' remarked the man across from me, genially, 'includin' swindles.'

The round-faced gentleman's eye kindled with new interest. 'Were you let in on those Kakeboygan Limiteds?' he said. 'By Jove!—abominable! Never knew a cooler thing! Must have scooped in fifty thousand!'

'It was ve'y painful,' said the other, unexcitedly. 'By th' way, what d'you think of Little Toledos?'

'Don't know anything about 'em. Bought a few—daresay I've dropped my money.'

'Wilkinson wanted me to buy. Lunched the beast last week, expectin' to get a pointer. Confounded sharp scoundrel, Wilkinson!' And this gentleman smiled quite seraphically. 'Still expectin'. I see Oneida Centrals have reached a premium. Bought a lot eight months ago for a song. Cheapah to buy 'em, I thought, than waste more money in somethin' I knew as little about! There's luck!' This stage of the conversation found me reflecting upon the degree of depravity involved in getting the better of the business capacity which made its investments on these principles. I did not meditate a defence for my fellow-countrymen, but I thought they had a pretty obvious temptation.

The talk drifted upon clubs, and the gentlemen expressed their preferences. 'Hear you're up for the Army and Navy,' said the rosy-faced one.

'Ye-es. Beastly bore getting in,' returned he of the aquiline nose, dreamily.

'How long?'

"Bout two years, I believe. I'm up again for the United Service, too. Had a fit of economy in '85—year of the Tarantillas smash—you were in that, too, wehn't you?—an' knocked off five o' six o' my clubs. They make no end of a wow about lettin' you in again.'

'Well, the Rag's good enough for me, and the Lyric's convenient to take a lady to. They say the Corinthian's the thing to belong to now, though,' said the round gentleman, tentatively.

'If you have a taste for actresses,' returned the other, with another tender glance at his boot.

Then it appeared, from a remark from the pink-eyed one, that he dined at the Carlton four nights out of seven—stood by the Carlton—hoped he might never enter a better club—never met a cad there in his life. Fairly lived there when he wasn't in Manchester.

'D'you live in Manchester?' drawled the thin gentleman, quite agreeably. Now, what was there in that to make the pink-eyed one angry? Is Manchester a disreputable place to live in? But he was—as angry as possible. The pink spread all over, under his close-trimmed whiskers and down behind his collar. He answered, in extremely rasping and sub-indignant tones, that he had a 'place near it,' and retired from the conversation.

Then the rotund gentleman stated that there were few better clubs than the Constitutional; and then, what a view you could get from the balconies! 'Tremendous fine view,' he said, 'I tell you, at night, when the place is lighted up, an' the river in the distance——'

'Moon?' inquired his companion, sweetly. But the stout gentleman's robust sentiment failed him at this point, and he turned the conversation abruptly to something else—a 'house-party' somewhere.

'Have you got what they call a pleasant invitation?' the other asked; and the portly one said Yes, in fact he had three, with a smile of great satisfaction. Just then the train stopped, and we all changed cars, and I, rejoining Lady

Torquilin, lost my entertaining fellow-passengers. I was sorry it stopped at that point, because I particularly wanted to know what a house-party and a pleasant invitation were—they seemed to me to be idiomatic, and I had already begun to collect English idioms to take home with me. In fact, I should have liked to have gone on observing the landscape from my unobtrusive corner all the way to Aldershot if I could—these gentlemen made such interesting incidents to the journey—though I know I have told you that two or three times before, without making you understand in the least, I am afraid, how or why they did. There was a certain opulence and indifference about them which differed from the kind of opulence and indifference you generally see in the United States in not being in the least assumed. They did not ignore the fact of my existence in the corner—they talked as if they were not aware of it. And they had worn the conventionalism of England so long that it had become a sort of easy uniform, which they didn't know they had on. They impressed you as having always before them, unconsciously, a standard of action and opinion—though their perception of it might be as different as possible—and as conducting themselves in very direct relation to that standard. I don't say this because none of them used bad language or smoked in my presence. The restraint was not to be defined—a delicate, all-pervasive thing; and it was closely connected with a lack of enthusiasm upon any subject, except the approach to it the rounded gentleman made with reference to the Constitutional view. They could not be considered flippant, and yet their talk played very lightly upon the surface of their minds, making no drafts upon any reserve store of information or opinion. This was odd to me. I am sure no three Americans who knew each, other could travel together in a box about six by eight without starting a theory and arguing about it seriously, or getting upon politics, or throwing themselves into the conversation in some way or other.

But I have no doubt that, to be impressed with such things as these, you must be brought up in Chicago, where people are different. Lady Torquilin was unable to tell me anything about the gentlemen from my description of them; she said they were exactly like anybody else, and as for gambling in stocks, she had no sympathy with anybody who lost—seeming to think that I had, and that that was what had attracted my attention.

The young officer was at Aldershot Station to meet us, looking quite a different person in his uniform. I can't possibly describe the uniform, or you would know the regiment, and possibly the officer, if you are acquainted with Aldershot—which he might not like. But I may say, without fear of identifying him, that he wore a red coat, and looked very handsome in it—red is such a popular colour among officers in England, and so generally becoming. He was a lieutenant, and his name was Oddie Pratte.

'ODDIE PRATTE'

By the time I found this out, which was afterwards, when Mr. Pratte had occasion to write two or three letters to me, which he signed in that way, I had noticed how largely pet names cling to gentlemen in England—not only to young gentlemen in the Army, but even to middle-aged family men. Mr. Winterhazel's name is Bertram, and I should be interested to hear what he would say if any one addressed him as 'Bertie.' I think he would be mad, as we say in America. If I had ever called him anything but Mr. Winterhazel— which I have not—I would do it myself when I return, just for an experiment. I don't think any gentleman in the United States, out of pinafores, could be called 'Bertie' with impunity. We would contract it into the brutal brevity of 'Bert,' and 'Eddie' to 'Ed,' and 'Willie' to 'Will,' and 'Bobby' to 'Bob.' But it is a real pleasing feature of your civilisation, this overlapping of nursery tenderness upon maturer years, and I hope it will spread. What 'Oddie.' was derived from I never got to know Mr. Pratte well enough to ask, but he sustained it with more dignity than I would have believed possible. That is the remarkable—at any rate a remarkable—characteristic of you English people. You sustain everything with dignity, from your Lord Mayor's Show to your farthing change. You are never in the least amused at yourselves.

XVIII

AWF'LY glad you've been able to come!' said Mr. Pratte, leading the way to his dogcart, 'quite a marked figure, in his broad red shoulders, among the dark-coloured crowd at the station. 'There's so much going on in the village I was afraid you'd change your mind. Frightful state of funk, I assure you, every time the post came in!' Mr. Pratte spoke to Lady Torquilin, but looked across at me. We are considerably more simple than this in America. If a gentleman wants to say something polite to you, he never thinks of transmitting it through somebody else. But your way is much the most convenient. It gives one the satisfaction of being complimented without the embarrassment of having to reply in properly negative terms. So it was Lady Torquilin who said how sorry we should have been to miss it, and I found no occasion for remark until we were well started. Then I made the unavoidable statement that Aldershot seemed to be a pretty place, though I am afraid it did not seriously occur to me that it was.

'Oh, it's a hole of sorts!' remarked Mr. Pratte. 'But to see it in its pristine beauty you should be here when it rains. It's adorable then!' By that time I had observed that Mr. Pratte had very blue eyes, with a great deal of laugh in them. His complexion you could find in America only at the close of the seaside season, among the people, who have just come home, and even then it would be patchy—it would not have the solid richness of tint that Mr. Pratte's had. It was a wholesome complexion, and it went very well with the rest of Mr. Pratte. I liked its tones of brown and red, and the way it deepened in his nose and the back of his neck. In fact, I might as well say in the beginning that I liked Mr. Pratte altogether—there was something very winning about him. His manner was variable: sometimes extremely flippant, sometimes—and then he let his eyeglass drop—profoundly serious, and sometimes, when he had it in mind, preserving a level of cynical indifference that was impressively interesting, and seemed to stand for a deep and unsatisfactory experience of life. For the rest, he was just a tall young subaltern, very anxious to be amused, with a dog.

Mr. Pratte went on to say that he was about the only man in the place not on parade. There was some recondite reason for this, which I have forgotten. Lady Torquilin asked him how his mother and sisters were, and he said: 'Oh, they were as fit as possible, thanks, according to latest despatches,' which I at once mentally put down as a lovely idiom for use in my next Chicago letter. I wanted, above all things, to convince them at home that I was wasting no time so far as the language was concerned; and I knew they would not understand it, which was, of course, an additional pleasure. I would express myself very clearly about it though, I thought, so as not to suggest epilepsy or anything of that sort.

Americans are nearly always interested in public buildings. We are very proud of our own, and generally point them out to strangers before anything else, and I was surprised that Mr. Pratte mentioned nothing of the sort as we drove through Aldershot. So the first one of any size or importance that met my eye I asked him about. 'That, I suppose, is your jail?' I said, with polite interest, as we came in sight of a long building with that simplicity of exterior that always characterises jails. Our subaltern gave vent to a suppressed roar. 'What is she saying now?' asked Lady Torquilin, who had not been paying attention.

'She says—oh, I say, Auntie, what a score! Miss Wick has just pointed out that building as Aldershot *jail!*'

'Isn't it?' said I.

'I'm afraid Miss Wick is pullin' our leg, Auntie!'

Now, I was in the back seat, and what could have induced Mr. Pratte to charge me with so unparalleled and impossible a familiarity I couldn't imagine, not being very far advanced in the language at the time; but when Mr. Pratte explained that the buildings I referred to were the officers' quarters, with his own colonel's at one end—and 'Great Scott!' said Mr. Pratte, going off again, 'What would the old man say to that?'—I felt too much overcome by my own stupidity to think about it. I have since realised that I was rather shocked. It was, of course, impossible to mention public buildings again in any connection, and, although I spent a long and agreeable day at Aldershot, if you were to ask me whether it had so much as a town pump, I couldn't tell you. But I must say I am not of the opinion that it had. To speak American, it struck me as being rather a one-horse town, though nothing could be nicer than I found it as a military centre.

'WE DROVE STRAIGHT OUT OF TOWN TO THE PARADE-GROUND'

We drove straight out of town to the parade-ground, over a road that wound through rugged-looking, broken fields, yellow with your wonderful flaming gorse and furze, which struck me as contrasting oddly with the neatness of your landscapes generally. When I remarked upon their uncultivated state, Mr. Pratte said, with some loftiness, that military operations were not advantageously conducted in standing corn—meaning wheat—and I decided for the rest of the day to absorb information, as far as possible, without inquiring for it.

It was a lovely day—no clouds, no dust, nothing but blue sky, and sunshine on the gorse; and plenty of people, all of whom seemed to have extreme views upon the extraordinary fineness of the weather, were on their way to the parade-ground, chiefly driving in dogcarts. Whenever we passed a lady in anything more ambitious, Mr. Pratte invariably saluted very nicely indeed, and told Lady Torquilin that she was the wife of Colonel So-and-so, commanding the somethingth something. And I noticed all through the day what a great deal of consideration these ladies received from everybody, and what extraordinary respect was accorded to their husbands. I have no doubt it is a class distinction of yours, and very proper; but I could not help thinking of the number of colonels and their families we have at home, and how little more we think of them on that account. Poppa's head man in the baking-powder business for years was a colonel—Colonel Canister; so is poppa himself—and I never knew either of them show that they thought anything of it. I suppose momma's greatest friend is Mrs. Colonel Pabbly, but that is because their tastes are similar and their families about the same age. For that matter, I daresay one-third of the visiting-cards momma receives have 'Colonel' between the 'Mrs.' and the last name. It is really no particular distinction in America.

We were rather late, and all the best places had been taken up by the dogcarts of other people. They formed an apparently unbroken front, or, more properly, back, wherever we wanted to get in. By some extraordinary means, however, more as a matter of course than anything else—it couldn't have been done in America—Mr. Pratte inserted his dogcart in an extremely advantageous position, and I saw opposite, and far off, the long, long double line of soldiers, stretching and wavering as the country dipped and swelled under the sky. 'In a minute,' said Mr. Pratte, 'you'll hear the "furious joy"'— and an instant later there came splitting and spitting against the blue, from east to west, and from west to east, the chasing white smoke-jets of the *feu de joie*. You have a few very good jokes in England.

It seemed to me that two of the bands which defied each other for the rest of the morning began playing at that instant to prevent any diminution in the furious joy, while the long line of soldiers broke up into blocks, each block going off somewhere by itself; and Mr. Pratte told Lady Torquilin about a dance in town the night before, where he met a lot of people he loved.

'Was the fair and only one there?' Lady Torquilin inquired with archness; and Mr. Pratte's countenance suddenly became rueful as he dropped his eyeglass. 'Yes,' he said; 'but there's a frost on—we don't play with each other any more!' And I believe other confidences followed, which I did not feel entitled to hear, so I divided my attention between the two bands and the parade. One band stood still at a little distance, and played as hard as possible continually, and every regiment sent its own band gloriously on ahead of it with the colonel, generally getting the full significance out of a Scotch jig, which Mr. Pratte said was the 'march-past.' It made a most magnificently effective noise.

I hope the person for whose benefit that parade was chiefly intended—I believe there is always some such person in connection with parades—was as deeply impressed with it as I was. It was the first time I had ever seen English soldiers in bulk, and they presented a threatening solidity which I should think would be very uninteresting to the enemy. There are more interstices in our regiments—I think it must be admitted that we are nationally thinner than you are. Besides, what we are still in the habit of calling 'our recent unpleasantness' happened about a quarter of a century ago, and I shouldn't think myself that a taste for blood could survive that period of peace and comfort, to be very obvious. Certainly, Chicago parades had not prepared me for anything so warlike as this. Not that I should encourage anybody to open hostilities with us, however. Though we are thin, we might be found lively.

The cavalry regiments were splendid, with the colonel's horse as conscious as anybody of what was expected of him, as the colonel's horse, stepping on ahead; and particularly the Lancers, with their gay little pennons flying; but there was not the rhythmic regularity in their movement that was so beautiful to see in the infantry coming after. "Lady Torquilin found it very absurd—there were so many points to notice that were more admirable—that the thing I liked best in the whole parade was that long, quick, instant crinkle that we saw from the rear as every man bent his knee at once; but it seemed to have the whole essence of martial order in it, and to hold great fascination. That, and the swing of the Highlanders' kilts, and the gleam of the sun on their philabegs, and the pride of their marching."

'WITH THEIR GAY LITTLE PENNONS FLYING'

That Aldershot Highland regiment, with its screaming bagpipes, seemed, to my Chicago imagination, to have marched straight out of Inkermann. Then came the South Wales Borderers, and I heard the story of the Isandula colours, with the Queen's little gold wreath above them, that went, preciously furled, in the middle. I wished then—though it is not consistent with the Monroe doctrine—that we had a great standing army, with traditions and a constant possibility of foreign fighting. It may be discouraging to the increase of the male population, but it encourages sentiment, and is valuable on that account.

So they all came and passed and went, and came and passed and went again, three times—the whole ten thousand cavalry, infantry, artillery, commissariat, ambulance, doctors, mules, and all—with a great dust, and much music, and a tremendous rattling and bumping when the long waggons came, at the rear of which a single soldier sat in each, with his legs hanging down looking very sea-sick and unhappy. And they showed me a prince-subaltern, walking through the dust beside his company with the others. Nobody seemed to see anything remarkable in this but me, so I thought it best to display no surprise. But the nominal nature of some privileges in England began to grow upon me. I also saw a mule—a stout, well-grown, talented mule—who did not wish to parade. I was glad of the misbehaviour of that mule. It reduced to some extent the gigantic proportions of my respect for the British Army.

I met some of the colonels, and their wives and daughters, afterwards, and in most cases I was lost in admiration of the military tone of the whole family.

Chicago colonels often have very little that is strikingly military about them, and their families nothing at all. But here the daughters carried themselves erect, moved stiffly but briskly, and turned on their heels as sharply as if they were on the parade-ground. I suppose it would be difficult to live in such constant association with troops and barracks, and salutes and sentries, and the word of command, without assimilating somewhat of the distinctive charm of these things; and the way some of the colonels' ladies clipped their sentences, and held their shoulders, and otherwise identified themselves with their regiments, was very taking. It explained itself further when I saw the 'quarters' in which one or two of them kept house—very pleasant quarters, where we received most interesting and delightful hospitality. But it would be odd if domesticity in a series of rooms very square and very similar, with 'C. O.' painted in black letters over all their doors, did not develop something a little different from the ordinary English lady accustomed to cornices and *portières*.

Then came lunch at the mess, at which, as the colonel took care of Lady Torquilin, I had the undivided attention of Mr. Oddie Pratte, which I enjoyed. Mr. Pratte was curious upon the subject of American girls at home—he told me he began to believe himself misinformed about them—seriously, and dropping his eyeglass. He would like to know accurately—under a false impression one made such awkward mistakes—well, for instance, if it were true that they were up to all sorts of games at home, how was it they were all so deucedly solemn when they came over here? Mr. Pratte hoped I wouldn't be offended—of course, he didn't mean that *I* was solemn—but—well, I knew what he meant—I *must* know! And wouldn't I have some more sugar for those strawberries? 'I like crowds of sugar, don't you?' said Mr. Oddie Pratte. Another thing, he had always been told that they immediately wanted to see Whitechapel. Now he had asked every American girl he'd met this season whether she had seen Whitechapel, and not one of 'em had.

He wasn't going to ask me on that account. They didn't, as a rule, seem to see the joke of the thing. Mr. Pratte would like to know if I had ever met the M'Clures, of New York—Nellie M'Clure was a great pal of his—and was disappointed that I hadn't. The conversation turned to India, whither Mr. Pratte's regiment was ordered to proceed immediately, and I received a good deal of information as to just how amusing life might be made there from Mr. Pratte. 'They say a man marries as soon as he learns enough Anglo-Indian to propose in!' he remarked, with something like anticipative regret. 'First dance apt to be fatal—bound to bowl over before the end of the season. Simla girl is known to be irresistible.' And Lady Torquilin, catching this last, put in her oar in her own inimitable way. 'You're no nephew of mine, Oddie,' said she, 'if you can't say "No."' Whereat I was very sorry for Oddie, and forgave him everything.

There was tea on the lawn afterwards, and bagpipes to the full lung-power of three Highlanders at once, walking up and down, and beating time on the turf with one foot in a manner that was simply extraordinary considering the nature of what they were playing; and conversation with more Aldershot ladies, followed by an inspection in a body of Mr. Pratte's own particular corner of the barracks, full of implements of war, and charming photographs, and the performance of Mr. Pratte's intellectual, small dog. That ended the Aldershot parade. We have so few parades of any sort in America, except when somebody of importance dies—and then they are apt to be depressing—that I was particularly glad to have seen it.

XIX

POPPA'S interests in London necessitated his having lawyers there—Messrs. Pink, Pink & Co., of Cheapside. If you know New York, you will understand me when I say that I had always thought Cheapside a kind of Bowery, probably full of second-hand clothing shops and ice-cream parlours—the last place I should think of looking for a respectable firm of solicitors in, especially after cherishing the idea all my life that London lawyers were to be found only in Chancery Lane. But that was Messrs. Pink & Pink's address, and the mistake was one of the large number you have been kind enough to correct for me.

It was a matter of some regret to poppa that Messrs. Pink & Pink were bachelors, and could not very well be expected to exert themselves for me personally on that account; two Mrs. Pinks, he thought, might have done a little to make it pleasant for me in London, and would, probably, have put themselves out more or less to do it. But there was no Mrs. Pink, so I was indebted to these gentlemen for money only, which they sent me whenever I wrote to them for it, by arrangement with poppa. I was surprised, therefore, to receive one morning an extremely polite note from Messrs. Pink & Pink, begging me to name an afternoon when it would be convenient for me to call at their office, in order that Messrs. Pink & Pink might have the honour of discussing with me a matter of private business important to myself. I thought it delightfully exciting, and wrote at once that I would come next day. I speculated considerably in the meantime as to what the important private matter could possibly be—since, beyond my address, Messrs. Pink & Pink knew nothing whatever of my circumstances in London—but did not tell Lady Torquilin, for fear she would think she ought to come with me, and nothing spoils an important private matter like a third person.

'1st Floor, Messrs. Dickson & Dawes, Architects; 2nd Floor, Norwegian Life Insurance Co.; 3rd floor, Messrs. Pink & Pink, Solicitors,' read the framed directory inside the door in black letters on a yellow ground. I looked round in vain for an elevator-boy, though the narrow, dark, little, twisting stairway was so worn that I might have known that the proprietors were opposed to this innovation. I went from floor to floor rejoicing. At last I had found a really antique interior in London; there was not a cobweb lacking in testimony. It was the very first I had come across in my own private investigations, and I had expected them all to be like this.

Four or five clerks were writing at high desks in the room behind the frosted-glass door with 'Pink & Pink' on it. There was a great deal of the past in this room also, and in its associations—impossible to realise in America—which I found gratifying. The clerks were nearly all elderly, for one thing—grey-headed men. Since then I've met curates of about the same date. The curates astonished me even more than the clerks. A curate is such a perennially young person with us. You would find about as many aged schoolboys as elderly curates in America. I suppose our climate is more favourable to rapid development than yours, and they become full-fledged clergymen or lawyers after a reasonable apprenticeship. If not, they must come within the operation of some evolutionary law by which they disappear. America is a place where there is very little room for anachronisms.

Beside the elderly clerks, the room had an air of old leather, and three large windows with yellow blinds *pinned up*—in these days of automatic rollers. Through the windows I noticed the cheerful chimneys and spires of London, E.C., rising out of that lovely atmospheric tone of yellow which is so becoming to them; and down below—if I could only have got near enough I am certain I should have seen a small dismantled graveyard, with mossy tombstones of different sizes a long way out of the perpendicular. I have become accustomed to finding graveyards in close connection with business enterprise in London, and they appeal to me. It is very nice of you to let them stay just where they were put originally, when you are so crowded.

'WITH AN AIR OF INQUIRY'

At home there isn't a dead person in existence, so to speak, that would have a chance in a locality like Cheapside.

And they must suggest to you all sorts of useful and valuable things about the futility of ambition and the deceitfulness of riches down there under your very noses, as it were, whenever you pause to look at them. I can quite understand your respect for them, even in connection with what E.C. frontage prices must be, and I hope, though I can't be sure, that there was one attached to the offices in Cheapside of Messrs. Pink & Pink.

The clerks all looked up with an air of inquiry when I went in, and I selected the only one who did not immediately duck to his work again for my interrogation. It was an awkward interrogation to make, and I made it awkwardly. 'Are the Mr. Pinks in?' I asked; for I did not know in the least how many of them wanted to see me.

'I believe so, miss,' said the elderly clerk, politely, laying down his pen. 'Would it be Mr. A. Pink, or Mr. W. W. Pink?'

I said I really didn't know.

'Ah! In that case it would be Mr. A. Pink. Shouldn't you say so?'—turning to the less mature clerk, who responded loftily, from a great distance, and without looking, 'Probably.' Whereupon the elderly one got down from his stool, and took me himself to the door with 'Mr. A. Pink' on it, knocked, spoke to someone inside, then ushered me into the presence of Mr. A. Pink, and withdrew.

The room, I regret to say, did not match its surroundings, and could not have been thought of in connection with a graveyard. It was quite modern, with a raised leather wall-paper and revolving chairs. I noticed this before I saw the tall, thin, depressed-looking gentleman who had risen, and was bowing to me, at the other end of it. He was as bald as possible, and might have been fifty, with long, grey side-whiskers, that fell upon a suit of black, very much wrinkled where Mr. Pink did not fill it out. His mouth was abruptly turned down at the corners, with lines of extreme reserve about it, and whatever complexion he might have had originally was quite gone, leaving only a modified tone of old-gold behind it. 'Dear me!' I thought, 'there can be nothing interesting or mysterious here.' Mr. Pink first carefully ascertained whether I was Miss Wick, of Chicago; after which he did not shake hands, as I had vaguely expected him to do, being poppa's solicitor, but said, 'Pray be seated, Miss Wick!'—and we both sat down in the revolving chairs, preserving an unbroken gravity.

'You have been in London some weeks, I believe, Miss Wick,' said Mr. A. Pink, tentatively. He did not know quite how long, because for the first month I had plenty of money, without being obliged to apply for it. I smiled, and said 'Yes!' with an inflection of self-congratulation. I was very curious, but saw no necessity for giving more information than was actually asked for.

'Your—ah—father wrote us that you were coming over alone. That must have required great courage on the part of'—here Mr. Pink cleared his throat—'so young a lady;' and Mr. Pink smiled a little narrow, dreary smile.

'Oh, no!' I said, 'it didn't, Mr. Pink.'

"You are—ah—quite comfortable, I hope, in Cadogan Mansions. I think it is Cadogan Mansions, is it not?—Yes.'

'Very comfortable indeed, thank you, Mr. Pink. They are comparatively modern, and the elevator makes it seem more or less like home.'

Mr. Pink brightened; he evidently wished me to be discursive. 'Indeed!' he said—'Ye-es?'

'Yes,' I returned; 'when I have time I always use the elevator.'

'That is not, I think, the address of the lady your father mentioned to us as your only relative in London, Miss Wick?' 'Oh no,' I responded, cheerfully; 'Mrs. Cummers Portheris lives in Half-Moon Street, Mr. Pink.'

'Ah, so I understand. Pardon the inquiry, Miss Wick, but was there not some expectation on your father's part that you would pass the time of your visit in London with Mrs. Portheris?'

'On all our parts, Mr. Pink. But it vanished the day after I arrived'—and I could not help smiling as I remembered the letter I had written from the Métropole telling the Wick family about my reception by my affectionate relation.

Mr. Pink smiled too, a little doubtfully as well as drearily this time. He did not seem to know quite how to proceed.

'Pardon me again, Miss Wick, but there must be occasions, I should think, when you would feel your—ah—comparative isolation'—and Mr. Pink let one of his grey whiskers run through his long, thin hand.

'Very seldom,' I said; 'there is so much to see in London, Mr. Pink. Even the store-windows are entertaining to a stranger'—and I wondered more than ever what was coming.

'I see—I see. You make little expeditions to various points of interest—the Zoological Gardens, the Crystal Palace, and so forth.'

It began to be like the dialogues in the old-fashioned reading-books, carefully marked I 'Q.' and 'A.'

'IT BEGAN TO BE LIKE THE DIALOGUES IN THE OLD-FASHIONED READING-BOOKS.'

'Yes,' I said, 'I do. I haven't seen the Zoo yet, but I've seen Mrs. Por———'; there I stopped, knowing that Mr. Pink could not be expected to perceive the sequence of my ideas.

But he seemed to conclude that he had ascertained as much as was necessary. 'I think, Miss Wick,' he said, 'we must come to the point at once. You have not been in England long, and you may or may not be aware of the extreme difficulty which attaches—er—to obtaining—that is to say, which Amer— *foreigners* find in obtaining anything like a correct idea of—of social institutions here. To a person, I may say, without excellent introductions, it is, generally speaking, impossible.'

I said I had heard of this difficulty.

'I do not know whether you, personally, have any curiosity upon this point, but——'

I hastened to say that I had a great deal.

'But I should say that it was probable. There are few persons of your intelligence, Miss Wick, I venture to hazard, by whom a knowledge of English society, gained upon what might be termed a footing of intimacy, would fail to be appreciated.'

I bowed. It was flattering to be thought intelligent by Mr. Pink.

'The question now resolves itself, to come, as I have said, straight to the point, Miss Wick, into whether you would or would not care to take steps to secure it.'

'That would depend, I should think, upon the nature of the steps, Mr. Pink. I may as well ask you immediately whether they have anything to do with Miss Purkiss.'

'Nothing whatever—nothing whatever!' Mr. Pink hastened to assure me. 'I do not know the lady. The steps which have recommended themselves to me for you would be taken upon a—upon a basis of mutual accommodation, Miss Wick, involving remuneration, of course, upon your side.'

'Oh!' said I, comprehendingly.

'And in connection with a client of our own—an old, and, I may say, a highly-esteemed'—and Mr. Pink made a little respectful forward inclination of his neck—'client of our own.' I left the burden of explanation wholly to Mr. Pink, contenting myself with looking amiable and encouraging.

'A widow of Lord Bandobust,' said Mr. Pink, with an eye to the effect of this statement. The effect was bad—I could not help wondering how many Lord Bandobust had, and said, 'Really!' with an effort to conceal it.

'Lady Bandobust, somewhat late in life—this, of course, is confidential, Miss Wick—finds herself in a position to—to appreciate any slight addition to her income. His lordship's rather peculiar will—but I need not go into that. It is, perhaps, sufficient to say that Lady Bandobust is in a position to give you every advantage, Miss Wick—*every* advantage.'

This was fascinating, and I longed to hear more. 'It seems, a little indefinite,' said I to Mr. Pink.

'It does, certainly—you are quite right, Miss Wick—it does. Beyond approaching you, however, and ascertaining your views, I am not instructed to act in the matter. Ascertaining your views in particular, I should say, as regards the sum mentioned by Lady Bandobust as a—a proper equivalent—ahem!'

'What is her ladyship's charge?' I inquired.

'Lady Bandobust would expect three hundred pounds. My client wishes it to be understood that in naming this figure she takes into consideration the fact that the season is already well opened,' Mr. Pink said. 'Of course, additional time must be allowed to enable you to write to your parents.'

'I see,' I said; 'it does not strike me as exorbitant, Mr. Pink, considering what Lady Bandobust has to sell.'

Mr. Pink smiled rather uncomfortably. 'You Americans are so humorous,' he said, with an attempt at affability.

'Well'—drawing both whiskers through his hand conclusively, and suddenly standing up—'will you step this way, Miss Wick? My client has done me the honour of calling in person about this matter, and as your visits, oddly enough, coincide, you will be glad of the opportunity of going into details with her.' And Mr. A. Pink opened the door leading into the room of Mr. W. W. Pink. I was taken by surprise, but am afraid I should have gone in even after time for mature deliberation, I was so deeply, though insincerely, interested in the details.

'I WAS TAKEN BY SURPRISE'

XX

'LADY BANDOBUST, may I have the honour of introducing Miss Wick, of Chicago?' said Mr. Pink, solemnly, bowing as if he himself were being introduced to somebody. 'I could not do better, I am sure, Miss Wick, than leave you in Lady Bandobust's hands'—with which master-stroke of politeness Mr. Pink withdrew, leaving me, as he said, in Lady Bandobust's hands. She was a little old woman in black, with sharp eyes, a rather large, hooked nose, and a discontented mouth, over which hovered an expression of being actively bored. She had sloping shoulders, and little thin fingers in gloves much too long for them, and her bonnet dated back five seasons. Her whole appearance, without offering any special point for criticism, suggested that appreciation of any pecuniary advantage of which Mr. Pink had spoken, though her manner gave me definitely to understand that she did not care one jot about it. She was looking out of the window when Mr. Pink and I came in, and after acknowledging my bow with a small perfunctory smile, a half-effort to rise, and a vague vertebral motion at the back of her neck, she looked out of the window again. I am convinced that there was nothing in the view that could possibly interest her, yet constantly, in the course of our conversation, Lady Bandobust looked out of the window. She was the most uninterested person I have had the pleasure of talking to in England.

'LADY BANDOBUST'

"SHE WAS THE MOST UNINTERESTED PERSON I HAVE HAD THE PLEASURE OF TALKING TO IN ENGLAND."

I said it was a lovely day.

'Yes,' said Lady Bandobust. 'Mr. Pink tells me you are an American, Miss Wick, though anybody could see that much. He knows your father, I believe?'

'Not personally, I think,' I returned. 'Poppa has never visited England, Lady Bandobust.'

'Perhaps we had better say "financially," then—knows him financially.'

'I daresay that is all that is necessary,' I said, innocently at the time, though I have since understood Lady Bandobust's reason for looking at me so sharply.

'You come from Chinchinnatti, I understand from Mr. Pink,' she continued.

'I beg your pardon? Oh, Cincinatti! No, from Chicago, Lady Bandobust.'

'*I understood* from Mr. Pink that you came from Chinchinnatti—the place where people make millions in tinned pork. I had a nephew there for seven years, so I ought to know something about it,' said Lady Bandobust, with some asperity. 'But if you say you are from Chickago, I have no doubt you are right.'

- 140 -

'Mr. Pink informed me,' continued Lady Bandobust, 'that he thought you might feel able to afford to see a little of English society. I've noticed that Americans generally like to do that if they can.'

I said I was sure it would be interesting.

'It is very difficult,' said Lady Bandobust—'extremely difficult. It is impossible that you should know how difficult it is.'

I remarked modestly, by way of reply, that I believed few things worth having were easy to get.

Lady Bandobust ignored the generalisation. 'As Mr. Pink has probably told you, it costs money,' said she, with another little concessive smile.

'Then, perhaps, it is not so difficult after all,' I replied, amiably.

Lady Bandobust gave me another sharp look. 'Only you rich Americans can afford to say that,' she said. 'But Mr. Pink has told me that the expense would in all likelihood be a matter of indifference to your people. That, of course, is important.'

'Poppa doesn't scrimp,' I said. 'He likes us to have a good time.'

'Regardless,' said Lady Bandobust—'regardless of the cost! That is very liberal.'

'Americans,' she went on, 'in English society are very fortunate. They are always considered as—as Americans, you understand——'

'I'm afraid I don't,' said I.

'And I think, on the whole, they are rather liked. Yes generally speaking, I think I may say they are liked.'

I tried to express my gratification.

'As a rule,' said Lady Bandobust, absently, 'they spend so much money in England.'

'There can be no doubt of the *advantages* of an experience of English society,' she continued, rather as if I had suggested one. 'To a young lady especially it is invaluable—it leads to so much. I don't know quite to what extent you would expect——' Here Lady Bandobust paused, as if waiting for data on which to proceed.

'I would expect——?' I repeated, not quite understanding.

'But I think I could arrange a certain number of balls, say four; one or two dinners—you wouldn't care much about dinners, though, I dare say; a few good 'at homes'; a Saturday or so at Hurlingham—possibly Ascot; but, of course, you know everything would depend upon yourself.'

'I could hardly expect you to make me enjoy myself, Lady Bandobust,' I said. 'That altogether depends upon one's own capacity for pleasure, as you say.'

'Oh, altogether!' she returned. 'Well, we might say six balls—thoroughly good ones'—and Lady Bandobust looked at me for a longer time together than she had yet—'and *possibly* the Royal Inclosure at Ascot. I say "possibly" because it is very difficult to get. And a house-party to finish up with, which really ought to be extra, as it doesn't properly belong to a London season; but if I can at all see my way to it,' Lady Bandobust went on, 'I'll put it into the three hundred. There are the Allspices, who have just bought Lord Frereton's place in Wilts—I could take anybody there!'

'Your friends must be very obliging, Lady Bandobust,' said I.

'The Private View is over,' said Lady Bandobust; 'but there is the Academy Soiree in June, and the Royal Colonial Institute, and a few things like that.'

'It sounds charming,' I remarked.

'We might do something about the Four-in-hand,' Lady Bandobust continued, with some impatience.

'Yes?' I said.

There was a pause, in which I cast about me for some way of escape. I felt that my interest in Lady Bandobust was exhausted, and that I could not pretend to entertain her scheme any longer with self-respect. Besides, by this time I cordially hated her. But I could think of no formula to retreat under, and resigned myself to sit there helplessly, and defend myself as best I could, until I was dismissed.

Lady Bandobust produced her last card. 'The Duchess of Dudlington gives a *fête* on the twelfth,' she said, throwing it, as it were, upon the table. 'I should probably be able to take you there.'

'The Duchess of Dudlington?' said I, in pure stupidity.

'Yes. And she is rather partial to Americans, for some extraordinary reason or another.' The conversation flagged again.

'Presentation—if that is what you are thinking of—would be extra, Miss Wick,' Lady Bandobust stated, firmly.

'Oh'—how much extra, Lady Bandobust?'

My prospective patroness did not hesitate a minute. 'Fifty pounds,' she said, and looked at me inquiringly.

'I—I don't think I was thinking of it, Lady Bandobust,' I said. I felt mean, as we say in America.

'You were not! Well,' said she, judicially, 'I don't know that I would advise the outlay. It is a satisfactory thing to have done, of course, but not nearly so essential as it used to be—nothing like. You can get on without it. And, as you say, fifty pounds is fifty pounds.'

I knew I hadn't said that, but found it impossible to assert the fact.

'Miss Boningsbill, whom I took out last season, I did present,' Lady Bandobust continued; 'but she went in for everything—perhaps more extensively than you would be disposed to do. It might facilitate matters—give you an idea, perhaps—if I were to tell you my arrangements with Miss Boningsbill.'

'I should like to hear them,' I said.

'She did not live with me—of course, chaperonage does not imply residence, you understand that. When she went out with me she called for me in her brougham. She had a brougham by the month, and a landau for the park. I should distinctly advise you to do the same. I would, in fact, make the arrangement for you. I know a very reliable man.' Lady Bandobust paused for my thanks.

'Generally speaking, Miss Boningsbill and I went out together; but when I found this particularly inconvenient, she took one carriage and I the other, though she always had her choice. I *stipulated* only to take her to the park twice a week, but if nothing interfered I went oftener. Occasionally I took her to the play—that bores me, though. I hope you are not particularly fond of the theatre. And then she usually found it less expensive to get a box, as there were generally a few other people who could be asked with advantage—friends of my own.' 'She had a box at Ascot, too, of course,' Lady Bandobust went on, looking down her nose at a fly in the corner of the window-pane; 'but that is a matter of detail.'

'Of course,' I said, because I could think of nothing else to say.

'I gave her a ball,' Lady Bandobust continued; 'that is to say, cards were sent out in my name. That was rather bungled, though—so many friends of mine begged for invitations for friends of theirs that I didn't know half the people. And Miss Boningsbill, of course, knew nobody. Miss Boningsbill was dissatisfied about the cost, too. I was foolish enough to forget to tell her beforehand. Everything came from my own particular tradespeople, and, naturally, nothing was cheap. I *never* niggle,' said Lady Bandobust, turning her two little indifferent black eyes full upon me.

'Miss Boningsbill insisted on having her name on the cards as well,' she said: '"Lady Bandobust and Miss Boningsbill," you understand. That I should not advise—very bad form, I call it.'

'She was married in October,' Lady Bandobust continued, casually. The second son of Sir Banbury Slatte—the eldest had gone abroad for his health. I knew the Banbury Slattes extremely well—excellent family.'

'Miss Boningsbill,' Lady Bandobust went on, absently, 'had nothing like your figure.'

'Was she an American?' I asked.

'No—Manchester,' answered Lady Bandobust, laconically.

'Cotton-spinners.'

'My dressmaker tells me she finds a marked difference between English and American figures.' I remarked; 'but I am afraid it is not to our advantage. We are not nearly so fine as you are.'

'Ah!' said Lady Bandobust. 'Who is your dressmaker?' she asked with interest.

'I spoke of the firm whose place of business, though not mentioned in any guide-book, I had found to repay many visits.

'Oh, those people!' said Lady Bandobust. 'Dear, I call them. Smart enough for evening frocks, but *certainly* not to be depended upon for anything else. I should strongly advise you to try Miss Pafty, in Regent Street, and say I sent you. And for millinery, do let me recommend Madame Marie. I would give you a note to her. An *excessively* clever woman—personal friend of my own. A husband and two sons to support, so she makes bonnets. I *believe* the Princess goes to her regularly. And you pay very little more than you do anywhere else. And now, with regard to our little scheme, what do you think, Miss Wick?'

'Really, Lady Bandobust,' said I, 'I am afraid I must think about it.' A decided negative was an utter impossibility at the time.

'Ah!' said Lady Bandobust, I perhaps you think my terms a little high—just a trifle more than you expected, perhaps. Well, suppose we say two hundred and fifty?'

'I had no expectations whatever about it, Lady Bandobust,' I said; 'I knew nothing of it up to about an hour ago.'

'Two hundred,' said Lady Bandobust.

'I am afraid I have no idea of the value of—of such things, Lady Bandobust,' I faltered.

'I *can* bring it as low as one hundred and fifty,' she returned, 'but it would not be quite the same, Miss Wick—you could not expect that.'

The rest of the conversation, which I find rather painful to call to memory, may perhaps be imagined from the fact that Lady Bandobust finally brought her offer down to seventy-five pounds, at which point I escaped, taking her address, promising to write her my decision in the course of a day or two, and feeling more uncomfortably contemptible than ever before in my life. We happened to be making visits in Park Lane next day, and as Lady Bandobust lived near there, I took the note myself, thinking it would be more polite. And I found the locality, in spite of its vicinity to Park Lane, quite extraordinary for Lady Bandobust to have apartments in.

I met Lady Bandobust once again. It was at an 'at home' given by Lord and Lady Mafferton, where everybody was asked 'to meet' a certain distinguished traveller. Oddly enough, I was introduced to her, and we had quite a long chat. But I noticed that she had not caught my name as my hostess pronounced it—she called me 'Miss Winter' during the whole of our conversation, and seemed to have forgotten that we had ever seen each other before; which was disagreeable of her, in my opinion.

XXI

I WENT to Ascot with the Bangley Coffins—Mr., Mrs., and the two Misses Bangley Coffin. I didn't know the Bangley Coffins very well, but they were kind enough to ask Lady Torquilin if I might go with them, and Lady Torquilin consented with alacrity. 'You *couldn't* go away from England without seeing Ascot,' said she. 'It would be a sin! It's far too much riot for me; besides, I can't bear to see the wretched horses. If they would only learn to race without beating the poor beasties! To say nothing of the expense, which I call enormous. So by all means go with the Bangley Coffins, child—they're lively people—I daresay you'll enjoy yourself.'

Lady Torquilin was surprised and disappointed, however, when she learned that the party would go by train. 'I wonder at them,' she said, referring to the Bangley Coffins; 'they know such a lot of people. I would have said they were morally certain to be on somebody's drag. Shall you care to go by train?' Whereupon I promptly assured Lady Torquilin that I was only too happy to go any way.

So we started, the morning of the Gold Cup day, I and the Bangley Coffins. I may as well describe the Bangley Coffins, in the hope that they may help to explain my experiences at Ascot. I have to think of Mrs. Bangley Coffin very often myself, when I try to look back intelligently upon our proceedings.

Mrs. Bangley Coffin was tall, with a beautiful figure and pale gold hair. The Misses Bangley Coffin were also tall, with prospectively beautiful figures and pale gold hair. I never saw such a resemblance between mother and daughters as there was between the Misses Bangley Coffin and their mamma. They sat up in the same way, their shoulders had the same slope, their elbows the same angle. The same lines developed on the countenance of Mrs. Bangley Coffin were undeveloped on the countenances of the Misses Bangley Coffin. Except in some slight matter of nose or eyes, Mr. Bangley Coffin hardly suggested himself in either of the young ladies. When they spoke, it was in their mother's voice and in their mother's manner—a manner that impressed you for the moment as being the only one in the world. Both they and their mamma had on dresses which it was perfectly evident they had never worn before, and of which they demanded my opinion with a frankness that surprised me. 'What do you think,' said they, 'of our Ascot frocks?' I admired them very much; they represented, amongst them, nearly all the fashionable novelties, and yet they had a sort of conventional originality, if I may say such a thing, which was extremely striking. They seemed satisfied with my applause, but promptly fell upon me for not meriting applause myself. 'We saw you,' they said unitedly, 'in that frock last Sunday in the park!'—and there was a distinct reproach in the way they said it. 'It's quite charming!' they assured me—and it was—'but it's not as if you hadn't *quantities* of them! Do you mean to say Lady Torquilin didn't tell you you ought to have a *special* frock for Ascot?' 'She said I should do very well in this,' I declared, 'and that it would be a sin to buy another; I had much better give the money to Dr. Barnardo!' Whereat Mrs. Bangley Coffin and the two Misses Bangley Coffin looked at one another and remarked, 'How like Lady Torquilin!'

'I didn't give it to Dr. Barnardo,' I continued—to which Mrs. Bangley Coffin rejoined, in parenthesis, 'I should hope not'—' but I'm glad Lady Torquilin did not advise me to get an Ascot frock, though yours are very pretty. I feel that I couldn't have sustained one—I haven't the personality!' And indeed this was quite true. It occurred to me often again through the day; I could not have gone about inside an Ascot frock without feeling to some extent the helpless and meaningless victim of it. The Bangley Coffin girls thought this supreme nonsense, and declared that I could carry anything off, and Mrs.

Bangley Coffin said, with pretended severity, that it was not a question of feeling but of *looking*; but they united in consoling me so successfully that I at last believed myself dressed to perfection for Ascot—if I had only worn something else to the park the Sunday before!

The husband and father of the Bangley Coffins was a short, square-shouldered gentleman with bushy eyebrows, a large moustache, plaid trousers, and a grey tail-coat that was a very tight fit round the waist. He had an expression of deep sagacity, and he took from an inner pocket, and fondled now and then, a case containing six very large brown cigars. His look of peculiar anticipative intelligence, combined with the cigars, gave me the idea that we should not be overburdened with Mr. Bangley Coffin's society during the day—which proved to be a correct one.

It did not seem to me, in spite of what Lady Torquilin had said, that it was at all unpopular to go to Ascot by rail. Trains were leaving the station every four or five minutes, all full of people who preferred that way of going; and our own car, which was what, I believe, you call a 'saloon carriage,' had hardly an empty seat. They looked nice respectable people, too, nearly all in Ascot frocks, though not perhaps particularly interesting. What surprised me in connection with the ride was the length of it; it was not a ride, as I had somehow expected, of twenty minutes or half an hour from London, but a journey of, I forget how many, interminable hours. And what surprised me in connection with the people was their endurance of it. They did not fuss, or grow impatient, or consult their watches as the time dragged by; they sat up, calm and placid and patient, and only looked occasionally, for refreshment, at their Ascot frocks. They seemed content to take an enormous amount of trouble for the amusement which might be supposed to be tickling their fancy at the other end of the trip—if there was any other end—to take it unshrinkingly and seriously. It gave me an idea of how difficult it is to be amused in England—unless you are a foreigner. Ascot to them was no light matter, and to me it was such a very light matter. I tried to imagine any fifty Americans of my acquaintance dressing up in their best clothes, and spending six or seven hours of a day in protracted railway journeys, for the sake of a little fun in between; and I failed. It's as much as we would do to inaugurate a president, or bury a general who saved the Union. We would consider the terms high. But, of course, it is impossible for me to say how we might behave if we had Distinguished Occasions, with Royal Inclosures inside them.

We started with a sense of disappointment, which seemed to come in through the windows and envelop the Bangley Coffins, because 'some people' they had expected failed to appear upon the platform. Mr. Bangley Coffin looked particularly depressed. 'Don't see how the deuce we're going to arrange!' he said to Mrs. Bangley Coffin, with unction. 'Oh, there's sure to be somebody, Joey, love!' she returned, cheerfully; 'and in any case, you see, we have you.' To which Mr. Bangley Coffin gave a dubious and indistinct assent. I did not get on well with Mr. Bangley Coffin. He seemed to mean well, but he had a great many phrases which I did not in the least understand, and to which he invariably added, 'As you say in America.' It was never by any chance a thing we did say in America, but nothing could make Mr. Bangley Coffin believe that. I can't say that we had much general conversation either, but in what there was I noticed great good-feeling between the Misses Bangley Coffins and their mamma.

'The bonnet of that Israelite at the other end of the carriage would suit you to a "T", mummie,' one of them remarked in joke. The bonnet was a terrible affair, in four shades of heliotrope.

'Yes,' replied Mrs. Bangley Coffin, smiling quite good-naturedly; 'that's about my form.'

The Bangley Coffins were all form. Form, for them, regulated existence. It was the all-compelling law of the spheres, the test of all human action and desire. 'Good form' was the ultimate expression of their respect, 'bad form' their final declaration of contempt. Perhaps I should misjudge the Bangley Coffins if I said form was their conscience, and I don't want to misjudge them—they were very pleasant to me. But I don't think they would have cared to risk their eternal salvation upon any religious tenets that were not entirely *comme il faut*—I mean the ladies Bangley Coffin. The head of their house twisted his moustache and seemed more or less indifferent.

There is no doubt that, in the end, we did get to Ascot, and left our dust-cloaks in charge of that obliging middle-aged person who is to be found in every ladies' waiting-room in England. There was some discussion as to whether we should or should not leave our dust-cloaks with her—they were obviously unbecoming, but, obviously also, it might rain. However, in the end we did. Mrs. Bangley Coffin thought we might trust to Providence, and Providence proved itself worthy of Mrs. Bangley Coffin's confidence.

Again, as we joined the crowd that surged out of the station, I noticed that look of anxious expectancy on the face of the Bangley Coffin family. It was keener than before, and all embracing. I even fancied I noticed an understood division of survey—an arrangement by which Mr. Bangley Coffin looked to the north, and Mrs. Bangley Coffin to the south, one young lady to the east, and the other to the west. 'We really must keep an eye open,' said Mr. Bangley Coffin. 'Coming this way? Oh! Hullo, Pipply, old man! H'are you?' with extreme cordiality, to a short, very stout gentleman in grey, with a pink face and a hooked nose, and a white moustache, and a blue-spotted necktie—a New Yorker, I was sure, before he spoke. Pipply responded with very moderate transports, and shook hands hastily with the ladies attached to Mr. Bangley Coffin. 'Mrs. Pipply's with you, I see,' continued Mr. Bangley Coffin, joyously, 'and that charming sister of hers! Kitty, we *must* see whether they have forgotten us, mustn't we?'—and he and Kitty advanced upon two very much-accented fair ladies in frilled muslins and large flowery hats. They were dressed as fashionably as Bond Street could dress them, and they were as plump and pretty as could be, but perhaps just a little too big and blue of eye and pink-and-white of complexion quite to satisfy the Bangley Coffin idea of 'form.' It would be difficult to account otherwise for what they did. For the Pipplys, they were very amiable, but, as you might say, at bay; and after reproaching the Bangley Coffins with having never, never, never come to see them, after promising *solemnly* to do so at Cannes, where they had all had *such* a good time together, Mrs. Pipply proceeded to say that she didn't know whether we were driving—if not, they had room for one, and we might arrange to meet again somewhere. 'How good of you!' said Mrs. Bangley Coffin, and looked at her two daughters. 'We're really obliged to you,' said Mr. Bangley Coffin, and bent a gaze of strong compulsion upon his wife. The young ladies smiled, hesitated, and looked at me. I couldn't go. I had not even been introduced. There was an awkward pause—the kind of pause you never get out of England—and as the Pipplys, rather huffed and rather in a hurry, were moving off, Mrs. Bangley Coffin covered their retreat, as it were, with the unblushing statement that she was afraid we must try to keep our little party together. And we lost the Pipplys; whereupon Mr. Bangley Coffin regarded his family with the air of a disciplinarian. 'They're *certain* to be on a drag,' said he, 'and no end of Pipply's clubs have tents. Why didn't one of you go? Not classy enough, eh?' Whereupon they all with one accord began to make excuse, after which we walked on in a troubled silence. It was very dusty and very steep, that narrow hill that so many people find fortune at the top or ruin at the bottom of, leading to the heart of Ascot. But the day had brightened, and the people—all going uphill—were disposed to be merry, and two one-armed sailors sat in the sun by the side of the road singing ballads and shouting, 'Good luck to you, ladies!' so that my spirits gradually rose. I didn't see how I could help enjoying myself.

'I always think it's such a frightful charge for admission to the Grand Stand,' said Mrs. Bangley Coffin, as we walked up the arboreal approach to it. 'A sovereign! Of course, they have to do it, you know, to keep the mob out; but really, when one thinks of it, it is too much!'

I thought this a real kindness of Mrs. Bangley Coffin, because if I had not known it was so much I might have let Mr. Bangley Coffin pay for my ticket too.

It was about this time that Mr. Bangley Coffin disappeared. He launched us, as it were, upon the crowded terrace in front of the Grand Stand, where at every turn the Misses Bangley Coffin expected to see a man they knew. He remained semi-detached and clinging for about a quarter of an hour, coming up with an agreeable criticism upon a particular costume, darting off again to talk to a large, calm man with an expansive checked shirt-front and a silk hat well on the back of his head, who carried a notebook. Then, once, Mrs. Bangley Coffin addressed him, thinking him behind her. 'Joey, love!' said she. 'Joey, love!' said she again, turning her head. But Joey was utterly and wholly gone. I believe he explained afterwards that he had lost us.

'There!' said Mrs. Bangley Coffin, with incisiveness; 'now we *must* see somebody we know! Pet, isn't that Sir Melville Cartus?' It was, and Sir Melville came up in response to Mrs. Bangley Coffin's eyeglass and bow and smile, and made himself extremely agreeable for about four minutes and a-quarter. Then he also took off his hat with much charm of manner and went away. So did a nervous little Mr. Trifugis, who joined us for a short time. He said he was on the Fitzwalters's drag, and it was so uncommon full he had apprehensions about getting back. Whose drag were we on? and didn't we think it was drawing near the halcyon hour of luncheon?

'Nobody's,' said Mrs. Bangley Coffin, pointedly. 'We came by train this year. Joey is suffering from a fit of economy—the result of Surefoot's behaviour at the Derby. It *is* about time for luncheon.'

Whereat Mr. Trifugis dropped his eyeglass and looked absently over his left shoulder, blushing hard. Then he screwed the eyeglass in again very tight, looked at us all with amiable indefiniteness, took off his hat, and departed. 'Little beast!' said Mrs. Bangley Coffin, candidly; 'there's not the slightest reason why he couldn't have given us all luncheon at the Lyric enclosure.'

Then I began to see why it was so necessary that we should meet somebody we knew—it meant sustenance. It was, as Mr. Trifugis had said, quite time for sustenance, and neither the Bangley Coffin family nor I had had any since breakfast, and if it had not been for that consideration, which was naturally a serious one, I, for my part, would have been delighted just to go round, as we seemed likely to do, by ourselves. There was no band, as there never is in England—I suppose because Edward the Confessor or somebody didn't like bands; but there was everything else that goes to give an occasion brilliance and variety—a mingling crowd of people with conventionally picturesque clothes and interesting manners, sunlight, flags, a race-course, open boxes, an obvious thrill of excitement, a great many novel noises. Besides, it was Ascot, and its interest was intrinsic.

'I think we must try the drags,' said Mrs. Bangley Coffin—and we defiled out into the crowd beyond the gates, whose dress is not original, that surges unremuneratively between the people who pay on the coaches and the people who pay on the Lawn. It was more amusing outside, though less exclusive—livelier, noisier. Men were hanging thick against the palings of the Lawn, with expressions of deep sagacity and coloured shirts, calling uninterruptedly, 'Two to one bar one!' 'Two to one Orveito!' and very well dressed young gentlemen occasionally came up and entered into respectful conference with them. We were jostled a good deal in the elbowing multitude, and it seemed to me to be always, as if in irony, by a man who sold gingerbread or boiled lobsters. We made our way through it, however, and walked slowly in the very shadow of the drags, on top of which people with no better appetites than we had were ostentatiously feasting. We were all to look out for the Pibbly hats, and we did—in vain. 'I can't imagine,' said Mrs. Bangley Coffin to each of her daughters in turn, 'why you didn't go with them!' We saw Mr. Trifugis, and noted bitterly that he had not been at all too late. An actress on the Lyric drag gave us a very frank and full-flavoured criticism of our dresses, but it was unsatisfying, except to the sensibilities.

'ALWAYS, AS IF IN IRONY, BY A MAN WHO SOLD GINGERBREAD.'

'Shall we try behind, mamma?' asked one of the young ladies. 'Who could possibly see us behind?' exclaimed Mrs. Bangley Coffin, who was getting cross. Nevertheless, we did try behind, and somebody did see us—several very intelligent footmen.

'Is there no place,' I inquired for the fourth or fifth time, 'where we could *buy* a little light refreshment?' Mrs. Bangley Coffin didn't say there was not, but seemed to think it so improbable that it was hardly worth our while to look. 'Nobody lunches at Ascot, Miss Wick,' she said at last, with a little asperity, 'except on the drags or at the club enclosures. It's—it's impossible.'

'Well,' I said, 'I think it's very unenterprising not to make provision for such a large number of people. If this were in America——' But just then we came face to face with Colonel and Mrs. B. J. Silverthorn, of St. Paul's, Minnesota. To say that I was glad to see these old friends in this particular emergency is to say very little. I knew the Colonel's theory of living, and I was quite sure that starving for six hours on an English racecourse had no place in it. I knew his generous heart, too, and was confident that any daughter of poppa's might rely upon it to the utmost. So, after introducing Mrs. and the Misses Bangley Coffin, I proceeded to explain our unfortunate situation. 'Can you tell us,' I begged, 'where we can get something to eat?'

The Colonel did not hesitate a moment. 'Come right along with me,' he said. 'It isn't just the Fifth Avenue Hotel, but it'll do if you're hungry, and I guess you are!' And we all followed him to the rather abridged seclusion of the restaurant behind the Grand Stand. The Colonel did it all very handsomely—ordered champagne, and more dishes than twice as many people could have disposed of; but the cloud that rested upon the brows of Mrs. and the Misses Bangley Coffin did not disperse with the comforting influence of food, and they kept a nervous eye upon the comers and goers. I suppose they had waited too long for their meal really to enjoy it.

We parted from Colonel and Mrs. Silverthorn almost immediately afterwards—they said they wanted to go and have another good look at the Royalties and Dukes in their own yard, and Mrs. Bangley Coffin thought it was really our duty to stay where Mr. Bangley Coffin might find us. So we went and sat in a row and saw the Gold Cup won, and shortly after took an early train for London, Mrs. Bangley Coffin declaring that she had no heart for another sovereign for the Paddock. On the way home she said she was sorry I had had such a dull day, and that it was her first and last attempt to 'screw' Ascot. But I had not had at all a dull day—it had been immensely interesting, to say nothing of the pleasure of meeting Colonel and Mrs. Silverthorn. I quite agreed with Mrs. Bangley Coffin, however, that it is better to make liberal arrangements for Ascot when you go as an Ascot person.

XXII

I DON'T know what we were about to let Miss Wick miss the Boats,' said Mr. Mafferton one day, over his after-noon-tea in Lady Torquilin's flat. I looked at Lady Torquilin, and said I thought Mr. Mafferton must be mistaken; I had never missed a boat in my life, and, besides, we hadn't been going anywhere by boat lately. The reason we had put off our trip to Richmond five times was invariably because of the weather. Peter Corke happened to be there that afternoon, too, though she didn't make much of a visit. Miss Corke never did stay very long when Mr. Mafferton was there—he was a person she couldn't bear. She never called him anything but 'That.' She declared you could see hundreds of him any afternoon in Piccadilly, all with the same hat and collar and expression and carnation in their button-holes. She failed to see why I should waste any portion of my valuable time in observing Mr. Mafferton, when I had still to see 'Dolly's Chop House,' and Guy the King-maker's tablet in Warwick Lane, and the Boy in Panyer Alley, and was so far unimproved by anything whatever relating to Oliver Goldsmith or Samuel Johnson. She could not understand that a profoundly uninteresting person might interest you precisely on that account. But, 'Oh you aborigine!' she began about the Boats, and I presently understood another of those English descriptive terms by which you mean something that you do not say.

The discussion ended, very happily for me, in an arrangement suggested jointly by Miss Corke and Mr. Mafferton. Lady Torquilin and I should go to Oxford to see 'the Eights.' Mr. Mafferton had a nephew at Pembroke, and no doubt the young cub would be delighted to look after us. Miss Corke's younger brother was at Exeter, and she would write to the dear boy at once that he must be nice to us. Peter was very sorry she couldn't come herself—nothing would have given her greater pleasure, she said, than to show me all I didn't know in the Bodleian.

I suppose we have rather a large, exaggerated idea of Oxford in America, thinking about it, as it were, externally. As a name it is so constantly before us, and the terms of respect in which the English despatches speak of it are so marked, that its importance in our eyes has become extremely great. We think it a city, of course—no place could grow to such fame without being a city—and with us the importance of a city naturally invests itself in large blocks of fine buildings chiefly devoted to business, in a widely-extended and highly-perfected telephone system, and in avenues of Queen Anne residences with the latest modern conveniences. And Lady Torquilin, on the way, certainly talked a great deal about 'the High'—which she explained to be Oxford's principal thoroughfare—and the purchases she had at one time or another made on it, comparing Oxford with London prices. So that I had quite an extensive State Street or Wabash Avenue idea of 'the High.' Both our young gentlemen friends were fractional parts of the Eights, and were therefore unable to meet us. It had been arranged that we should lunch with one at two, and take tea with the other at five, but Lady Torquilin declared herself in urgent need of something sustaining as soon as we arrived, and 'Shall we go to the Clarendon to get it?' said she, 'or to Boffin's?'

'What is Boffin's?' I inquired. It is not safe, in English localisms, to assume that you know anything.

'Boffin's is a pastry-cook's,' Lady Torquilin informed me, and I immediately elected for Boffin's. It was something idyllic, in these commonplace days, when Dickens has been so long dead, that Boffin should be a pastry-cook, and that a pastry-cook should be Boffin. Perhaps it struck me especially, because in America he would have been a 'confectioner,' with some aesthetic change in the spelling of the original Boffin that I am convinced could not be half so good for business. And we walked up a long, narrow, quiet street, bent like an elbow, lined with low-roofed little shops devoted chiefly, as I remember them, to the sale of tennis-racquets, old prints, sausages, and gentlemen's neckties, full of quaint gables, and here and there lapsing into a row of elderly stone houses that had all gone to sleep together by the pavement, leaving their worldly business to the care of the brass-plates on their doors. Such a curious old street we went up to Boffin's, so peaceful, nothing in it but inoffensive boys pushing handcarts, and amiable gentlemen advanced in years with spectacles—certainly more of these than I ever saw together in any other place—never drowsing far from the shadow of some serious grey pile, ivy-bearded and intent, like a venerable scholar—oh, a very curious old street!

'Shall we get,' said I to Lady Torquilin, 'any glimpse of the High before we reach Boffin's?' Dear Lady Torquilin looked at me sternly, as if to discover some latent insincerity. 'None of your impertinence, miss,' said she; 'this is the High!'

I was more charmed and delighted than I can express, and as Lady Torquilin fortunately remembered several things we urgently needed, and could buy to much better advantage in Oxford than in 'Town,' I had the great pleasure of finding out what it was like to shop in the High, and the other queer little streets which are permitted to run—no, to creep—about the feet of the great wise old colleges that take such kindly notice of them. It was very nice, to my mind, that huddling together of pastry-cooks and gargoyles, of chapels and old china shops, of battered mediæval saints and those little modern errand-boys with their handcarts—of old times and new, preponderatingly old and respectfully new. Much more democratic, too, than a seat of learning would be in America, where almost every college of reputation is isolated in the sea of 'grounds,' and the only sound that falls upon the academic ear is the clatter of the lawn-mower or the hissing of the garden-hose. Nor shall I soon forget the emotions with which I made a perfectly inoffensive purchase in a small establishment of wide reputation for petty wares, called, apparently from time immemorial, 'The Civet Cat'—not reproachfully, nor in a spirit of derision, but bearing the name with dignity in painted letters.

People who know their way about Oxford will understand how we found ours to Pembroke from the High. I find that I have forgotten. We stood at so many corners to look, and Lady Torquilin bade me hurry on so often, that the streets and the colleges, and the towers and the gardens, are all lost to me in a crowded memory that diverges with the vagueness of enchantment from Carfax and Boffin's. But at last we walked out of the relative bustle of the highways and byways into the quietest place I ever saw or felt, except a graveyard in the Strand—a green square hedged in with buildings of great dignity and solidity, and very serious mind. I felt, as we walked around it to ask a respectable-looking man waiting about on the other side where Mr. Sanders Horton's rooms were, as if I were in church.

'I FELT AS IF I WERE IN CHURCH'

'Yes'm! This way'm, if you please,' said the respectable-looking man. 'Mr.'Orton's rooms is on the first floor h'up, 'm'; and as Mr. Horton himself had come out on the landing to receive us, and was presently very prettily shaking hands with us, we had no further difficulty. Our host had not considered himself equal to lunching two strange ladies unassisted, however, and as he looked a barely possible nineteen, this was not remarkable, Lady Torquilin thought afterwards. He immediately introduced his friend, Lord Symonds, who seemed, if anything, less mature, but whose manners were quite as nice. Then we all sat down in Mr. Sanders Horton's pretty little room, and watched the final evolution of luncheon on the table, and talked about the view. 'You have a lovely lawn,' said I to Mr. Horton, who responded that it wasn't a bad quad; and when I asked if the respectable-looking man downstairs was the caretaker of the college: 'Oh, nothing so swagger!' said Lord Symonds; 'probably a scout!' And the presence of a quad and a scout did more than all the guide-books I read up afterwards to give me a realising sense of being in an English university centre. We looked at Mr. Horton's pictures, too, and examined, complimentarily, all his decorative effects of wood-carving and old china, doing our duty, as is required of ladies visiting the *menage* of a young gentleman, with enthusiasm. I was a little disappointed, personally, in not finding the initials of Byron or somebody cut on Mr. Horton's window-sill, and distinctly shocked to hear that this part of Pembroke College had been built within the memory of living man, as Mr. Horton was reluctantly obliged to admit. He apologised for its extreme modernness on the ground of its comparative comfort, but seemed to feel it, in a subdued way, severely, as was eminently proper. Among the various photographs of boat-races upon the wall was one in which Mr. Horton pointed out 'the Torpids,' which I could not help considering and remarking upon as a curious name for a boating-crew. 'Why are they called that?' I asked; 'they seem to be going pretty fast.'

'Oh, rather!' responded Mr. Horton. 'Upon my word, I don't know. It does seem hard lines, doesn't it? Symonds, where did these fellows get their name?' But Lord Symonds didn't know exactly either—they'd always had it, he fancied; and Lady Torquilin explained that 'this young lady'—meaning me— could never be satisfied with hearing that a thing was so because it was so— she must always know the why and wherefore of everything, even when there was neither why nor wherefore; at which we all laughed and sat down to luncheon. But I privately made up my mind to ask an explanation of the Torpids from the first Oxford graduate with honours that I met, and I did. He didn't know either. He was not a boating-man, however; he had taken his honours in Classics.

XXIII

I HAD heard so much from English sources of the precocity and forwardness of very young people in America, that I was quite prepared to find a commendably opposite state of things in England, and I must say that, generally speaking, I was not disappointed. The extent to which young ladies and gentlemen under twenty-two can sit up straight and refrain from conversation here, impressed me as much as anything I have seen in society. I have not observed any of this shyness in married ladies or older gentlemen; and that struck me oddly, too, for in America it is only with advancing years that we become conscious of our manners.

I have no doubt that, if the Eights had been in America—where they would probably be called the Octoplets—and Mr. Sanders Horton had been a Harvard Sophomore, and Lord Symonds's father had made his fortune out of a patent shoe-lace-tag, and we had all been enjoying ourselves over there, we might have noticed a difference both in the appearance and the behaviour of these young gentlemen. They would certainly have been older for their years, and more elaborately dressed. Their complexions would probably not have been so fresh, nor their shoulders so broad, and the pencilling on Mr. Horton's upper lip, and the delicate, fair marking on Lord Symonds's, would assuredly have deepened into a moustache. Their manners would not have been so negatively good as they were in Oxford, where they struck me as expressing an ideal, above all things, to avoid doing those things which they ought not to do. Their politeness would have been more effusive, and not the least bit nervous; though I hope neither Mr. Horton nor Lord Symonds will mind my implying that in Oxford they were nervous. People can't possibly help the way they have been brought up, and to me our host's nervousness was interesting, like his English accent, and the scout and the quad. Personally, I liked the feeling of superinducing bashfulness in two nice boys like those—it was novel and amusing—though I have no doubt they were much more afraid of Lady Torquilin than of me. I never saw a boy, however, from twelve to twenty-three—which strikes me as the span of boyhood in England—that was not Lady Torquilin's attached slave after twenty minutes' conversation with her. She did not humour them, or flatter them, or talk to them upon their particular subjects; she was simply what they called 'jolly' to them, and their appreciation was always prompt and lively. Lady Torquilin got on splendidly with both Mr. Sanders Horton and Lord Symonds. The only reason why Mr. Horton's lunch was not an unqualifiedly brilliant success was that, whenever she talked to one of our hosts, the other one was left for me to talk to, which was usually distressing for both of us.

It was an extremely nice lunch, served with anxious deference by the respectable-looking little man who had come upstairs, and nervously commanded by Mr. Horton at one end with the cold joint, and Lord Symonds at the other with the fowl. It began, I remember, with *bouillon*. Lady Torquilin partook of *bouillon*, so did I; but the respectable scout did not even offer it to the young gentlemen. I caught a rapid, inquiring glance from Lady Torquilin. Could it be that there was not *bouillon* enough? The thought checked any utterance upon the subject, and we finished our soup with careful indifference, while Lord Symonds covered the awkwardness of the situation by explaining to me demonstratively the nature of a Bump. I did not understand Bumps then, nor did I succeed during the course of the afternoon in picking up enough information to write intelligently about them. But this was because Lord Symonds had no *bouillon*. Under the circumstances, it was impossible for me to put my mind to it.

Presently Mr. Horton asked us if he might give us some salmon—not collectively, but individually and properly, Lady Torquillin first; and we said he might. He did not help Lord Symonds, and relapsed himself, as it were, into an empty plate. It was Lady Torquilin's business to inquire if the young gentlemen were not well, or if salmon did not agree with them, and not mine; but while I privately agitated this matter, I unobservantly helped myself to *mayonnaise*. 'I—I beg your pardon,' said Mr. Sanders Horton, in a pink agony; 'that's cream!' So it was, waiting in a beautiful old-fashioned silver pitcher the advent of those idylls that come after. It was a critical moment. Only one thing occurred to me to say, for which I hope I may be forgiven.

'THE RESPECTABLE SCOUT.'

'Yes,' I returned, 'we like it with fish in America. At which Mr. Horton looked interested and relieved. And I ate as much of the mixture as I could with a smile, though the salmon had undergone a vinegar treatment which made this difficult. 'It is in Boston, is it not,' remarked Lord Symonds politely, 'that the people live almost entirely upon beans?' And the conversation flowed quite generally until the advent of the fowl. It was a large, well-conditioned chicken, and when the young gentlemen, apparently by mutual consent, refrained from partaking of it, the situation had reached a degree of unreasonableness which was more than Lady Torquilin could endure.

'Do you intend to eat?'

'Oh, we'd like to, but we can't,' they replied, earnestly and simultaneously.

'We're still in training, you know,' Lord Symonds went on. 'Fellows have got to train pretty much on stodge.' And at this juncture Mr. Horton solemnly cut two slices of the cold beef, and sent them to his friend, helping himself to the same quantity with mathematical exactness. Then, with plain bread, and gravity which might almost be called severe, they attacked it.

Lady Torquilin and I looked at each other reproachfully. This privation struck us as needless and extreme, and it had the uncomfortable moral effect of turning our own repast into a Bacchanalian revel. We frowned, we protested, we besought. We suggested with insidious temptation that this was the last day of the races, and that nobody would know. We commended each particular dish in turn, in terms we thought most appetising. It was very wrong, and it had the sting which drives wrong-doing most forcibly home to the conscience, of being entirely futile, besides engendering the severe glances of the respectable scout. The young gentlemen were as adamant, if adamant could blush. They would not be moved, and at every fresh appeal they concentrated their attention upon their cold beef in a manner which I thought most noble, if a trifle ferocious. At last they began to look a little stern and disapproving, and we stopped, conscious of having trenched disrespectfully upon an ideal of conduct. But over the final delicacy of Mr. Horton's lunch, the first of the season, Lady Torquilin regarded them wistfully. 'Not even gooseberry tart?' said she. And I will not say that there was no regret in the courageous rejoinder:

'Not even gooseberry tart.'

I am not pretending to write about the things that ought to have impressed me most, but the things that did impress me most, and these were, at Mr. Sanders Horton's luncheon, the splendid old silver college goblets into which our host poured us lavish bumpers of claret-cup, the moral support of the respectable scout, and the character and dignity an ideal of duty may possess, even in connection with cold beef. I came into severe contact with an idiom, too, which I shall always associate with that occasion. Lord Symonds did not belong to Pembroke College, and I asked him, after we had exchanged quite a good deal of polite conversation, which one he did belong to.

'How lovely these old colleges are,' I remarked, 'and so nice and impressive and time-stained. Which one do you attend, Lord Symonds?'

'Maudlin,' said Lord Symonds, apparently taking no notice of my question, and objecting to the preceding sentiment.

'Do you think so?' I said. I was not offended. I had made up my mind some time before never to be offended in England until I understood things. 'I'm very sorry, but they do strike an American that way, you know.'

Lord Symonds did not seem to grasp my meaning. 'It is jolly old,' said he. 'Not so old as some of 'em. New, for instance. But I thought you asked my college. Maudlin, just this side of Maudlin bridge, you know.'

'Oh!' I said. 'And will you be kind enough to spell your college, Lord Symonds? I am but a simple American, over here partly for the purpose of improving my mind.'

'Certainly. "M-a-g-d-a-l-e-n,"' returned Lord Symonds, very good-naturedly. 'Now that you speak of it, it is rather a rum way of spelling it. Something like "Cholmondeley." Now, how would you spell "Cholmondeley?"'

I was glad to have his attention diverted from my mistake, but the reputation of 'Cholmondeley' is world-wide, and I spelled it triumphantly. I should like to confront an American spelling-match with 'Magdalen,' though, and about eleven other valuable orthographical specimens that I am taking care of.

In due course we all started for the river, finding our way through quads even greyer and greener and quieter than Exeter, and finally turning into a pretty, wide, tree-bordered highway, much too well trodden to be a popular Lovers' Walk, but dustily pleasant and shaded withal. We were almost an hour too early for the races, as Mr. Horton and Lord Symonds wished to take us on the river before they were obliged to join their respective crews, and met hardly anybody except occasional strolling, loose-garmented undergraduates with very various ribbons on their round straw hats, which they took off with a kind of spasmodic gravity when they happened to know our friends. The tree-bordered walk ended more or less abruptly at a small stream, bordered on its hither side by a series of curious constructions reminding one of all sorts of things, from a Greek warship to a Methodist church in Dakota, and wonderfully painted. These, Mr. Horton explained, were the College barges, from which the race was viewed, and he led the way to the Exeter barge. There is a stairway to these barges, leading to the top, and Mr. Horton showed us up, to wait until he and Lord Symonds got out the punt.

The word 'punting' was familiar to me, signifying an aquatic pursuit popular in England, but I had never even seen a punt, and was very curious about it. I cannot say, however, that the English punt, when our friends brought it round, struck me as a beautiful object. Doubtless it had points of excellence, even of grace, as compared with other punts—I do not wish to disparage it—but I suffered from the lack of a standard to admire it by. It seemed to me an uninteresting vessel, and I did not like the way it was cut off at the ends. The mode of propulsion, too, by which Mr. Horton and Lord Symonds got us around the river—poking a stick into the mud at the bottom and leaning on it—did not impress me as being dignified enough for anybody in Society. Lord Symonds asked me, as we sat in one end enjoying the sun— you get to like it in England, even on the back of your neck—what I thought of punting. I told him I thought it was immoderately safe. It was the most polite thing I could think of at the spur of the moment. I do not believe punting would ever become popular in America. We are a light-minded people; we like an element of joyous risk; we are not adapted to punt.

The people were beginning to come down upon the barges when we returned from this excursion, and it was thought best that we should take our places. The stream was growing very full, not only of laborious punts containing three brightly-dressed ladies and one perspiring young man, but of all kinds of craft, some luxuriously overshadowed with flounced awnings, under which young gentlemen with cigarette-attachments reposed, protecting themselves further with Japanese paper umbrellas. The odd part of this was that both they and their umbrellas seemed to be taken by themselves and everybody else quite *au sérieux*. This, again, would be different in America.

Mr. Horton left us with Lord Symonds, who had not to row, he explained to us, until later in the day; and presently we saw our host below, with the rest of his bare-legged, muscular crew, getting gingerly into the long, narrow outrigger lying alongside. They arranged themselves with great care and precision, and then held their oars, looking earnestly at a little man who sat up very straight in the stern—the cox. He was my first cox, for I had never seen a boat-race before, excepting between champions, who do not row with coxes, and I was delighted to find how accurately he had been described in the articles we read about English boating—his size, his erect-ness and alertness, and autocratic dignity. At a word from the cox every man turned his head half-way round and back again; then he said, in the sternest accents I had ever heard, 'Are—you—ready?' and in an instant they were off.

'Where are they going?' Lady Torquilin asked.

'Oh, for a preliminary spin,' said Lord Symonds, 'and then for the starting-point.'

'And when do the barges start?' I inquired, without having given the matter any kind of consideration.

'The barges!' said Lord Symonds, mystified. 'Do you mean these? They don't start; they stay here.'

'But can we see the race from here?' I asked.

'Beautifully! They come past.'

'Do I understand, Lord Symonds, that the Oxford boat-race takes place *out there?*'

'Certainly,' said he. 'Why not?'

'Oh, no particular reason,' I returned—'if there is room.'

'Rather!' the young gentleman explained. 'This is the noble river Isis, Miss Wick.'

'It may not be so big as the Mississippi, but it's worthy of your respectful consideration, young lady,' put in Lady Torquilin. Thus admonished, I endeavoured to give the noble river Isis my respectful consideration, but the barges occupied so much space in it that I was still unable to understand how a boat-race of any importance could come between us and the opposite bank without seriously inconveniencing somebody.

It did, however, and such was the skill displayed by the coxes in charge that nobody was hurt. It came off amid demonstrations of the most extraordinary nature, tin whistles predominating, on the opposite bank, where I saw a genuine bishop capering along with the crowd, waving his hat on his stick. It came off straight and tense and arrowy, cheered to the last stroke.

'A GENUINE BISHOP.'

'So near it!' said Lord Symonds, after shouting 'Well rowed, Pembroke!' until he could shout no longer.

'Near what?' I asked.

'A bump,' said he, sadly; 'but it was jolly well rowed!' and for the moment I felt that no earthly achievement could compare with the making of bumps.

Such excitement I never saw, among the Dons on the barges—my first Dons, too, but they differed very much; I could not generalise about them—among their wives, who seemed unaggressive, youngish ladies, as a rule, in rather subdued gowns; among the gay people down from 'Town,' among the college men, incorrigibly uproarious; among that considerable body of society that adds so little to the brilliance of such an occasion but contributes so largely to its noise. And after it was over a number of exuberant young men on the other side plunged into the noble river Isis and crossed it with a few well-placed strides, and possibly two strokes. None of them were drowned.

After that we had a joyous half-hour in the apartments, at Exeter, of Mr. Bertie Corke, whose brown eyes had Peter's very twinkle in them, and who became established in our affections at once upon that account. Mr. Corke was one of the Exeter Eight, and he looked reproachfully at us when we inadvertently stated that we had lingered to congratulate Pembroke.

'Pembroke got a bump, you know, yesterday,' I remarked, proud of the technicality.

'Yes,' returned Mr. Bertie Corke, ruefully, 'bumped *us*.'

This was an unfortunate beginning, but it did not mar our subsequent relations with Miss Peter Corke's brother, which were of the pleasantest description. He told us on the way down once more to the noble river Isis the names of all those delightful elderly stone images that had themselves put over the college doors centuries ago, when they were built, and he got almost as many interiors into half an hour as his sister could. He explained to us, too, how, by the rules of the University, he was not allowed to play marbles on the college steps, or to wear clothes of other than an 'obfusc hue,' which was exactly the kind of thing that Peter would tell you—and expect you to remember. He informed us, too, that according to the pure usage of Oxonian English he was a 'Fresher,' the man we had just passed being an unattached student, a 'tosher,' probably walking for what in the vulgar tongue might be called exercise, but here was 'ekker.' In many ways he was like Peter, and he objected just as much to my abuse of the English climate.

The second race was very like the first, with more enthusiasm. I have a little folding card with 'The Eights, May 22 to 28, 1890,' and the names of the colleges in the order of starting, printed in blue letters on the inside. The 'order of finish' from 'B. N. C.' to 'St. Edm. Hall' is in Mr. Bertie Corke's handwriting. I'm not a sentimentalist, but I liked the Eights, and I mean to keep this souvenir.

XXIV.

THE records of my experiences in London would be very incomplete without another chapter devoted to those Miss Peter Corke arranged for me. Indeed, I would need the license of many chapters to explain at any length how generously Miss Corke fulfilled to me the offices of guide, philosopher, and friend; how she rounded out my days with counsel, and was in all of them a personal blessing.

Dispensing information was a habit which Peter Corke incorrigibly established—one of the things she could not help. I believe an important reason why she liked me was because I gave her such unlimited opportunities for indulging it, and she said I simulated gratitude fairly well. For my own part, I always liked it, whether it was at the expense of my accent or my idioms, my manners or my morals, my social theories or my general education, and encouraged her in it. I was pleased with the idea that she found me interesting enough to make it worth while, for one thing, and then it helped my understanding of the lady herself better than anything else would have done. And many voyages and large expense might go into the balance against an acquaintance with Peter Corke.

Miss Corke was more ardently attached to the Past than anybody I have ever known or heard of that did not live in it. Her interest did not demand any great degree of antiquity, though it increased in direct ratio with the centuries; the mere fact that a thing was over and done with, laid on the shelf, or getting mossy and forgotten, was enough to secure her respectful consideration. She liked old folios and prints—it was her pastime to poke in the dust of ages; I've seen her placidly enjoying a graveyard—with no recent interments—for half an hour at a time. She had a fine scorn of the Present in all its forms and phases. If I heard her speak with appreciation of anybody with whose reputation I was unacquainted, I generally found it safe to ask, intelligently, 'When did he die?' She always knew exactly, and who attended the funeral, and what became of the children, and whether the widow got an annuity from the Government or not, being usually of the opinion that the widow should have had the annuity.

Of course, it was Miss Corke who took me down into Fleet Street to see where Dr. Johnson used to live. I did not hear the name of Dr. Johnson from another soul in London during the whole of my visit. My friend bore down through the Strand, and past that mediæval griffin where Temple Bar was, that claws the air in protection of your placid Prince in a frock-coat underneath—stopping here an instant for anathema—and on into the crook of Fleet Street, under St. Paul's, with all the pure delight of an enthusiastic cicerone in her face. I think Peter loved the Strand and Fleet Street almost as well as Dr. Johnson did, and she always wore direct descendants of the seven-league boots. This was sometimes a little trying for mine, which had no pedigree, though, in other respects——; but I must not be led into the statement that shoemaking is not scientifically apprehended in this country. I have never yet been able to get anybody to believe it.

'This,' said Miss Corke, as we emerged from a dark little alley occupied by two unmuzzled small boys and a dog into a dingy rectangle, where the London light came down upon unblinking rows of windows in walls of all colours that get the worse for wear—'this is Gough Court. Dr. Johnson lived here until the death of his wife. You remember that he had a wife, and she died?'

'I have not the least doubt of it,' I replied.

'I've no patience with you!' cried Miss Corke, fervently. 'Well, when she died he was that disconsolate, in spite of his dictionaries, that he couldn't bear it here any longer, and moved away.'

'I don't think that was remarkable,' I said, looking round; to which Miss Corke replied that it was a fine place in those days, and Johnson paid so many pounds, shillings, and pence rent for it every Lady Day. 'I am waiting,' she said, with ironical resignation, 'for you to ask me which house.'

'Oh!' said I. 'Which house?'

'That yellowish one, at the end, idjit!' said Peter, with exasperation. 'Now, if you please, we'll go!'

I took one long and thoughtful look at the yellowish house at the end, and tried to imagine the compilation of lexicons inside its walls about the year 1748, and turned away feeling that I had done all within my personal ability for the memory of Dr. Johnson. Miss Corke, however, was not of that opinion. 'He moved to Johnson's Court somewhat later,' she said, 'which you must be careful to remember was *not* named from him. We'll just go there now.'

'Is it far?' I asked; 'because there must be other celebrities——'

'*Far*!' repeated Miss Corke, with a withering accent; 'not ten minutes' walk! Do the trams run *everywhere* in America? There may be other celebrities—London is a good place for them—but there's only one Samuel Johnson.'

We went through various crooked ways to Johnson's Court, Miss Corke explaining and reviling at every step. 'We *hear*' she remarked with fine scorn, 'of intelligent Americans who come over here and apply themselves diligently to learn London! And I've never met a citizen of you yet,' she went on, ignoring my threatening parasol, 'that was not quite satisfied at seeing one of Johnson's houses—houses he lived in! You are a nation of tasters, Miss Mamie Wick of Chicago!' At which I declared myself, for the honour of the Stars and Stripes, willing to swallow any quantity of Dr. Johnson, and we turned into a little paved parallelogram seven times more desolate than the first. Its prevailing idea was soot, relieved by scraps of blackened ivy that twisted along some of the window-sills. I once noticed very clever ivy decorations in iron upon a London balcony, and always afterwards found some difficulty in deciding between that and the natural vine, unless the wind blew. And I would not like to commit myself about the ivy that grew in Johnson s Court. 'Dear me!' said I; 'so he lived here, too! 'I do not transcribe this remark because it struck me as particularly clever, but because it seems to me to be the kind of thing anybody might have said without exciting indignation. But Peter immediately began to fulminate again. 'Yes,' she said, 'he lived here too, miss, at No. 7, as you don't appear to care to know. A little intelligent curiosity.' she continued, apparently appealing to the Samuel Johnson chimneys, 'would be gratifying!'

We walked around these precincts several times, while Miss Corke told me interesting stories that reminded me of Collier's 'English Literature' at school, and asked me if by any chance I had ever heard of Boswell. I loved to find myself knowing something occasionally, just to annoy Peter, and when I said certainly, he was the man to whom Dr. Johnson owed his reputation, it had quite the usual effect.

'We shall now go to Bolt Court,' said my friend, 'where Samuel spent the last of his days, surrounded by a lot of old ladies that I don't see how he ever put up with, and from which he was carried to Westminster Abbey in 1784. Hadn't you better put that down?'

Now Peter Corke would never have permitted me to call Dr. Johnson 'Samuel.'

I looked round Johnson's Court with lingering affection, and hung back. 'There is something about this place,' I said, 'some occult attraction, that makes me hate to leave it. I believe, Peter, that the Past, under your influence, is beginning to affect me properly. I dislike the thought of remaining for any length of time out of reach, as it were, of the memory of Dr. Johnson.'

Peter looked at me suspiciously. 'He lived at Bolt Court as well,' she said.

'Nowhere between here and there?' I asked. 'No friend's house, for instance, where he often spent the night? Where did that lady live who used to give him nineteen cups of tea at a sitting? Couldn't we pause and refresh ourselves by looking at her portals on the way?'

'Transatlantic impertinence,' cried Miss Corke, leading the way out, 'is more than I can bear!'

'But,' I said, still hanging back, 'about how far———?'

When my dear friend gave vent to the little squeal with which she received this, I knew that her feelings were worked up to a point where it was dangerous to tamper with them, so I submitted to Bolt Court, walking with humility all the way. When we finally arrived I could see no intrinsic difference between this court and the others, except that rather more—recently—current literature had blown up from an adjacent news-stall. For a person who changed his residence so often, Dr. Johnson's domestic tastes must have undergone singularly little alteration.

'He went from here to Westminster Abbey, I think you said,' I remarked, respectfully, to Peter.

'In 1784,' said Peter, who is a stickler for dates.

'And has not moved since!' I added, with some anxiety, just to aggravate Peter, who was duly aggravated.

'Well,' I responded, 'we saw Westminster Abbey, you remember. And I took particular notice of the monument to Dr. Johnson. We needn't go *there*.'

'It's in St. Paul's!' said Peter, in a manner which wounded me, for if there is an unpleasant thing it is to be disbelieved.

'And which house did Dr. Johnson live in here?' I inquired.

'Come,' said Peter, solemnly, 'and I'll show you.'

'It has been lost to posterity,' she continued, with depression—'burnt in 1819. But we have the site—there!'

'Oh!' I replied. 'We have the site. That is—that is something, I suppose. But I don't find it very stimulating to the imagination.'

'You haven't any!' remarked Miss Corke, with vehemence; and I have no doubt she had reason to think so. As a matter of fact, however, the name of Samuel Johnson is not a household word in Chicago. We don't govern our letter-writing by his Dictionary, and as to the 'Tatler' and the 'Rambler,' it is impossible for people living in the United States to read up the back numbers of even their own magazines. It is true that we have no excuse for not knowing 'Rasselas,' but I've noticed that at home hardly any of the English classics have much chance against Rider Haggard, and now that Rudyard Kipling has arisen it will be worse still for elderly respectable authors like Dr. Johnson. So that while I was deeply interested to know that the great lexicographer had hallowed such a considerable part of London with his residence, I must confess, to be candid, that I would have been satisfied with fewer of his architectural remains. I could have done, for instance, without the site, though I dare say, as Peter says, they were all good for me.

Before I reached Lady Torquilin's flat again that day, Peter showed me the particular window in Wine Office Court where dear little Goldsmith sat deploring the bailiff and the landlady when Dr. Johnson took the 'Vicar' away and sold it for sixty pounds—that delightful old fairy godfather whom everybody knows so much better than as the author of 'Rasselas.' And the 'Cheshire Cheese,' on the other side of the way, that quaintest of low-windowed taverns, where the two sat with their friends over the famous pudding that is still served on the same day of the week. Here I longed in especial to go inside and inquire about the pudding, and when we might come down and have some; but Peter said it was not proper for ladies, and hurried me on. As if any impropriety could linger about a place a hundred and fifty years old!

The Temple also we saw that day, and Goldsmith's quiet, solitary grave in the shadow of the old Knights' Church, more interesting and lovable there, somehow, than it would be in the crowd at Westminster. Miss Peter Corke was entirely delightful in the Temple, whether she talked of Goldsmith's games and dancing over Blackstone's sedate head in Brick Court, or of Elizabeth sitting on the wide platform at the end of the Middle Temple Hall at the first performance of 'Twelfth Night,' where, somewhere beneath those dusky oak rafters, Shakespeare made another critic. Peter never talked scandal in the present tense, on principle, but a more interesting gossip than she was of a century back I never had a cup of tea with, which we got not so very far from the Cock Tavern in Fleet Street; and I had never known before that Mr. Pepys was a flirt.

XXV

MR. MAFFERTON frequently expressed his regret that almost immediately after my arrival in London—in fact, during the time of my disappearance from the Métropole, and just as he became aware of my being with Lady Torquilin—his mother and two sisters had been obliged to go to the Riviera on account of one of the Misses Mafferton's health. One afternoon—the day before they left, I believe—Lady Torquilin and I, coming in, found a large assortment of cards belonging to the family, which were to be divided between us, apparently. But, as Mr. Charles Mafferton was the only one of them left in town, my acquaintance with the Maffertons had made very little progress, except, of course, with the portly old cousin I have mentioned before, who was a lord, and who stayed in London through the entire session of Parliament. This cousin and I became so well acquainted, in spite of his being a lord, that we used to ask each other conundrums. 'What do they call a black cat in London?' was a favourite one of his. But I had the advantage of Lord Mafferton here, for he always forgot that he had asked the same conundrum the last time we met, and thought me tremendously clever when I answered, 'Puss, puss!' But, as I have said before, there were very few particulars in which this nobleman gratified my inherited idea of what a lord ought to be.

One of the Misses Mafferton—the one who enjoyed good health—had very kindly taken the trouble to write to me from the Riviera a nice friendly letter, saying how sorry they all were that we did not meet before they left Town, and asking me to make them a visit as soon as they returned in June. The letter went on to say that they had shared their brother's anxiety about me for some time, but felt quite comfortable in the thought of leaving me so happily situated with Lady Torquilin, an old friend of their own, and was it not singular? Miss Mafferton exclaimed, in her pointed handwriting, signing herself mine ever affectionately, E. F. Mafferton. I thought it was certainly singularly nice of her to write to me like that, a perfect stranger; and while I composed an answer in the most cordial terms I could, I thought of all I had heard about the hearty hospitality of the English—'when once you know them.'

When I told Mr. Mafferton I had heard from his sister, and how much pleasure the letter had given me, he blushed in the most violent and unaccountable manner, but seemed pleased nevertheless. It was odd to see Mr. Mafferton discomposed, and it discomposed me. I could not in the least understand why his sister's politeness to a friend of his should embarrass Mr. Mafferton, and was glad when he said he had no doubt Eleanor and I would be great friends, and changed the subject. But it was about this time that another invitation from relatives of Mr. Mafferton's living in Berkshire gave me my one always-to-be-remembered experience of the country in England. Lady Torquilin was invited too, but the invitation was for a Tuesday and Wednesday particularly full of engagements for her.

'Couldn't we write and say we'd rather come next week?' I suggested.

Lady Torquilin looked severely horrified. 'I should think *not!*' she replied. 'You're not in America, child. I hardly know these people at all; moreover, it's you they want to see, and not me in the least. So I'll just send my apologies, and tell Mrs. Stacy you're an able-bodied young woman who gets about wonderfully by herself, and that she may expect you by the train she proposes—and see that you don't outstay your invitation, young lady, or I shall be in a fidget!' And Lady Torquilin gave me her cheek to kiss, and went away and wrote to Mrs. Stacy as she had said.

An hour or two beyond London the parallel tracks of the main line stretched away in the wrong direction for me, and my train sped down them, leaving me for a few minutes undecided how to proceed. The little station seemed to have nothing whatever to do with anything but the main line. It sat there in the sun and cultivated its flower-beds, and waited for the big trains to come thundering by, and had no concern but that. Presently, however, I observed, standing all by itself beside a row of tulips under a clay bank on the other side of the bridge, the most diminutive thing in railway transport I had ever seen. It was quite complete, engine and cab, and luggage-van and all, with its passenger accommodation properly divided into first, second, and third class, and it stood there placidly, apparently waiting for somebody. And I followed my luggage over the bridge with the quiet conviction that this was the train for Pinbury, and that it was waiting for me.

There was nobody else. And after the porter had stowed my effects carefully away in the van he also departed, leaving the Pinbury train in my charge. I sat in it for a while and admired the tulips, and wondered how soon it would rain, and fixed my veil, and looked over the 'Daily Graphic' again, but nothing happened. It occurred to me that possibly the little Pinbury train had been forgotten, and I got out. There was no one on the platform, but just outside the station I saw a rusty old coachman seated on the box of an open landau, so I spoke to him. 'Does that train go to Pinbury?' I asked. He said it did. 'Does it go to-day?' I inquired further. He looked amused at my ignorance. 'Oh yes, lady,' he replied; 'she goes every day—twice. But she 'as to wait for two hup trains yet. She'll be hoff in about 'alf an hour now!'—this reassuringly.

When we did start it took us exactly six minutes to get to Pinbury, and I was sorry I had not tipped the engine-driver and got him to run down with me and back again while he was waiting. Whatever they may say to the contrary, there are few things in England that please Americans more than the omnipotence of the tip.

Two of the Stacy young ladies met me on the Pinbury platform, and gave me quite the most charming welcome I have had in England. With the exception of Peter Corke—and Peter would be exceptional anywhere—I had nearly always failed to reach any sympathetic relation with the young ladies I had come in contact with in London. Perhaps this was because I did not see any of them very often or very long together, and seldom without the presence of some middle-aged lady who controlled the conversation; but the occasions of my meeting with the London girl had never sufficed to overcome the natural curiosity with which she usually regarded me. I rejoiced when I saw that it would be different with Miss Stacy and Miss Dorothy Stacy, and probably with the other Misses Stacy at home. They regarded me with outspoken interest, but not at all with fear. They were very polite, but their politeness was of the gay, unconscious sort, which only impresses you when you think of it afterwards. Delightfully pretty, though lacking that supreme inertia of expression that struck me so often as the finishing touch upon London beauty, and gracefully tall, without that impressiveness of development I had observed in town, Miss Dorothy Stacy's personality gave me quite a new pleasure. It was invested in round pink cheeks and clear grey eyes, among other things that made it most agreeable to look at her; and yellow hair that went rippling down her back; and the perfect freshness and unconsciousness of her beauty, with her height and her gentle muscularity, reminded one of an immature goddess of Olympia, if such a person could be imagined growing up. Miss Dorothy Stacy was sixteen past, and in a later moment of confidence she told me that she lived in dread of being obliged to turn up her hair and wear irretrievably long 'frocks.' I found this unreasonable, but charming. In America all joys are grown up, and the brief period of pinafores is one of probation.

We drove away in a little brown dogcart behind a little brown pony into the English country, talking a great deal. Miss Stacy drove, and I sat beside her, while Miss Dorothy Stacy occupied the seat in the rear when she was not alighting in the middle of the road to pick up the Pinbury commissions, which did not travel well, or the pony's foot, to see if he had a stone in it. The pony objected with mild viciousness to having his foot picked up; but Miss Dorothy did not take his views into account at all; up came the foot and out came the stone. The average American girl would have driven helplessly along until she overtook a man, I think.

I never saw a finer quality of mercy anywhere than the Stacy young ladies exhibited toward their beast. When we came to a rising bit of road Miss Dorothy invariably leaped down and walked as well as the pony, to save him fatigue; when a slight declivity presented itself he walked again solemnly to the bottom, occasionally being led. He expected this attention always at such times, pausing at the top and looking round for it, and when it was withheld his hind-quarters assumed an aggrieved air of irresponsibility. When Miss Stacy wished to increase his rate of going by a decimal point, she flicked him gently, selecting a spot where communication might be made with his brain at least inconvenience to himself; but she never did anything that would really interfere with his enjoyment of the drive.

Of course, Miss Stacy wanted to know what I thought of England in a large general way, but before I had time to do more than mention a few heads under which I had gathered my impressions she particularised with reference to the scenery. Miss Stacy asked me what I thought of English scenery, with a sweet and ladylike confidence, including most of what we were driving through, with a graceful flourish of her whip. She said I might as well confess that we hadn't such nice scenery in America. 'Grander, you know—more mountains and lakes and things,' said Miss Stacy, 'but not *really* so nice, now, have you?' No, I said; unfortunately it was about the only thing we couldn't manage to take back with us; at which Miss Stacy astonished; me with the fact that she knew I was going to be a treat to her—so original—and I must be simply craving my tea, and it was good of me to come, and flicked the pony severely, so that he trotted for almost half a mile without a pause.

But we returned to the scenery, for I did not wish to be thought unappreciative, and the Misses Stacy were good enough to be interested in the points that I found particularly novel and pleasing—the flowering hedges that leaned up against the fields by the wayside, and the quantities of little birds that chirruped in and out of them, and the trees, all twisted round with ivy, and especially the rabbits, that bobbed about in the meadows and turned up their little white tails with as much *naivete* as if the world were a kitchen-garden closed to the public. The 'bunnies,' as Miss Dorothy Stacy called them, were a source of continual delight to me. I could never refrain from exclaiming, 'There's another!' much to the young ladies' amusement. 'You see,' explained Miss Dorothy in apology, 'they're not new to us, the dear sweet things! One might say one has been brought up with them, one knows all their little ways. But they are loves, and it is nice of you to like them.'

The pony stopped altogether on one little rise, as if he were accustomed to it, to allow us to take a side-look across the grey-green fields to where they lost themselves in the blue distance, in an effort to climb. It was a lovely landscape, full of pleasant thoughts, ideally still and gently conscious. There was the glint of a river in it, white in the sun, with twisting lines of round-headed willows marking which way it went; and other trees in groups and rows threw soft shadows across the contented fields. These trees never blocked the view; one could always see over and beyond them into other peaceful stretches, with other clumps and lines, greyer and smaller as they neared the line where the low, blue sky thickened softly into clouds and came closer down. An occasional spire, here and there a farmhouse, queer, old-fashioned hayricks gossiping in the corners of the fields, cows, horses, crows. All as if it had been painted by a tenderly conscientious artist, who economised his carmines and allowed himself no caprices except in the tattered hedge, full of May, in the foreground; all as if Nature-had understood a woman's chief duty to be tidy and delectable, except for this ragged hem of her embroidered petticoat. I dare say it would not seem so to you; but the country as I had known it in America had been an expanse of glowing colour, diversified by a striking pattern of snake-fences, relieved by woods that nobody had ever planted, and adorned by the bare, commanding brick residences of the agricultural population. Consequently, delightful as I found this glimpse of English scenery, I could not combat the idea that it had all been carefully and beautifully made, and was usually kept under cottonwool. You would understand this if you knew the important part played in our rural districts by the American stump.

'Isn't it lovely?' asked Miss Stacy, with enthusiasm. Two cows in the middle distance suddenly disappeared behind a hayrick, and for a moment the values of the landscape became confused. Still, I was able to say that it was lovely, and so neat—which opinion I was obliged to explain to Miss Stacy, as I have to you, while the brown pony took us thoughtfully on.

XXVI

I DROVE in at the gates of Hallington House as one might drive into the scene of a dear old dream—a dream that one has half-believed and half-doubted, and wholly loved, and dreamed again all one's life long. There it stood, as I had always wondered if I might not see it standing in that far day when I should go to England, behind its high brick wall, in the midst of its ivies and laburnums and elms and laurel-bushes, looking across where its lawns dipped into its river at soft green meadows sloping to the west—a plain old solid grey stone English country-house so long occupied with the birthdays of other people that it had quite forgotten its own. Very big and very solid, without any pretentiousness of Mansard roof, or bow window, or balcony, or verandah its simple story of strength and shelter and home and hospitality was plain to me between its wide-open gates and its wide-open doors, and I loved it from that moment.

It was the same all through—the Stacys realised the England of my imagination to me most sweetly and completely; I found that there had been no mistake. Mrs. Stacy realised it, pretty and fresh and fair at fifty, plump and motherly in her black cashmere and lace, full of pleasant greetings and responsible inquiries. So did the Squire, coming out of his study to ask, with courteous old-fashioned solicitude, how I had borne the fatigue of the journey—such a delightful old Squire, left over by accident from the last century, with his high-bred phraseology and simple dignity and great friendliness. So did the rest of the Stacy daughters, clustering round their parents and their guest and the teapot, talking gaily with their rounded English accent of all manner of things—the South Kensington Museum, the Pinbury commissions, the prospects for tennis. Presently I found myself taken through just such narrow corridors and down just such unexpected steps as I would have hoped for, to my room, and left there. I remember how a soft wind came puffing in at the little low, tiny-paned window flung back on its hinges, swelling out the muslin curtains and bringing with it the sweetest sound I heard in England—a cry that was quite new and strange, and yet came into me from the quiet hedges of the nestling world outside, as I sat there bewitched by it, with a plaintive familiarity—*'Cuckoo!*... *'Cuckoo!* I must have heard it and loved it years ago, when the Wicks lived in England, through the ears of my ancestors. Then I discovered that the room was full of a dainty scent that I had not known before, and traced it to multitudinous little round flower-bunches, palest yellow and palest green, that stood about in everything that would hold them—fresh and pure and delicious, all the tender soul of the spring in them, all the fairness of the meadows and the love of the shy English sun. Ah, the charm of it! It is almost worth while being brought up in Chicago to come fresh to cuckoos and cowslips, and learn their sweet meaning when you are grown up and can understand it. I mean, of course, entirely apart from the inestimable advantages of a Republican form of Government, female emancipation, and the climate of Illinois. We have no cowslips in Chicago, and no cuckoos; and the cable cars do not seem altogether to make up for them. I couldn't help wishing, as I leaned through my low little window into the fragrant peace outside, that Nature had taken a little more time with America.

'Cuckoo!' from the hedge again! I could not go till the answer came from the toppling elm-boughs in the field corner, 'Cuckoo!' And in another minute, if I listened, I should hear it again.

'TWO TIDY LITTLE MAIDS.'

Down below, in the meantime, out came two tidy little maids in cap and apron, and began to weed and to potter about two tidy little plots—their own little gardens anybody might know by the solicitude and the comparisons they indulged in—the freedom, too, with which they pulled what pleased themselves. It was pretty to see the little maids, and I fell to conjecturing such a scene in connection with the domestic duchess of Chicago, but without success. Her local interest could never be sufficiently depended upon, for one thing. Marguerite might plant, and Irene might water, but Arabella Maud would certainly gather the fruits of their labour, if she kept her place long enough. And I doubt if the social duties of any of these ladies would leave them time for such idylls.

'Cuckoo!' The bird caught it from the piping of the very first lover's very first love-dream. How well he must have listened!... 'Cuckoo!'

I bade Miss Dorothy Stacy come in when I heard her knock and voice; and she seemed to bring with her, in her innocent strength and youth and pinkness, a very fair and harmonious counterpart of the cowslips and the cuckoos. She came to know if I wasn't coming down to tea. 'Listen!' I said, as the sweet cry came again. 'I was waiting till he had finished.' It was better than no excuse at all.

'I think I can show you from here where I suspect they have stolen a nest, lazy things!' answered Miss Dorothy, sympathetically, and she slipped her arm round my waist as we looked out of the window together in the suspected direction. 'Then you don't find them tiresome? Some people do, you know.' 'No,' I said, 'I don't,' And then Miss Dorothy confided to me that she was very glad; 'for, you know,' she said, I one *can't* like people who find cuckoos tiresome,' and we concluded that we really must go down to tea. At that point, however, I was obliged to ask Miss Dorothy to wait until I did a little towards improving my appearance. I had quite forgotten, between the cuckoos and the cowslips, that I had come up principally to wash my face.

'You met our cousin on the ship crossing the Atlantic, didn't you?' the third Miss Stacy remarked, enthusiastically, over the teapot. 'How delightfully romantic to make a—a friend—a friend like *that*, I mean, on a ship in the middle of the ocean! Didn't you always feel perfectly comfortable afterwards, as if, no matter what happened, he would be sure to save you?'

'*Kitty!*' said Mrs. Stacy from the sofa, in a tone of helpless rebuke. 'Mother, darling!' said Kitty, 'I do beg your pardon! Your daughter always speaks first and thinks afterwards, doesn't she, sweetest mother! But you must have had that feeling,' Miss Stacy continued to me; 'I know you had!'

'Oh, no!' I returned. It was rather an awkward situation

—I had no wish to disparage Miss Stacy's cousin's heroism, which, nevertheless, I had not relied upon in the least. 'I don't think I thought about being drowned,' I said.

'That proves it!' she cried in triumph. 'Your confidence was so perfect that it was unconscious! Sweetest mother—there, I won't say another word; not another syllable, mother mine, shall pass your daughter's lips! But one *does* like to show one's self in the right, doesn't one, Miss Wick?'—and Mrs. Stacy surrendered to an impulsive volume of embraces which descended from behind the sofa, chiefly upon the back of her neck.

How pleasant it was, that five o'clock tea-drinking in the old-fashioned drawing-room, with the jessamine nodding in at the window and all the family cats gathered upon the hearthrug—five in number, with one kitten. The Stacy's compromise in the perpetually-recurring problem of new kittens was to keep only the representative of a single generation for family affection and drawing-room privileges. The rest were obscurely brought up in the stables and located as early as was entirely humane with respectable cottagers, or darkly spoken of as 'kitchen cats.' There had been only one break in the line of posterity that gravely licked itself on the rug, or besought small favours rubbingly with purrs—made by a certain Satanella, who ate her kittens! and suffered banishment in consequence. But this was confided to me in undertones by the second Miss Stacy, who begged me not to mention the matter to Dorothy. 'We don't talk about it often, for Satanella was her cat, you know, and she can't get over her behaving so dreadfully.' Each cat had its individual history, and to the great-great-grandmother of them attached the thrilling tale, if I remember rightly, of having once only escaped hanging by her own muscular endurance and activity; but none bore so dark a blot as covered the memory of Satanella. Perhaps it is partly owing to my own fondness for pussies, but ever since I made the acquaintance of the Stacys I must confess to disparaging a family with no cats in it.

It was naturally Dorothy who took me out to see the garden—sweet, shy Dorothy, who seemed so completely to have grown in a garden that Lady Torquilin, when she brought her pink cheeks afterwards to gladden the flat in Cadogan Mansions, dubbed her 'the Wild Rose' at once. At any rate, Dorothy had always lived just here beside her garden, and never anywhere else, for she told me so in explaining her affection for it. I thought of the number of times we had moved in Chicago, and sighed.

It was not a very methodical garden, Dorothy remarked in apology—the dear sweet things mostly came up of their own accord year after year, and the only ambition Peter entertained towards it was to keep it reasonably weeded. A turn in the walk disclosed Peter at the moment with a wheelbarrow—the factotum of garden and stable, a solemn bumpkin of twenty, with a large red face and a demeanour of extreme lethargy. His countenance broke into something like a deferential grin as he passed us. 'Can you make him understand?' I asked Miss Dorothy. 'Oh, I should think so!' she replied. 'He is very intelligent!' From his appearance I should not have said so. There was nothing 'sharp,' as we say in America, about Peter, though afterwards I heard him whistling 'Two lovely black eyes' with a volume of vigorous expression that made one charge him with private paradoxical sweethearting. But I was new to the human product after many generations of the fields and hedges.

It was a square garden, shut in from the road and the neighbours by that high old red-brick wall. A tennis-court lay in the middle in the sun; the house broke into a warmly-tinted gable, red-roofed and plastered and quaint, that nestled over the little maids in the larder, I think, at one end; a tall elm and a spreading horse-chestnut helped the laurestinus bushes to shut it in from the lawns and the drive and any eyes that might not fall upon it tenderly. We sat down upon the garden-seat that somebody had built round the elm, Dorothy and I, and I looked at the garden as one turns the pages of an old storybook. There were the daisies in the grass, to begin with, all over, by hundreds and thousands, turning their bright little white-and-yellow faces up at me and saying something—I don't know quite what. I should have had to listen a long time to be sure it was anything but 'Don't step on me!' but I had a vague feeling that every now and then one said, 'Can't you remember?' Dorothy remarked it was really disgraceful, so many of them, and Peter should certainly mow them all down in the morning—by which her pretty lips gave me a keen pang. 'Oh!' I said, I what a pity!' 'Yes,' she said, relentingly, 'they *are* dear things, but they're very untidy. The worst of Peter is,' she went on, with a shade of reflection, 'that we are obliged to keep *at* him.'

I dare say you don't think much of daisies in the grass—you have always had so many. You should have been brought up on dandelions instead—in Chicago!

Then there were all the sweet spring English flowers growing in little companies under the warm brick wall—violets and pansies and yellow daffodils, and in one corner a tall, brave array of anemones, red and purple and white. And against the wall rose-bushes and an ancient fig-tree; and farther on, all massed and tangled in its own dark-green shadows, the ivy, pouring out its abundant heart to drape and soften the other angle, and catch the golden rain of the laburnum that hung over. And this English Dorothy, with her yellow hair and young-eyed innocence, the essence and the flower of it all.

Near the stables, in our roundabout ramble to the kitchen-garden, Dorothy showed me, with seriousness, a secluded corner, holding two small mounds and two small wooden tablets. On one the head of a spaniel was carved painstakingly and painted, with the inscription, 'Here Lies a Friend.' The second tablet had no bas-relief and a briefer legend: 'Here Lies Another.' 'Jack,' said she, with a shade of retrospection, and Jingo. Jack died in—let me see—eighteen eighty-five. Jingo two years later, in eighteen eighty-seven. I didn't do Jingo's picture,' Miss Dorothy went on, pensively. 'It wasn't really necessary, they were so very much alike.'

About the kitchen-garden I remember only how rampant the gooseberry-bushes were, how portentous the cabbages, and how the whole Vegetable Kingdom combined failed to keep out a trailing company of early pink roses that had wandered in from politer regions to watch the last of the sunset across the river and beyond the fields.

'I have a letter to send,' said Miss Dorothy, 'and as we go to the post-office you shall see Hallington.' So we went through the gates that closed upon this dear inner world into the winding road. It led us past 'The Green Lion,' amiably *couchant* upon a creaking sign that swung from a yellow cottage, past a cluster of little houses with great brooding roofs of straw, past the village school, in a somewhat bigger cottage, in one end whereof the schoolmistress dwelt and looked out upon her lavender and rue, to the post-office at the top of the hill, where the little woman inside, in a round frilled cap and spectacles, and her shawl pinned tidily across her breast, sold buttons and thread, and 'sweeties' and ginger ale, and other things. My eye lighted with surprise upon a row of very familiar wedgeshaped tins, all blue and red. They contained corned beef, and they came from Chicago. 'I know the gentleman who puts those up very well,' I said to Miss Dorothy Stacy; 'Mr. W. P. Hitt, of Chicago. He is a great friend of poppa's. 'Really!' said she, with slight embarrassment. 'Does he—does he do it himself? How clever of him!'

On the way back through the village of Hallington we met several stolid little girls by ones and twos and threes, and every little girl, as we approached, suddenly lowered her person and her petticoats by about six inches and brought it up again in a perfectly straight line, and without any change of expression whatever. It seemed to me a singular and most amusing demonstration, and Miss Dorothy explained that it was a curtsey—a very proper mark of respect. 'But surely,' she said, 'your little cottager girls in America curtsey to the ladies and gentlemen they meet!' And Miss Dorothy found it difficult to understand just why the curtsey was not a popular genuflection in America, even if we had any little cottager girls to practise it, which I did not think we had, exactly.

'MISS DOROTHY EXPLAINED THAT IT WAS A CURTSEY.'

Later on we gathered round a fire, with the cats, under the quaint old portraits of very straight-backed dead-and-gone ladies Stacy in the drawing-room, and I told all I knew about the Apache Indians and Niagara Falls. I think I also set the minds of the Stacy family at rest about the curious idea that we want to annex Canada—they had some distant relations there, I believe, whom they did not want to see annexed—although it appeared that the relations had been heterodox on the subject, and had said they wouldn't particularly mind! I suggested that they were probably stock-raising in the Northwest out there, and found our tariff inconvenient; and the Stacys said Yes, they were. I continued that the union they would like to see was doubtless commercial, and not political; and the Stacys, when they thought of this, became more cheerful. Further on, the Squire handed me a silver candlestick at the foot of the stairs with the courtliness of three generations past; and as I went to bed by candle-light for the first time in my life, I wondered whether I would not suddenly arrive, like this, at the end of a chapter, and find that I had just been reading one of Rhoda Broughton's novels. But in the morning it came in at the window with the scent of the lilacs, and I undoubtedly heard it again—'Cuckoo!'...'Cuckoo!'

XXVII

'HAVEN'T you some letters, child, to your Ambassador, or whatever he is, here in London?' asked Lady Torquilin one morning.

'Why, yes,' I said, 'I have. I'd forgotten about them. He is quite an old friend of poppa's—in a political way; but poppa advised me not to bother him so long as I wasn't in any difficulty—he must have such lots of Americans coming over here for the summer and fussing round every year, you know. And I haven't been.'

'Well, you must now,' declared Lady Torquilin, 'for I want you to go to Court with me a fortnight from to-day. It's five years since I've gone, and quite time I should put in an appearance again. Besides, the Maffertons wish it.'

'The Maffertons wish it?' I said. 'Dear me! I consider that extremely kind. I suppose they think I would enjoy it very much. And I dare say I should.'

'Lady Mafferton and I talked it over yesterday,' Lady Torquilin continued, 'and we agreed that although either she or I might present you, it would be more properly done, on account of your being an American, by your American man's wife. Indeed, I dare say it's obligatory. So we must see about it.' And Lady Torquilin and Lady Mafferton, with very little assistance from me, saw about it.

In the moment that succeeded the slight shock of the novel idea, I found a certain delirium in contemplating it that I could not explain by any of the theories I had been brought up upon. It took entire possession of me—I could not reason it away. Even in reading my home letters, which usually abstracted mo altogether for the time, I saw it fluttering round the corners of the pages. 'What would they say,' I thought, 'if they knew I was going to be presented to the Queen—their daughter, Mamie Wick, of Illinois?' Would they consider that I had compromised the strict Republican principles of the family, and reprobate the proceeding! The idea gave me a momentary conscience-chill, which soon passed off, however, under the agreeable recollection of poppa's having once said that he considered Her Majesty a very fine woman, and for his part he would be proud to be introduced to her. After all, being presented was only a way of being introduced to her—the way they do it in England. I felt pretty sure the family principles could stand that much. As a matter of fact, you know, very few Americans have any personal objection to royalty. And I dismissed the idea, abandoning myself to the joy of preparation, which Lady Torquilin decreed should begin the very next day. I thought this, though pleasurable, rather unnecessary at first. 'Dear Lady Torquilin,' said I, in the discussion of our Court dresses, 'can't we see about them next week?—we planned so many other things for this one!'

'Child, child,' returned Lady Torquilin, impressively, 'in the coming fortnight we have *barely time!* You must know that we don't do things by steam and electricity in this country. You can't go to Court by pressing a button. We haven't a moment to lose. And as to other arrangements, we must just give everything up, so as to have our minds free and comfortable till we get the whole business over.' Afterwards, about the seventh time I had my Court dress tried on, I became convinced that Lady Torquilin was right. You do nothing by steam and electricity in this country. I found that it took ten days to get a pair of satin slippers made. Though, 'of course, if you were not *quite* so particular, miss, about that too, or if you 'ad come about them *sooner*, we could 'ave obliged you in less time,' the shoemaker said. In less time! A Chicago firm would have made the slippers, gone into liquidation, had a clearing sale, and reopened business at the old stand in less time!

"'WHOEVER HEARD OF ATTENDING ONE OF HER MAJESTY'S DRAWING-ROOMS IN A FROCK MADE IN NEW YORK!'"

I like to linger over that fortnight's excitement—its details were so novel and so fascinating. First, the vague and the general, the creation of two gowns for an occasion extraordinary, mentioned by head ladies, in establishments where a portrait of Her Majesty hung suggestively on the wall, almost with bated breath. Lady Torquilin for once counselled a mild degree of extravagance, and laughed at my ideas—though she usually respected them about clothes—when I laid out for her inspection three perfectly fresh New York dresses, quite ideal in their way, and asked her if any of thom would 'do.' You have a great deal to learn, child!' she said. 'No, they won't, indeed! Who ever heard of attending one of Her Majesty's Drawing-Rooms in a frock made in New York! I'm not saying you haven't very nice taste over there, my dear, for that you have; but it stands to reason that your dressmakers, not having Court instructions, can't be expected to know anything about Court trains, *doesn't it?*' From which there was no appeal, so that the next day or two went in deep conferences with the head ladies aforesaid and absorbed contemplation of resultant patterns—which Lady Torquilin never liked to hear me call 'samples.' I was spared the trial of deciding upon a colour combination; being a young lady I was to go in white, Lady Torquilin gave me to understand, by edict of the Court. But should I have the train or the petticoat of the brocade, or would I prefer a bengaline train with a bodice and petticoat of *crêpe de chine?* Should the train come from the shoulder or be 'fulled' in at the waist; and what did I really think myself about ostrich tips grouped down one side, or bunches of field flowers dispersed upon the petticoat, or just a *suggestion* of silver embroidory gleaming all through; or perhaps mademoiselle might fancy an Empress gown, which would be thoroughly good style—they had made three for the last Drawing-Room? I had never been so wrought up about any dress before. Privately, I compared it to Lady Torquilin with the fuss that is made about a wedding-dress. 'My dear,' she exclaimed, candidly, 'a wedding-dress is *nothing* to it; as I dare say,' she added, roguishly pinching my cheek in a way she had, 'it won't be long before you find out!' But I don't think Lady Torquilin really know at the time anything about this.

It was not too much to say that those two Court dresses—Lady Torquilin was going in a cheme of pansy-coloured velvet and holiotrope—haunted our waking and sleeping hours for quite five days. Peter Corke, dropping in almost at the beginning, declared it a disgraceful waste of time, with the whole of Chelsea a dead-letter to me, and came again almost every afternoon that week to counsel and collaborate for an hour and a half. I may say that Miss Corke took the matter in hand vigorously. It was probably a detail in the improvement of my mind and my manners which she could not conscientiously overlook. 'Since you *have* the audacity to wish to kiss the hand of a sovereign who is none of yours,' said she, with her usual twinkle, 'you'll kindly see that you do it properly, miss!' So she gave us explicit instructions as to the right florist, and glover, and laceman, and hairdresser, to which even Lady Torquilin listened with respect; 'and *do not be persuaded*,' said she, with mock-severe emphasis, 'to go to anybody else. These people are dear, but you are perfectly safe with them, and that's important, don't you think?' Peter even brought over a headdress she wore herself the season before, to get the American effect, she said, and offered to lend it to me. It consisted of three white ostrich feathers and a breadth of Brussels net about a yard and a half long hanging down behind, and I found it rather trying as an adornment. So

I told her I was very much obliged, but I didn't consider it becoming, and I thought I would go with nothing on my head. At which she screamed her delightful little scream, and said indeed I wouldn't, if the Lord Chamberlain had anything to say in the matter. And when I found out just how much the Lord Chamberlain had to say in the matter—how he arranged the exact length of my train and cut of my bodice, and what I wore in my hair—the whole undertaking, while it grew in consequence, grew also in charm. It was interesting in quite a novel way to come within the operation of these arbitrary requirements connected with the person of royalty. I liked getting ready to go to Court infinitely better than if I had been able to do it quite my own way, and the Lord Chamberlain had had nothing to do with it. I enjoyed his interference. This was hard to reconcile with democratic principles, too. I intend to read up authorities in Anglo-American fiction who may have dealt with the situation when I get home, to see if they shed any light upon it, just for my own satisfaction. But I think it is a good thing that the Lord Chamberlain's authority stops where it does. It would be simple tyranny if he were allowed to prescribe colours for middle-aged ladies, for instance, and had commanded Lady Torquilin to appear in yellow, which is almost the only colour she can't wear. As it was, he was very nice indeed about it, allowing her to come in a V-shaped bodice on account of her predisposition to bronchitis; but she had to write and ask him very politely indeed. He told her by return post—of course it was not a private letter, but a sort of circular—just which dressmakers had the V shaped patterns the Queen liked best in such cases as hers, and Lady Torquilin at once obtained them. After that she said she had no further anxiety—there was nothing like going straight to the proper sources for information to have a comfortable mind. With that letter, if anything went wrong, the Lord Chamberlain could clearly be made responsible—and what did one want more than that?

One thing that surprised me during that fortnight of preparation was the remarkable degree of interest shown in our undertaking by all our friends. I should have thought it an old story in London, but it seemed just as absorbing a topic to the ladies who came to see Lady Torquilin on her 'day,' and who had lived all their lives in England, as it was to me. They were politely curious upon every detail; they took another cup of tea, and said it was really an ordeal; they seemed to take a sympathetic pleasure in being, as it were, in the swirl of the tide that was carrying us forward to the Royal presence. If the ladies had been presented themselves they gave us graphic and varying accounts of the occasion, to which we listened with charmed interest; if not, they brought forth stories, if anything more thrilling, of what had happened to other people they knew or had heard of—the lady whose diamond necklace broke as she bent; the lady who forgot to take the silver paper out of her train at home, and left it in the arms of the Gentlemen of the Court as she sailed forward; the lady who was attacked by violent hysteria just as she passed the Duke of Edinburgh. Miss Corke's advice—though we relied upon nobody else—was supplemented fifty times; and one lady left us at half-past six in the afternoon, almost in tears, because she had failed to persuade me to take a few lessons, at a guinea a lesson, from a French lady who made a specialty of *debutante* presentations. I think I should have taken them, the occasion found me with so little self-reliance, if it had not been for Lady Torquilin. But Lady Torquilin said No, certainly not, it was a silly waste of money, and she could show me everything that was necessary for all practical purposes as well as Madame Anybody. So several mornings we had little rehearsals, Lady Torquilin and I, after breakfast, in my room, by which I profited much. We did it very simply, with a towel and whatever flowers were left over from dinner the night before. I would pin the towel to my dress behind and hold the flowers, and advance from the other end of the room to Lady Torquilin, who represented Her Majesty, and gave me her hand to kiss. I found the curtsey difficult at first, especially the getting up part of it, and Lady Torquilin was obliged to give me a great deal of practice.

'I FOUND THE CURTSEY DIFFICULT AT FIRST.'

'Remember one thing about the Queen's hand absolutely, child,' said she. 'You're not, under any circumstances whatever, *to help yourself up by it!* And then I would be the Queen, and Lady Torquilin, just to get into the way of it again, would pin on the towel and carry the roses, and curtsey to me.

XXVIII

I KNOW I shall enjoy writing this chapter, I enjoyed its prospective contents so much. To be perfectly candid, I liked going to Court better than any other thing I did in England, not excepting Madame Tussaud's. or the Beefeaters at the Tower, or even 'Our Flat' at the Strand. It did a great deal to reconcile me, practically, with monarchical institutions, although, chiefly on poppa's account, I should like it to be understood that my democratic theories are still quite unshaken in every respect.

It seems to me, looking back upon it, that we began to go very early in the morning. I remember a vision of long white boxes piled up at the end of the room through the grey of dawn, and a very short nap afterwards, before the maid came knocking with Lady Torquilin's inquiries as to how I had slept, and did I remember that the hairdresser was coming at nine sharp? It was a gentle knock, but it seemed to bristle with portent as I heard it, and brought with it the swift realisation that this was Friday at last—the Friday on which I should see Queen Victoria. And yet, of course, to be quite candid, that was only half the excitement the knock brought; the other half was that Queen Victoria should see me, for an instant and as an individual. There was a very gratifying flutter in that.

The hairdresser was prompt. She came just as Charlotte was going out with the tray, Lady Torquilin having decreed that we should take our morning meal in retirement. She was a kind, pleasant, loquacious hairdresser.

'I'm glad to see you've been able to take a good breakfast, miss,' she said, as she puffed and curled me. 'That's 'alf the battle!' She was sorry that she had to come to us so early, 'but not until two o'clock, miss, do I expect to be for one moment off my feet, what with Ontry ladys who don't wish to be done till they're just getting into their carriages—though for that I don't blame them, miss, and nobody could. I'm afraid you'll find these lappits very wearing on the nerves before the day is out. But I'll just pin them up so, miss—and of course you must do as best pleases you, but my *advice* would be, don't let them down for *anybody*, miss, till you start.' But I was not sorry the hairdresser came so early. It would have been much more wearing on the nerves to have waited for her.

Perhaps you will find it difficult to understand the interest with which I watched my own development into a lady dressed for Court. Even the most familiar details of costume seemed to acquire a new meaning and importance, while those of special relevance had the charm that might arise from the mingling of a very august occasion with a fancy-dress ball. When I was quite ready, it seemed to me that I was a different person, very pretty, very tall, with a tendency to look backward over my shoulder, wearing, as well as a beautiful sweeping gown, a lofty and complete set of monarchical prejudices, which I thought becoming in masquerade. I was too much fascinated with my outward self. I could have wished, for an instant, that the Declaration of Independence was hanging about somewhere framed.

Then the advent of the big square wooden box from the florist's, and the gracious wonder of white roses and grasses inside, with little buds dropping and caught in its trailing ribbons—there is a great deal of the essence of a Royal function in a Drawing-Room bouquet. And then Lady Torquilin, with a new graciousness and dignity, quite a long way off if I had not been conscious of sharing her state for the time. Lady Torquilin's appearance gave me more ideas about my own than the pier-glass did. 'Dear me!' I thought, with a certain rapture, 'do I really look anything like *that?*'

'WE WENT DOWN IN THE LIFT, ONE AT A TIME, WITH CHARLOTTE AS TRAIN-BEARER.'

We went down in the lift one at a time, with Charlotte as train-bearer, and the other maids furtively admiring from the end of the hall. Almost everybody in Cadogan Mansions seemed to be going out at about the same time, and a small crowd had gathered on each side of the strip of carpet that led from the door to the carriage. It was Lady Mafferton's carriage, lent for the occasion, and the footman and coachman were as impressive as powder and buff and brass buttons would make them. In addition, they wore remarkable floral designs about the size and shape of a cabbage-leaf upon their breasts immediately under their chins. That was another thing that could not have been done with dignity in America.

The weather looked threatening as we drove off, precisely at twelve o'clock, and presently it began to rain with great industry and determination. The drops came streaming down outside the carriage windows; fewer people as we passed leaned out of hansoms to look at us. Inside the Mafferton carriage we were absurdly secure from the weather; we surveyed our trains, piled up on the opposite seat, with complacency; we took no thought even for the curl of our feathers. We counted, as we drove past them to take our place, and there were forty carriages in line ahead of us. Then we stopped behind the last, in the middle of a wide road, heavily bordered under the trees with damp people and dripping umbrellas—there for the spectacle. All kinds of people and all kinds of umbrellas, I noticed with interest—ladies and gentlemen, and little seamstresses, and loafers and ragamuffins, and apple-women, and a large proportion of your respectable lower middle-class. We sat in state amongst them in the rain, being observed, and liking it. I heard my roses approved, and the nape of my neck, and Lady Torquilin's diamonds. I also heard it made very unpleasant for an elderly young lady in the carriage in front of ours, whose appearance was not approved by a pair of candid newsboys. The policemen kept the people off, however; they could only approach outside a certain limit, and there they stood, or walked up and down, huddled together in the rain, and complaining of the clouded carriage windows. I think there came to me then, sitting in the carriage in the warmth and pride and fragrance and luxuriance of it all, one supreme moment of experience, when I bent my head over my roses and looked out into the rain—one throb of exulting pleasure that seemed to hold the whole meaning of the thing I was doing, and to make its covetable nature plain. I find my thoughts centre, looking back, upon that one moment.

It was three o'clock before we moved again. In the hours that came between we had nothing to do but smell our flowers, discuss the people who drove past to take places farther down the line, congratulate ourselves upon being forty-first, and eat tiny sandwiches done up in tissue paper, with serious regard for the crumbs; yet the time did not seem at all long. Mr. Oddie Pratte, who was to escort us through the palace and home again, made an incident, dashing up in a hansom on his way to the club to dress, but that was all. And once Lady Torquilin had the footman down to tell him and his brother-functionary under the big umbrella to put on their rubber coats. 'Thank you, my lady!' said the footman, and went back to the box; but neither of them took advantage of the permission. They were going to Court too, and knew what was seemly. And the steamy crowd stayed on till the last.

XXIX

PRESENTLY, when we were not in the least expecting it, there came a little sudden jolt that made us look at each other precipitately. Lady Torquilin was quite as nervous as I at this point. 'What *has* become of Oddie?' she exclaimed, and descried a red coat in a cab rolling up beside us with intense relief. As we passed through the Palace gates the cab disappeared, and chaos came again.

'AND CHAOS CAME AGAIN.'

'Naughty boy!' said Lady Torquilin, in bitterness of spirit. 'Why, in the name of fortune, couldn't he have come with us in the carriage? Men have *no* nerves, my dear, none whatever; and they can't understand our having them!' But at that moment we alighted, in a maze of directions, upon the wide, red-carpeted steps, and whisked as rapidly as possible through great corridors with knots of gentlemen in uniform in them to the cloak-room. 'Hurry, child!' whispered Lady Torquilin, handing our wraps to the white-capped maid. 'Don't let these people get ahead of us, and keep close to me!'—and I observed the same spasmodic haste in everybody else. With our trains over our arms we fled after the others, as rapidly as decorum would permit, through spacious halls and rooms that lapse into a red confusion in my recollection, leaving one of my presentation cards somewhere on the way, and reaching the limit of permitted progress at last with a strong sense of security and comfort. We found it in a large pillared room full of regularly-curving lines of chairs, occupied by the ladies of the forty carriages that were before us. Every head wore its three white feathers and its tulle extension, and the aggregation of plumes and lappets and gentle movements made one in the rear think of a flock of tame pigeons nodding and pecking—it was very 'quaint,' as Lady Torquilin said when I pointed it out. The dresses of these ladies immediately became a source of the liveliest interest to us, as ours were apparently to those who sat near us. In fact, I had never seen such undisguised curiosity of a polite kind before. But then I do not know that I had ever been in the same room with so many jewels, and brocades, and rare orchids, and drooping feathers, and patrician features before, so perhaps this is not surprising. A few gentlemen were standing about the room, holding fans and bouquets, leaning over the backs of the ladies' chairs, and looking rather distraught, in very becoming costumes of black velvet and silk stockings and shoe-buckles, and officers in uniform were scattered through the room, looking as if they felt rather more important than the men in black; as I dare say they did, representing that most glorious and impressive British institution, the Army, while the others were only private gentlemen, their own property, and not connected with her Majesty in any personal way whatever.

'Here you are,' said somebody close behind us. 'How d'ye do, Auntie? How d'ye do, Miss Wick? 'Pon my word, I'm awfully sorry I missed you before; but you're all right, aren't you? The brute of a policeman at the gates wouldn't pass a hansom.' It was Mr. Oddie Pratte, of course, looking particularly handsome in his red-and-plaid uniform, holding his helmet in front of him in the way that people acquire in the Army, and pleased, as usual, with the world at large.

'Then may I ask how you came here, sir?' said Lady Torquilin, making a pretence of severity.

'Private *entree!*' responded Mr. Pratte, with an assumption of grandeur. 'Fellow drove me up as a matter of course—no apologies! They suspected I was somebody, I guess, coming that way, and I gave the man his exact fare, to deepen the impression. Walked in. Nobody said anything! It's what you call a game o' bluff, Auntie dear!'

'A piece of downright impertinence!' said Lady Torquilin? pleasantly. 'It was your red coat, boy. Now, what do you think of our gowns?'

Mr. Pratte told us what he thought of them with great amiability and candour. I had seen quite enough of him since the day at Aldershot to permit and enjoy his opinion, which even its frequent use of 'chic' and 'rico' did not make in any way irreverent. This young gentleman was a connoisseur in gowns; he understood them very well, and we were both pleased that he liked ours. As we criticised and chaffed and chatted a door opened at the farther end of the room, and all the ladies rose precipitately and swept forward.

It was like a great, shimmering wave, radiant in colour, breaking in a hundred places into the foam of those dimpling feathers and streaming lappets, and it rushed with unanimity to the open door, stopping there, chafing, on this side of a silk rope and a Gentleman of the Court. We hurried on with the wave—Lady Torquilin and Mr. Oddie Pratte and I—and presently we were inextricably massed about half-way from its despairing outer edge, in an encounter of elbows which was only a little less than furious. Everybody gathered her train over her left arm—it made one think of the ladies of Nepaul, who wear theirs in front, it is said—and clung with one hand to her prodigious bouquet, protecting her pendent head-dress with the other. 'For pity's sake, child, take care of your lappets,' exclaimed Lady Torquilin. 'Look at that!' I looked at 'that'; it was a ragged fragment of tulle about a quarter of a yard long, dependent from the graceful head of a young lady immediately in front of us. She did not know of her misfortune, poor thing, but she had a vague and undetermined sense of woe, and she turned to us with speaking eyes. 'I've lost mamma,' she said, unhappily.

'Where is mamma? I *must* go to mamma.' And she was not such a very young lady either. But Lady Torquilin, in her kindness of heart, said, 'So you shall, my dear, so you shall!' and Mr. Pratte took his aunt's bouquet and mine, and held them, one in each hand, above the heads of the mob of fine-ladyhood, rather enjoying the situation, I think, so that we could crowd together and allow the young lady who wanted her mamma to go and find her. Mr. Oddie Pratte took excellent care of the bouquets, holding them aloft in that manner, and looked so gallantly handsome doing it that other gentlemen immediately followed his example, and turned themselves into flowery candelabra, with great effect upon the brilliancy of the scene.

A sudden movement among the ladies nearest the silken barrier—a sudden concentration of energy that came with the knowledge that there was progress to be made, progress to Royalty! A quick, heaving rush through and beyond into another apartment full of emptiness and marble pillars, and we were once more at a standstill, having conquered a few places—brought to, a masterly inactivity by another silken cord and another Gentleman of the Court, polite but firm. In the room beyond we could see certain figures moving about at their ease, with no crush and no struggle—the ladies and gentlemen of the Private Entrée. With what lofty superiority we invested them! They seemed, for the time, to belong to some other planet, where Royal beings grew and smiled at every street-corner, and to be, on the other side of that silken barrier, an immeasurable distance off. It was a distinct shock to hear an elderly lady beside us, done up mainly in amethysts, recognise a cousin among them. It seemed to be self-evident that she had no right to have a cousin there.

'I'll see you through the barrier,' said Mr. Oddie Pratte, 'and then I'll have to leave you. I'll bolt round the other way, and be waiting for you at the off-door, Auntie. I'd come through, only Her Maj. does hate it so. Not at all nice of her, I call it, but she can't bear the most charming of us about on these occasions. We're not good enough.' A large-boned lady in front—red velvet and cream—with a diminutive major in attendance, turned to him at this, and said with unction, 'I am sure, Edwin, that is not the case. I have it on excellent authority that the Queen is *pleased* when gentlemen come through. Remember, Edwin, I will not face it alone.'

'I think you will do very well, my dear!' Edwin responded. 'Brace up! 'Pon my word, I don't think I ought to go. I'll join you at——'

'If you desert me, Edwin, *I shall die!*' said the bony lady, in a strong undertone; and at that moment the crowd broke again. Oddie slipped away, and we went on exultantly two places, for the major had basely and swiftly followed Mr. Pratte, and his timid spouse, in a last clutching expostulation, had fallen hopelessly to the rear.

About twenty of us, this time, were let in at once. The last of the preceding twenty were slowly and singly pacing after one another's trains round two sides of this third big room towards a door at the farther corner. There was a most impressive silence. As we got into file I felt that the supreme moment was at hand, and it was not a comfortable feeling. Lady Torquilin, in front of me, put a question to a gentleman in a uniform she ought to have been afraid of—only that nothing ever terrified Lady Torquilin, which made it less comfortable still. 'Oh, Lord Mafferton,' said she—I hadn't recognised him in my nervousness and his gold lace—'How many curtseys are there to make?'

'Nine, dear lady,' replied this peer, with evident enjoyment. 'It's the most brilliant Drawing-Room of the season. Every Royalty who could possibly attend is here. Nine, at the least!'

Lady Torquilin's reply utterly terrified me. It was confidential, and delivered in an undertone, but it was full of severe meaning. 'I'm full of rheumatism,' said she, 'and I shan't do it.'

The question as to what Lady Torquilin would do, if not what was required of her, rose vividly before me, and kept me company at every step of that interminable round. 'Am I all right?' she whispered over her shoulder from the other end of that trailing length of pansy-coloured velvet. 'Perfectly,' I said. But there was nobody to tell *me* that I was all right—I might have been a thing of shreds and patches. Somebody's roses had dropped; I was walking on pink petals. What a pity! And I had forgotten to take off my glove; would it ever come unbuttoned? How deliberately we were nearing that door at the farther end! And how could I possibly have supposed that my heart would beat like this! It was all very well to allow one's self a little excitement in preparation; but when it came to the actual event I reminded myself that I had not had the slightest intention of being nervous. I called all my democratic principles to my assistance—none of them would come. 'Remember, Mamie Wick,' said I to myself, 'you don't believe in queens.' But at that moment I saw three Gentlemen of the Household bending over, and stretching out Lady Torquilin's train into an illimitable expanse. I looked beyond, and there, in the midst of all her dazzling Court, stood Queen Victoria. And Lady Torquilin was bending over her hand! And in another moment it would be—it was my turn!

'IT WAS MY TURN.'

I felt the touches on my own train, I heard somebody call a name I had a vague familiarity with—'Miss Mamie Wick.' I was launched at last towards that little black figure of Royalty with the Blue Ribbon crossing her breast and the Koh-i-nor sparkling there! *Didn't* you believe in queens, Miss Mamie Wick, at that moment? I'm very much afraid you did.

And all that I remember after was going down very unsteadily before her, and just daring the lightest touch of my lips upon the gracious little hand she laid on mine. And then not getting nearly time enough to make all of those nine curtseys to the beautiful sparkling people that stood at the Queen's left hand, before two more Gentlemen of the Court gathered up my draperies from behind my feet and threw them mercifully over my arm for me. And one awful moment when I couldn't quite tell whether I had backed out of all the Royal presences or not, made up my mind that I had, then unmade it, and in agony of spirit turned *and backed again!*

It was over at last. I had kissed the hand of the Queen of Great Britain and Ireland, and—there's no use in trying to believe anything to the contrary—I was proud of it. Lady Torquilin and I regarded each other in the next room with pale and breathless congratulation, and then turned with one accord to Oddie Pratte.

'On the whole,' said that young gentleman, blandly, 'you did me credit!'

XXX

I AM writing this last chapter in the top berth of a saloon cabin on board the Cunard s.s. 'Etruria.' which left Liverpool June 25, and is now three days out. From which it will be seen that I am going home.

Nothing has happened there, you will be glad to hear, perhaps. Poppa and Momma, and all the dear ones of Mrs. Portheris's Christmas card, are quite in their usual state of health. The elections are not on at present, so there is no family depression in connection with poppa's political future. I am not running away from the English climate either, which had begun, shortly before I left, to be rather agreeable. I have been obliged to leave England on account of a Misunderstanding.

In order that you should quite see that nobody was particularly to blame, I am afraid I shall have to be very explicit, which is in a way disagreeable. But Lady Torquilin said the day I came away that it would have been better if I had been explicit sooner, and I shall certainly never postpone the duty again. So that, although I should much prefer to let my English experiences close happily and gloriously with going to Court, I feel compelled to add here, in the contracted space at my disposal, the true story of how I went to dine with Mr. Charles Mafferton's father and mother and brother and sisters in Hertford Street, Mayfair.

It occurred almost as soon as the family returned from the South of France, where they had been all spring, you remember, from considerations affecting the health of the eldest Miss Mafferton—with whom I had kept up, from time to time, a very pleasant correspondence. One day, about three weeks after the Drawing-Room, when Lady Torquilin and I could scarcely ever rely upon an afternoon at home, we came in to find all the Mafferton cards again in. There was a note, too, in which Mrs. Mafferton begged Lady Torquilin to waive ceremony and bring me to dine with them the following evening. 'You can guess,' said Mrs. Mafferton, 'how anxious we must be to see her.' There was a postscript to the invitation, which said that although Charlie, as we probably knew, was unfortunately out of town for a day or two, Mrs Mafferton hoped he would be back in the course of the evening.

'Well, my dear,' said Lady Torquilin, 'it's easily seen that I can't go, with those Watkins people coming here. But you shall—I'll let you off the Watkinses. It isn't really fair to the Maffertons to keep them waiting any longer. I'll write at once and say so. Of course,' Lady Torquilin went on, 'under ordinary circumstances I shouldn't think of letting you go out to dinner alone, but in this case—there is sure to be only the family, you know—I don't think it matters.'

So Lady Torquilin wrote, and when the time came lent me Charlotte to go with me in a hansom to Hertford Street, Mayfair. 'Be sure you bring me back a full and particular account of how they all behave, child,' said she, as she looked me over after my toilette was made; 'I shall be interested to hear.'

A massive butler let me into the usual narrow, high-ceiled Mayfair hall, richly lighted and luxurious; the usual convenient maid in a white cap appeared at the first landing to show the way to the proper room for my wraps. After Lady Torquilin's expression of interest in how they behaved, I had been wondering whether the Maffertons had any idiosyncrasies, and I did not waste any unnecessary time in final touches before going down to see. I like people with idiosyncrasies, and lately I had been growing accustomed to those of the English nation; as a whole they no longer struck me forcibly. I quite anticipated some fresh ones, and the opportunity of observing them closely.

The drawing-room seemed, as I went in, to be full of Maffertons. There were more Maffertons than china plates on the wall, than patterns on the carpet. And yet there were only the four young ladies and their mother and father. The effect was produced, I think, by the great similarity between the Misses Mafferton. Not in actual face or figure; there were quite perceptible differences there. The likeness lay in an indefinable shade of manner and behaviour, in the subdued and unobtrusive way in which they all got up and looked at me and at their mamma, waiting until it should be entirely proper for them to come forward. They were dressed a good deal alike, in low tones of silk, high necked, rather wrinkling at the shoulders, and finished with lace frills at the throat and wrists, and they all wore their hair parted in the middle, brushed smoothly back over their ears, and braided neatly across and across behind. I have never been sure about their ages—they might have been anything from twenty-five to forty; but Isabella, whom they spoke of as the youngest, seemed to me to be the most serious and elderly of all.

Mrs. Mafferton was a very stout old lady, with what is called a fine face. She wore a good many old-fashioned rings, and a wide lace collar over her expansive black silk, and as she came heavily forward to meet me she held out both her hands, and beamed upon me—not an impulsive beam, however, rather a beam with an element of caution in it.

'You are very welcome, Miss Wick. Indeed, we have been looking forward to this. I think you ought to let me give you a kiss!'

Of course I did let Mrs. Mafferton give me a kiss—it was impossible to refuse. But I thought myself singularly favoured; it did not seem at all in accordance with the character of the family to fall upon the neck of a stranger and embrace her by way of welcoming her to dinner. I was still further of that opinion when each of the Misses Mafferton followed the example of their mamma, and saluted me tenderly on the same cheek. But I immediately put it down to be an idiosyncrasy. 'We are so glad to see you at last,' said the eldest. 'Yes, indeed!' said the second. 'We began to think we never should,' said the third. 'We really did!' said the fourth.

'Papa,' said Mrs. Mafferton, 'this is Miss Wick, of whom we have all heard so much.' She spoke very close to the ear of an old gentleman in an arm-chair screened from the fire, with one leg stretched out on a rest; but he did not understand, and she had to say it over again: 'Miss Wick, of whom we have all heard so much. Poor dear! he does not hear very well,' Mrs. Mafferton added to me. 'You must use the speaking-trumpet, I fear, Miss Wick.' 'Well,' said old Mr. Mafferton, after shaking hands with me and apologising for not rising, 'if this is Miss Wick, I don't see why I shouldn't have a kiss too.' At which Mrs. Mafferton and all the young ladies laughed and protested, 'Oh, fie, papa!' For my part I began to think this idiosyncrasy singularly common to the family.

"'IF THIS IS MISS WICK, I DON'T SEE WHY I SHOULDN'T HAVE A KISS TOO.'"

Then the eldest Miss Mafferton put one end of a long black speaking-trumpet into my hand, and Mr. Mafferton, seeing her do this, applied the other to his ear. I had nothing whatever to say, but, overcome with the fear of seeming rude, I was raising it to my lips and thinking hard when I felt two anxious hands upon my arm. 'Do excuse us!' exclaimed a Miss Mafferton, 'but if you wouldn't mind holding it just a little farther from your lips, please! We are obliged to tell everybody. Otherwise the voice makes quite a distressing noise in his poor ears.' At which every semblance of an idea left me instantly. Yet I must say something—Mr. Mafferton was waiting at the other end of the tube. This was the imbecility I gave expression to. 'I came here in a cab!' I said. It was impossible to think of anything else.

That was not a very propitious beginning; and Mr. Mafferton's further apology for not being able to take me down to dinner, on the ground that he had to be taken down by the butler himself, did not help matters in the very least. At dinner I sat upon Mr. Mafferton's right, with the coiling length of the speaking-trumpet between us. The brother came in just before we went down—a thin young man with a ragged beard, a curate. Of course, a curate being there, we began with a blessing.

Then Mrs. Mafferton said, 'I hope you won't mind our not having asked any one else, Miss Wick. We were selfish enough to want you, this first evening, all to ourselves.'

It was certainly the Mafferton idiosyncrasy to be extravagantly kind. I returned that nothing could have been more delightful for me.

'Except that we think that dear naughty Lady Torquilin should have come too!' said the youngest Miss Mafferton. It began to seem to me that none of these young ladies considered themselves entitled to an opinion in the first person singular.

An idea appeared to be, as it were, a family product. 'She was very sorry,' I said.

'And so, I am sure, are we,' remarked Mrs. Mafferton, graciously, from the other end of the table. 'It was through dear Lady Torquilin, I believe, that you first met our son, Miss Wick?'

I began to feel profoundly uncomfortable—I scarcely knew exactly why. It became apparent to me that there was something in the domestic atmosphere with which I was out of sympathy. I thought the four Miss Maffertons looked at me with too much interest, and I believed that the curate was purposely distracting himself with his soup. I corroborated what Mrs. Mafferton had said rather awkwardly, and caught one Miss Mafferton looking at another in a way that expressed distinct sympathy for me.

I was quite relieved when Mrs. Mafferton changed the subject by saying, 'So you are an American, Miss Wick?' and I was able to tell her something about Chicago and our methods of railway travelling. Mrs. Mafferton was very pleasant about Americans; she said she always found them nice, kind-hearted people. The curate said, thoughtfully, crumbling his bread, that we had a vast country over there.

'Francis!' exclaimed the Miss Mafferton who sat next to him, playfully abstracting the crumbs, 'you know that's naughty of you! I'm afraid you've come to a very nervous family, Miss Wick.'

I felt myself blushing abominably. The situation all at once defined itself and became terrible. How could I tell the Maffertons, assembled there around their dinner-table, that I was *not* coming to their family!

'Burgundy, miss?'

How could I do anything but sip my claret with immoderate absorption, and say that nervous disorders did sometimes run in families, or something equally imbecile!

'But Charlie's nerves are as strong as possible!' said another Miss Mafferton, reproachfully, to her sister.

We had other general conversation, and I spoke into Mr. Mafferton's trumpet several times with a certain amount of coherence; but I remember only the points which struck me as of special interest at the time. Among them was the proposal that, if I were willing, Mrs. Mafferton should drive me on Tuesday week—that would be to-day—to see an invalid married sister living in Hampstead who was most anxious to welcome me. How could I say I was not willing!

Then, after dinner, in the drawing-room, Mrs. Mafferton took me aside 'for a little chat,' and told me what a good son Charles had always been, and showed me several photographs of him at earlier stages, from the time he wore a sash and pinafore. Even then, I remember, he looked a serious person.

'EVEN THEN, I REMEMBER, HE LOOKED A SERIOUS PERSON.'

After which I had another little chat with two of the Misses Mafferton together, who explained what a devoted brother they had always had in Charlie. 'We *are* so glad you've been kind to him,' they said, impulsively. 'Of course we haven't seen him yet since our return, but his letters have told us *that* much.' I tried in vain to rack my brain for occasions on which I had been kind to Mr. Charles Mafferton, and longed for an attack of faintness or a severe headache.

'Indeed,' I said, 'it was always your brother who was kind—to Lady Torquilin and to me.' At which the young ladies smiled consciously, and said something about *that* being perfectly natural. Then, just as I was wondering whether I absolutely must wait for Charlotte to arrive in a cab to take me home as Lady Torquilin had arranged, and as the third Miss Mafferton was telling me how noble but how uninteresting it was of Francis to take up extreme Ritualistic views and vow himself to celibacy, the door-bell rang.

'There's Charlie now!' exclaimed the Misses Mafferton all together.

'I must really go!' I said precipitately. 'I—I promised Lady Torquilin to be home early '—noting with despair by the gold clock under glass on the mantel that it was only a quarter to ten—'and the American mail goes out to-morrow—at least, I *think* it does—and—and Good-night, Mrs. Mafferton! Good*night*, Mr. Mafferton!' I said it very rapidly, and although they were all kind enough to meet my departure with protest, I think it was evident to them that for some reason or other I really must go. The young ladies exchanged glances of understanding. I think their idea was that I dreaded the embarrassment of meeting Mr. Charles Mafferton before his family. Two of them came upstairs with me to get my wraps, and assured me in various indirect ways that they quite understood—it was awkward.

'THE MISSES MAFFERTON, WHO ACCOMPANIED ME, TURNED QUITE PALE.'

Coming down, we met Mr. Charles Mafferton at the door of the drawing-room. The Misses Mafferton, who accompanied me, turned quite pale when they heard me assure their brother that there was not the slightest necessity that he should accompany me home. I could not persuade him of this, however, and we drove away together.

I am afraid I cannot possibly report the conversation that took place between Mr. Mafferton and myself in the cab. Looking back upon it, I find it difficult to understand clearly, as I dare say he does if he ever thinks about it. After I had made him see quite plainly that it was utterly, absolutely impossible, which was not easy, he left me to infer that I had been inconsistent, though I am sure I could make no self-accusation which would be more baseless. Privately, I thought the inconsistency was his, and that it was of the most glaring description. I am of opinion, with all due respect to your English customs, that if Mr. Mafferton desired to marry me, he should have taken me, to some extent, into his confidence about it. He should not have made Lady Torquilin the sole repository of the idea. A single bunch of roses, or basket of fruit, or box of candy addressed to me specially, would have been enough to give my thoughts a proper direction in the matter. Then I would have known what to do. But I always seemed to make an unavoidable second in Mr. Mafferton's attentions, and accepted my share of them generally with an inward compunction. And I may say, without any malice at all, that to guess of one's own accord at a developing sentiment within the breast of Mr. Mafferton would be an unlikely thing to occupy the liveliest imagination.

Perhaps Mr. Mafferton did not know how his family had intended to behave to me. At all events, he offered no apology for their conduct. I may say that the only thing of any consequence that resulted from our drive was the resolution which I am carrying out on board the s.s. 'Etruria' to-day.

The ladies' steward of the 'Etruria,' a little fellow with large blue eyes and spectacles and a drooping moustache, is very polite and attentive. His devotion, after Mr. Mafferton's, seems the embodiment of romance. I shall hesitate about tipping him. He has just brought me some inspiring beef-tea, which accounts for those asterisks.

think that I had treated Lady Torquilin badly. She seemed to think that I should have told her in the very beginning that I was engaged to Mr. Arthur Greenleaf Page, of the Yale University Staff. She seemed to think that I should have told everybody. I don't see why, especially as we are not to be married until Christmas, and one never can tell what may happen. Young ladies do not speak of these things quite so much in America as you do in England, I think. They are not so openly known and discussed. I must apologise to myself for bringing Mr. Page in even at this stage, but it seemed to be unavoidable.

I don't know at all, by the way, what Arthur will say to this last of my English experiences. He may not consider it as 'formative' as he hoped the others would be. There is only one thing that

'THE LADIES' STEWARD.'

The worst of it was Lady Torquilin's scolding next morning—not that she said anything unkind, but because it gave me the idea that I had treated her badly too. I should be so sorry to think that I had treated Lady Torquilin badly. She seemed to think that I should have told her in the very beginning that I was engaged to Mr. Arthur Greenleaf Page, of the Yale University Staff. She seemed to think that I should have told everybody. I don't see why, especially as we are not to be married until Christmas, and one never can tell what may happen. Young ladies do not speak of these things quite so much in America as you do in England, I think. They are not so openly known and discussed. I must apologise to myself for bringing Mr. Page in even at this stage, but it seemed to be unavoidable.

I don't know at all, by the way, what Arthur will say to this last of my English experiences; he may not consider it as 'formative' as he hoped the others would be. There is only one thing that makes the thought endurable for an instant—it would have been nice to be related to the Stacys.

Just before sailing the purser supplied me with dear consolation in the shape of a letter from Miss Peter Corke. It was a 'characteristic' letter, as we say when we want to say a thing easily—bewailing, advising, sternly questioning, comically reprobating, a little sad and deprecating by accident, then rallying to herself again with all sorts of funny reproaches. 'I meant to have done so much, and I've done so little!' was the burden of it, recurring often—'I meant to have done so much, and I've done so little!' Dear Peter! She can't possibly know how much she did do, though I'm taking my unformed mind back to a comparatively immature civilisation, and shall probably continue to attend a church where they use spring-edged cushions and incandescent burners. Peter's England will always be the true England to me. I shall be able to realise it again easily with some photographs and Hare's 'Walks in London,' though I am afraid I have got all her delightful old moss-grown facts and figures mixed up so that I couldn't write about them over again without assistance as intelligently as before. And Peter says she doesn't mind going on in my second volume, if only I won't print it; which is very good of her when one thinks that the second volume will be American, and never written at all, but only lived, very quietly, under the maples at Yale. I hope she may be found in the last chapter of that one too. Dear Peter!

www.ingramcontent.com/pod-product-compliance
Ingram Content Group UK Ltd.
Pitfield, Milton Keynes, MK11 3LW, UK
UKHW031350260325
456749UK00003B/504